WINNER OF THE
1993
NORTH AMERICAN
INDIAN PROSE AWARD

K. Tsianina Lomawaima

They Called It
Prairie Light

*The Story of Chilocco
Indian School*

University of Nebraska Press

Lincoln and London

First Bison Books printing: 1995
Most recent printing indicated by the last digit below:
10   9   8   7   6   5   4
Library of Congress Cataloging-in-Publication Data
Lomawaima, K. Tsianina, 1955–
They called it prairie light: the story of Chilocco
Indian School / K. Tsianina Lomawaima. p. cm.
Includes bibliographical references and index.
ISBN 0-8032-2904-6 (cl.: alk. paper)
ISBN 0-8032-7957-4 (pa.)
1. Chilocco Indian School – History.
2. Indians of North America – Education.
3. Indians of North America – Cultural assimilation.
4. Indians of North America – Biography.   I. Title.
E97.6.C4L65   1994   370'.08997 – dc20   93-30255   CIP

Chilocco

Oh Chilocco! Oh Chilocco!
Where the prairies never end,
Oh Chilocco! Oh Chilocco!
You are still our famous friend.
School of schools you are the best,
You're the school that stands the test,
You're the school that brings us fame,
Ever we'll revere thy name.

Oh Chilocco! Oh Chilocco!
We love your campus grand,
We love your lawns and shady walks
Where graceful maples stand.
We love the sunsets and the stars at night,
Reflected by the lake so bright.
We love the cardinal's cheery call,
And the bright red maples in the fall.

Oh Chilocco! Oh Chilocco!
Where your old stone buildings stand.
Oh Chilocco! Oh Chilocco!
Ivy covered they are grand.
They are monuments of hope
As we on learning's ladder grope,
School that makes our dreams come true,
We are ever loyal to you.

Oh Chilocco! Oh Chilocco!
When the morning bugle calls,
Oh Chilocco! Oh Chilocco!
We are glad to fill your halls.
We come here that we may learn,
Life's great secret to discern,
Teach us how to work and play,
Bring us something new each day.

Chilocco School song
Chilocco: School of Opportunity, 1938

Contents

Maps

Illustrations

Following Page 96

At the heart of all literature, oral and written, we find the effort of human memory, a recapitulation of event or of feeling that binds us again to our history.
Barry Lopez, *Bighorse the Warrior*

Preface

This is a story of Chilocco Indian Agricultural School, a federal off-reservation boarding school for Indian people. Chilocco was a federal school, so this is a story of an educational crusade—vast in scope, military in organization, fervent in zeal, and violent in method—to transform young Indian people. As in many crusades, its leaders could not accurately predict all of its astonishing results. Chilocco was an Indian school, so this is a story of Indian creativity, adaptability, and resistance to the federal agenda of transformation. Chilocco alumni reveal in their memories of school life how they created a school culture influenced but not determined by the bounds of federal control. This is a story of Indian students—loyal to each other, linked as family, and subversive in their resistance.

A history of Indian education based on the documentary remains of policy statements and school records might summarize the federal crusade as follows: The United States government established off-reservation boarding schools in the late 1800s as part of its grand civilizing plan to transform Native American people. Federal policymakers and administrators cooperated to remove thousands of Native American children and young adults from their families, homes, and tribes in order to educate them in a new way of life. Indian education flowed far beyond academic or vocational boundaries, soaking the child's growing up in the cleansing bath of Christian labor. Tribal/communal identity, primitive language, heathen religion: these pernicious influences would be rooted out and effaced in the construction of a new kind of American citizen.

Commentators have alternately glorified and vilified this educational crusade in the course of a full century; its history has been probed, researched, written, and rewritten.[1] The historical narrative manufactured in the process, laudatory or critical, begins with *federal* as the subject and encodes *Native American* or *Indian* as its object, mirroring the crusade even as it strives to delineate it.[2] The narrative corpus has, with few exceptions, been resurrected from the bones of official archival documents. The spoken, individual voice occasionally augments the inscribed voice of authority, but it still speaks from a position of power: the commissioner of Indian Affairs, the superintendent of Indian Schools, school administrators and teachers, the researcher as expert witness.[3]

What has become of the thousands of Indian voices who spoke the breath of boarding-school life? They have surrounded the historical narrative, speaking around it and under it, and even talking back to it.[4] The crafters of the historical narrative have, on occasion, bent an ear to listen to Indian voices, but they discern no pattern in the message, only variegated opinion.[5] As a result, scholars have exhaustively detailed federal policy and practice in the off-reservation boarding schools, whereas the process of life within them has been relatively unexamined until recent years.[6]

Native Americans who attended boarding schools are living archives, storehouses of memory and experience. Their memories and experiences, shaped into spoken narratives, continue to shape families, communities, and educational endeavors among Indian people. One of the astonishing results of boarding-school life, in light of federal goals, has been Indian students' stubborn refusal to jettison their Indian identity. The perseverance, even intensification, of ethnic identification associated with boarding-school life today was anticipated in the nineteenth century by R. H. Pratt, founder of Carlisle, the first off-reservation boarding school: "The great powers of schools, especially when located among the Indians and administratively utilized to that end [that is, maintaining segregated status on reservations], have easily become potential racial and tribal promoters of cohesion" (Utley 1964, 271).

The experiences of children and young adults at Chilocco illuminate the present scholarly discussion of ethnicity in the modern nation state and resistance to forced acculturation.[7] Ethnicity theory has been marked by an opposition between authors interested in how people manipulate the markers of ethnic solidarity in the pursuit of some economic or political gain and those who are concerned with the "primordial" emotional ties forged and reinforced in the development of personal identity.[8] Despite their differences, authors share an assumption about ethnic phenomena—that ethnic group formation and persistence are a consequence of the natural opposition of human groups.[9] Scholars of ethnicity theory might be tempted to gloss over the internal complexities of boarding school student life and assume student Indian identity "emerged" in natural opposition to non-Indian authority, but information from Chilocco suggests a more profitable avenue of analysis. We can focus at Chilocco on the specific circumstances of identity formation that many authors leave unexamined in the premise of ethnic "emergence."[10] Personal narratives provide the concrete details of how children, separated from home, viewed and used the markers of identity inherited from home and learned at the school—tribal background, language, degree of blood, physical appearance—to delineate peer groups (gangs among the boys) and forge bonds that have survived over decades and generations.

The government established boarding schools according to a nineteenth-century version of ethnicity theory, which ranked races along an evolutionary staircase ascending to a Christian heaven attainable by hard labor and acceptance of one's lot on earth. Federal educators assumed they could erase tribal identity by separating Indian children from Indian adults. It seemed logical that this would be more easily accomplished with younger children than with older. Chilocco students turned this assumption on its head, as the youngest boys formed gangs along tribal lines, whereas older students often downplayed intertribal boundaries in their peer groups. Even, or perhaps especially, the most vulnerable groups within the boarding school—the youngest, the most estranged from tribal background—were brought together and protected in the folds of tribal identity. For many students, a pan-tribal "Indian" identity also evolved in opposition to school authority. Through strict regimentation, non-Indian authority mobilized and strengthened Indian resistance, expressed as loyalty to fellow students as well as by covert and overt rule-breaking.

The fact that schools often strengthened rather than dissolved tribal identity is not the only surprise tucked within alumni reminiscence. The idealized school society envisioned in federal policy often bore little resemblance to reality. Federal practice in the schools more frequently subverted the idealism of policy than supported it. The military methods, for example, used to organize and control students were incapable of encouraging individuality or creativity and were ill-suited to produce independent citizens, the avowed goal of federal educational policy. These methods were necessary, however, to the efficient administration of many students by few, often minimally trained personnel. Interwoven oral and documentary sources build an image of a boarding-school culture that was created and sustained by students much more than by teachers or staff. Ironically, the practical realities of adapting to institutional life did foster self-sufficiency in many students.

Chilocco students defined successful adaptation to the boarding school in terms of their own experience, creating an honor code of admirable behavior that stressed peer group loyalty in kinship terms: "We were brothers and sisters." Successful adaptation meant different things to male and female students and to older and younger students. Individual remembrance provides the solid details of how each student adapted to and/or rebelled against the boarding school's strict regimentation.

This study examines the relations of power within the school to comprehend federal disciplinary practice and to situate the strategies Indian children devised to escape it. Boarding-school training for Indian girls in the arts of domesticity and rules of proper dress for female students reflect the power relations that permeated Chilocco. Wearing the uniform was a battleground for the contest of power between students and authorities. Alumni tell many stories about school days, and one—the bloomer story—documents female students' resistance to uniform dress and targets the peer group solidarity essential to student resistance. My analysis of the bloomer story depends upon a critical analysis of the boarding school as an institutional training ground for the subservience of the colonized.[11]

Bureau of Indian Affairs boarding schools, especially in the years before World War II, were often harsh and repressive institutions. Students were not allowed to speak their own language or practice their own religion. Their contact with home and family was severely restricted. In many ways they were made to feel inferior. Yet, boarding-school students had the resilience of children, and in many cases, found happiness in their surroundings. Some people hated and endured their boarding-school years; others hated and did not endure: they ran away. Some count their years away at school among the happiest and most carefree of their lives. This story speaks of a few social and cultural variables that made a difference to Chilocco students in the 1920s and 1930s. The students' age when entering boarding school and the stability of their home lives emerge as important influences on their response to the boarding-school environment.

This study does not pretend to be an exhaustive analysis of all the effects of boarding-school attendance on later life. Conversations and recollections about boarding school are emotionally charged and encompass many sensitive issues.

Boarding schools had a tremendous impact on language use and retention, religious conservatism and conversion, attitudes toward education and feelings of self-esteem, to name but a few influences. Schools also varied over time and over space as federal policies evolved, were interpreted by local staff, and were applied to ethnically and linguistically diverse Indian students. Chilocco in 1935, with more than a thousand students drawn from Oklahoma, was a vastly different world than Chilocco in 1972, with 460 students, 61 percent from the Northwest, Alaska, the Southwest, and other distant states.

The people whose lives are recorded in this book describe one school in one era: Chilocco Indian Agricultural School from 1920 to 1940. They tell us what resulted from the dynamic processes of interethnic and intertribal communication, cooperation, and conflict within that school. The view of boarding-school life constructed from their words portrays how an institution founded to transform Indian youth was paradoxically given life by the very people whose tribal identities it was committed to erase.

The Story

My father, Curtis Carr, remembers student life at Chilocco in the 1920s and 1930s. His reminiscences, and the thoughts and memories of sixty other Chiloccoans, anchor this narrative.[12] These men and women speak to us, recalling the voices of childhood that echoed down Chilocco's highly polished corridors. They instruct us in adaptation, accommodation, resistance, and revolt. They hone and polish their stories, distilling the essence of past experience. Stories keep the memory fresh and laughter keen at the frequent gatherings, formal and informal, of boarding-school alumni.[13]

Barbara Myerhoff eloquently frames the nature of retrospection, the act of reminiscence, and the benefits accruing to the performer in the act of "re-membering" as she presents the life histories of elderly Eastern European Jews living in California. Those survivors of a society extinguished by the Holocaust have, in Myerhoff's words, a heightened "sense of being memory bearers, carriers of a precious, unique cargo" (1980, 23). Memory bearers use two strategies in their recollection and performance of their own life histories: they deliver themselves of their memories, and by that process establish and make visible their own identities: "They become active participants in their own history; they provide their own sharp, insistent definitions of themselves, their own explanations for their past and their destiny" (1980, 22).

Myerhoff also focuses on the role of the listener as a recipient of information, as shaper of the interview process, and as a fellow mortal marked inalterably by the communion of shared experience: "A story told aloud . . . is more than a text. It is an event. When it is done properly, the listener is more than a passive receiver or validator, he is changed" (1980, 27). In the interchange between researcher and memory bearer, each one is enriched. Experience shared with another is not merely transmission of information along linguistic circuits. Once undertaken, the memories one has been entrusted with cannot be laid aside or relegated to the attic of the soul or mind.

The generational cohort of Chilocco alumni from the 1920s and 1930s *want* to share their experiences, to contribute to the chronicles of a way of life that is no more, for which they are the memory bearers. Alumni narrate the history of Chilocco not only to transmit information that would otherwise be lost but also to contribute to a definition of themselves. In this respect, boarding-school attendance functions as an important marker of ethnic and social identity for Chilocco alumni. As alumni review their lives, as they share and speak history in informal gatherings of friends or formal alumni association meetings and reunions, their pride and self-esteem are renewed and restored. In these gatherings, alumni continually define and redefine their memories and the meanings of those memories.

I tell a story that belongs to the narrators—it is essentially their property—but it does not represent them anymore than the documentary history of Chilocco represents its individual papers. I collect, record, transcribe, edit, analyze, order, construct an argument, and write.[14] The personal narratives transcribed in the following chapters are my best effort to render accurately and truthfully the opinions, feelings, and experiences of sixty-one people, "memory bearers" for themselves and for Chilocco Indian Agricultural School. In addition to presenting these narratives, I muster the evidence embedded in them to serve my purposes and my interpretations, to see the boarding school more clearly as a lived reality of Indian experience. I know that some alumni disagree vigorously with some of my interpretations, but I hope that the story told here is a faithful rendering of the many voices I have heard and that the story of Chilocco rings true to their ears.

One more word about the Chilocco alumni who speak within these pages. They are united by more than the shared school experience. They are also united by the distinction of survival.[15] They have worked, raised families, and arrived at a point in their lives when they wish to deliver themselves of their memories in a generous effort to contribute to a history of Chilocco. Their voices speak to us powerfully but should not lead us to forget the voices that we do not, or cannot, hear.

The narrative excerpts included in the following chapters have been lightly edited with two goals in mind: preserving as much as possible of the narrator's individual style and enhancing readability. Excerpts are identified by a pseudonym for each narrator (with one exception) and some basic information. Curtis, my father, is the only participant referred to by his real name. Each narrative tag indicates the year the narrator came to Chilocco, his or her age or grade when he or she first entered, and his or her tribal affiliation.

The entry "Edgar 1929/10 Creek" identifies Edgar (pseudonym) as a Creek who started school at Chilocco in 1929 at age 10. If age is uncertain, the grade when school was started at Chilocco is indicated: for example, 1929/5th indicates a student who enrolled in 1929 in the fifth grade. Students and employees referred to in any narrative by name are indicated by initials. Certain staff by virtue of their position are difficult to disguise, and they are named: Superintendent L. E. Correll, boys' dormitory staff Harry Kellar, Sam Lincoln, and Rose Daugherty; and girls' matron, Elizabeth McCormick.

Material of an intimate or confidential nature has been kept confidential. Editing followed these guidelines:

1. Extraneous interjections (*uh, so, and, you know*), false starts, and repeated words are not indicated in the text.

2. Elision of a few words is indicated by three dots, and longer elisions of one or more phrases or sentences are indicated by four dots.

3. When necessary to preserve sense, words are added: these are demarcated by brackets.

4. Explanatory notes of the editor are also enclosed in square brackets.

5. Braces surround comments that narrators added when editing the first drafts of their interview transcripts.

6. An asterisk in the line of text indicates a break in the narrative, that is, the sections preceding and following the asterisk come from separate portions of an individual's interview(s).[16]

Acknowledgments

This book and the research it is based upon would not have been possible without the generous support and cooperation of many individuals and institutions. All have my heartfelt thanks. Field and archival research in 1983–84 was supported by the National Institute of Mental Health, Department of Health and Human Services, Research Fellowship Grant for 1983–84 (#F31 MH09016–01); the Phillips Fund, American Philosophical Society; and the L. J. Skaggs and Mary C. Skaggs Foundation. Additional archival research in 1990 was supported by the Institute for Ethnic Studies in the United States (University of Washington).

My first thanks are due to my father, Curtis Carr, who attended Chilocco from 1927 to 1935. His faith in me and this project can never be repaid. To the alumni, staff, teachers, and other "Chiloccoans" by interest, marriage, or association who contributed to this history I owe a tremendous debt. Every one of you made a great contribution, and I hope that this work goes a small way toward meeting your expectation. Special thanks to the officers and members of the Chilocco Alumni Association, who were unstinting in their offers of assistance, and to Cedric Starr for his outstanding aid and words of encouragement. To all of those who took me into their homes and treated me like family, you have my love as well as my thanks: Cedric and Dee Starr, Lorraine Cummings, Clem and Joyce Griffin and all Griffins everywhere, Tom and Helen Whitewater, Janet Pasqua, Okemah Arey, Christine Scroggins, Leonard and Susan Harjo, Ben and Mary Arkeketa, Freeman Zunigha, Helen Sherline, and Susan Lankford and family.

For assistance with the archival portions of this research I am indebted to the staff members and librarians of the Oklahoma Historical Society in Oklahoma City; the Western History Collections at the University of Oklahoma in Norman, Oklahoma; the Federal Archives and Records Center in Fort Worth, Texas, especially Jeanette Ford, archivist; and the Museum of Native American Cultures in Spokane, Washington.

Of course, the views expressed within this work are mine, and all errors of fact or interpretation are mine alone.

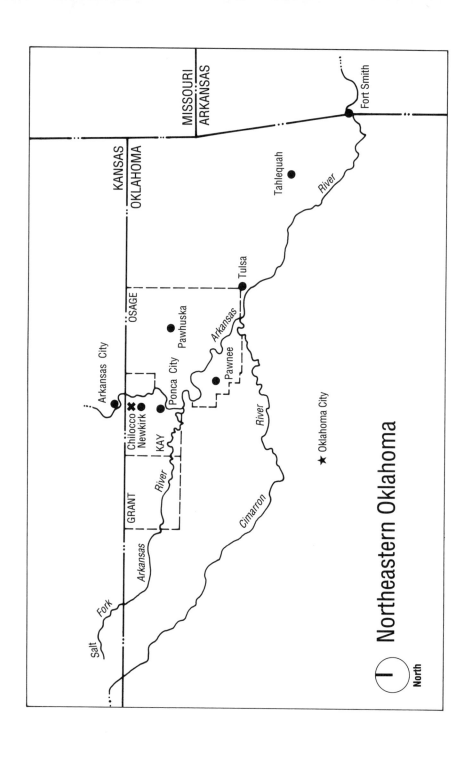

Northeastern Oklahoma

I

'They Called It
Prairie Light'

On 17 May 1882, the United States Congress authorized the construction of an Indian boarding school on a "suitable" section of land in the Indian Territory (present Oklahoma), adjacent to the Kansas state line and the Ponca and Pawnee reservations (Kappler 1975, 1:198). Major James N. Haworth, superintendent of Indian Schools, reluctantly selected a site for the school on the banks of Chilocco Creek in north-central Oklahoma. Haworth later wrote, "At that time I was not favorably impressed with the idea of a school in that neighborhood, thinking trouble would arise from pupils running off."[1]

Major Haworth and his wife planned one large building to house 150 students, plus employees, classrooms, kitchen, and dining rooms. Haworth, in fine federal tradition, overspent his construction budget by $3,000 but with impressive results (Wall and Wall 1979, 11a). A straight flight of steps rose to a roofed entry porch, elevated eight feet above the prairie. The open porch softened the bulk of three-and-one-half stories of native limestone blocks, quarried from the school reservation. In the evening, light shone through the tall windows across a prairie unblemished by hedgerows or trees, a beacon and landmark for travelers headed west. The Light on the Prairie was ready for its first class.

History of Indian Education

It is expected that all who borrow our opportunities shall return to the United States both principal and interest in intelligent and patriotic service as the result of an improved quality of citizenship. In such service alone can the debt be paid.   *The Chiloccoan*, 1926

Federal commitment to boarding schools and their "appropriate" education for Native Americans sprouted from the enduring rootstock of European misperceptions of America's natives. Europeans were at first skeptical of the humanity of the inhabitants of the American continents, but most were soon persuaded that these so-called Indians had souls worthy of redemption. Proselytization entailed communication, the basic tool of instruction, and Christian missionaries were the first to school American natives. They were not as concerned with academic instruction as bringing heathen brethren into the fold of Christianity, which included the accoutrements of Western civilization. The helping hand of the church was also the hand of the state, in so much as a Christian life was perceived to be a working life. Missionaries of all denominations hoped to convert and to civilize. Indians would surrender their particular religion, language, and culture and become Christian rural farmers and laborers. After the formation of the new republic, America's political leaders left the education of Indians in the hands of the clergy, who were deemed most fit to oversee this moral and practical transformation.

On 3 March 1819, the U.S. Congress passed an act to provide education "for the purpose of providing against further decline and final extinction of the Indian tribes . . . to instruct them in the mode of agriculture suited to their situation, and for teaching their children in reading, writing and arithmetic" (Tyler 1973, 45). The act authorized appropriations in 1819 of $10,000. By 1842, $214,000 in federal funds had been directed to missionary organizations maintaining 37 schools, employing 85 teachers and serving 1,283 students. The appropriation was commonly known as the "Civilization Fund."

Before 1900, the federal government subsidized church and mission schools on a per capita student basis. Different regions and tribes were franchised to competing denominations. The dissent fostered by this competition, the changing role of the federal government in Indian affairs, and the pressures exerted by powerful political factions in the East led the government to take a more active role in the administration of Indian education.[2] In the 1880s and 1890s, the government decreased aid to mission schools and eliminated aid entirely by the first decade of this century. The government built schools of its own on the foundation of religious instruction inherited from schools for Indians and blacks, such as the Hampton Normal Institute in Virginia,[3] although particular attention was paid that government instruction remain nondenominational (that is, Protestant). Mission and government manual labor schools emphasized agricultural and manual skills for boys and domestic skills for girls over academic training.[4]

Acculturation to and assimilation into the dominant white society remained the explicit goal of policy and practice. In 1887, this political ideology produced the General Allotment (Dawes) Act, or the "Indian Emancipation Act." Indians were to be divested of their tribal, communally held lands and introduced, forcefully if necessary, to individual land ownership. Special government obligations to Indian groups as sovereign entities would be dissolved, and Indian individuals would be no more or less privileged than any other American citizen. Government schools were responsible for preparing Indians for the independence envisioned in the Dawes Act.

The act targeted private land ownership as the essential force to civilize Indians. The president was authorized to survey reservations and allot quarter sections of land (160 acres) to individuals; allotments were larger or smaller depending on the marital and age status of the allottees, and suitability of land for farming or grazing. Allottees were issued a patent and allotted lands were held in trust, usually for twenty-five years, at which time the allottee (or heirs) received fee simple title to the land, as well as U.S. citizenship (Prucha 1986, 224–241).

Lands remaining after allotment could be purchased by the U.S. government and then opened for homesteading by non-Indians. Ultimately, allotment proved disastrous for Indian land tenure: "An enormous loss of Indian land followed, with total Indian landholdings falling from 138 million acres in 1887 to 52 million acres in 1934. More than 26 million acres of allotted land was transferred out of Indian hands after it passed out of trust" (Wilkinson 1987, 20).

Mission schools and the government schools that followed them were often situated close to the communities they served. Many educators viewed this proximity as a disadvantage. Attempts to teach children English, Christianity, and the moral superiority of a clean life of honest labor were constantly undermined by the so-called bad influences of family and tribe. It seemed a natural solution to separate children from such negative influences in order to insure their eventual success as citizens of the American nation. The solution took the form of the off-reservation boarding school.[5] General Richard H. Pratt, a staunch nineteenth-century assimilationist, vigorously campaigned for off-reservation boarding schools.

Pratt's personal philosophy of assimilation sprang from his Civil War command experience with Negro troops.

In Pratt's mind the Negro furnished the example. Slavery transplanted him from his native habitat and tribal affiliation into a new cultural environment, where he had to adapt to a new language, new dress, and new customs. As a result, in a span of several generations he had been shorn of his primitivism and elevated to American citizenship. Pratt believed profoundly that as the Negro had been civilized, so could the Indian be civilized (Utley 1964, xiv).

Pratt insisted that the best way to civilize the Indian was to "immerse him in civilization and keep him there until well soaked" (Utley 1964, xxi).

Pratt implemented his ideas of Indian education at Fort Marion, Florida, where he was in charge of Cheyenne, Kiowa, and Comanche hostiles captured after the Red River War. Pratt instituted an honor system of self-guard for the prisoners of war and undertook their training in trades and their employment in town. This daring educational venture met with astonishing (to Pratt's superiors) success, when his prisoners requested the Indian Office to allow their wives and children to join them in Florida so that they could settle down and learn to live as white men (Utley 1964, 128). Ironically, their request was denied by the Indian agent Haworth, who as superintendent of Indian schools, established Chilocco Indian School less than ten years later.

Armed with the success of his Florida experiment, Pratt went to Washington to garner support for a school where Indian children could be brought for an uninterrupted period of immersion in civilization. He had already been approached by General Samuel Armstrong, of the Hampton Agricultural School for Negroes, who wanted Pratt to direct an affiliated Indian school. Pratt declined, for he wanted no part of Armstrong's racial education. He was firmly committed to a school that would aid Indian assimilation into white society, not perpetuate their segregation outside of it. After a long and sometimes bitter battle with federal officials, Pratt was allowed to found such a school in 1879 at the site of unused cavalry barracks at Carlisle, Pennsylvania. Carlisle was the first, and perhaps the most famous, of the off-reservation boarding schools established by the U.S. Office of Indian Affairs (later the Bureau of Indian Affairs, or BIA).

Pratt organized Carlisle along strict, often harsh, military lines. In the interest of economy and with the rationale of teaching basic skills, the school depended on student labor in the kitchens, laundries, and sewing rooms. Students spent half a day in the classroom, and half a day working at various trades. They were responsible for campus maintenance, construction and repair, and raising and caring for crops and livestock. All the students worked, down to the youngest six- and seven-year-olds. Discipline was strict and the children's time completely scheduled. They were not allowed to speak their native languages or practice native singing, dancing, or religion.

At Carlisle, the *outing* was a cornerstone of Pratt's plan of education. Instead of returning home in the summer, students were placed with white farming families for three months and in some cases for up to three years after graduation. Here they could experience firsthand the responsibilities and amenities of civilized life. The outing was acknowledged as a strong and effective part of Pratt's educational strategy and was continued at other off-reservation schools through World War II, although it was discontinued at Chilocco before 1920.

Pratt's ideal of Indian education reiterated in philosophy and practice the ideals of the mission and government schools devoted to the acculturation of Native Americans:

I suppose the end to be gained, however far away it may be, is the complete civilization of the Indian and his absorption into our national life, with all the rights and privileges guaranteed to every other individual, the Indian to lose his identity as such, to give up his tribal relations and to be made to feel that he is an American citizen. If I am correct in this supposition, then the sooner all tribal relations are broken up; the sooner the Indian loses all his Indian ways, even his language, the better it will be for him and for the government and the greater will be the economy to both. Now, I do not believe that amongst his people an Indian can be made to feel all the advantages of a civilized life, nor the manhood of supporting himself and of standing out alone and battling for life as an American citizen. To accomplish that, his removal and personal isolation is necessary. One year in the midst of a civilized community where, whichever way he may turn he can see the industrious farmer plowing his fields or reaping his grain, and the industrious mechanic building houses or engaged in other manufactures, with all the realities of wealth and happiness which these efforts bring to the farmer and mechanic is worth more as a means of implanting such aspirations as these you desire for him in his mind than ten years, nay, than a whole life time of camp surroundings with the best Agency school work that can be done (Utley 1964, 266).

Schools devoted to the cultural quarantine of children away from their homes and families were not without detractors, even in the 1880s. Despite crit

5

Table 1. National Indian Student Enrollment, 1931–1932

Federal schools	No. (1932)	Enrollment (1931)
Off-reservation boarding	21	12,650
Reservation/tribal boarding	51	11,590
Sanatorium[a]	12	2,000
Day (elementary)	124	4,684
Total (federal)	208	30,924
Other schools		
Mission or private	——	8,403
Public (rural)	——	43,562
Total (other)		51,965
Total		82,889[b]

Source: Compiled from data in *Indian Schools and Education*, U.S. Bureau of Indian Affairs.
a. Sanatorium schools were established by the government for the seclusion, treatment, and continuing education of the many boarding school students diagnosed with tuberculosis.
b. Total no. of Indian children (age 6–18) in school. The total no. of Indian children (age 6–18) is 94,612.

icism and Pratt's frequent clashes with bureaucratic superiors, his successes were sufficient to prompt the government to found more schools patterned after Carlisle. By 1885, the government opened Chemawa School in Oregon; Chilocco in Oklahoma; Albuquerque Indian School in New Mexico; Haskell at Lawrence, Kansas; and Genoa Indian School in Nebraska. By 1899, twenty-four off-reservation boarding schools were in operation, with an average daily attendance overall of 6,263 students (Indian Affairs Bureau 1899, 69–72). The large industrial schools were intended to siphon older children from reservation day and boarding schools. In 1889, superintendant of Indian Schools S. H. Albro objected to "irregularities" in enrolling too many young children in the large schools. He felt that young children could not adequately learn a trade, and that they returned home too young to resist the temptations of their "savage parents and kinsmen."[6]

The 1890s through the 1930s were the heyday of the off-reservation boarding schools, and the majority saw their highest enrollments during the 1930s as a result of the economic conditions of the Depression. In 1931, 29 percent of Indian children in school were in boarding schools (see table 1). Off-reservation boarding schools housed 15 percent of all Indian children in school.

For a variety of social, economic, and political reasons, boarding schools were never as popular after World War II as they had been in the first three decades of the twentieth century. The 1920s and 1930s marked crucial milestones in United States Indian policy and administration. In the 1920s, liberal interest

groups in the East that had been founded in the late 1800s and early 1900s to pro-
mote Native American rights and education began in earnest a movement to reform the U.S. Office of Indian Affairs. The Indian Rights Association and the
Board of Indian Commissioners published articles in popular journals such as
Sunset; and they were instrumental in the defeat of the Bursum Bill (an act designed to undermine Pueblo legal title to their land grants), the establishment of
the Pueblo Lands Board in 1924, and passage of the Osage Guardianship Act in
1925. Criticism of Indian policy and administration culminated in 1928 with the
publication of *The Problem of Indian Administration,* commonly known as the
Meriam report. The Meriam report's criticism of the Indian Bureau was all en-
compassing and devastating. Health and education services were judged
harshly, and off-reservation boarding schools drew heavy fire, fueled by find-
ings of severe malnutrition, poor health care, overcrowding, unsanitary living
conditions, restrictive discipline, low quality of teaching staff, and inordinate
dependence on student labor (Meriam 1928, 11–12).[7]

In 1933 President Franklin D. Roosevelt appointed John Collier, ardent and
zealous leader of the liberal reform movement of the 1920s, as commissioner of
Indian Affairs.[8] Collier did not support the educational philosophy of complete
acculturation. He was an anomaly in the smooth course of Indian administration up to 1928: a man with an intellectual and spiritual commitment to Indian
tribal society, rooted in and flourishing on a communal land base. Collier, in
turn, worked with education director Will Carson Ryan, Jr. (1930–36) and his
successor, Willard Walcott Beatty (1936–52) to transform Indian education.

Ryan and Collier set out to strengthen and expand the reforms begun under
the Hoover administration in response to the Meriam report. Collier's prede-
cessor, Charles Rhoads, had initiated measures to alleviate the problems of inadequate food, overcrowding, and child labor that were typical of some of the
federal boarding schools in the 1920s (Tyler 1973, 121–22). Boarding schools,
especially those located away from reservation areas, were phased out, and
those kept open were instructed to implement reforms recommended by the
Meriam report survey staff. The number of boarding schools dropped from 76
to 65 between 1928 and 1933. Inspired by the political philosophy of Roosevelt's New Deal, Collier hoped to replace Indian boarding schools with day
schools, nourished by the heritage of their communities.

Collier was appointed in April of 1933, and by July, six boarding schools had
been closed and the enrollment at others reduced. Collier redirected Works Project Administration (WPA) funds to the construction of one hundred day

schools. He believed it was the government's duty to bring education and modern scientific knowledge to Indian communities and to reawaken Indian pride (Philp 1977, 212–13). Collier took even more radical steps in federal policy toward native religions. He firmly opposed interference with Indian religious beliefs and practices, and he issued one of his most controversial executive orders in 1934, curtailing missionary activity at day and boarding schools and prohibiting compulsory attendance at religious services (Philp 1977, 131).

Will Carson Ryan, Collier's education director, had supervised the educational section of the Meriam report and had authored many of the charges filed against boarding schools. He issued a number of directives aimed at improving conditions in the schools, as did Collier. Ryan replaced the obsolete "Uniform Course of Study" with a program oriented to practical and vocational education, at the same time reducing the amount of menial labor, such as scrubbing floors, that previously had passed as vocational training. He added a high school program to some boarding schools and abolished the positions of girls' matron and boys' disciplinarian (in name at least).[9]

In 1936 Willard Beatty replaced Ryan as director of education. Beatty rejected the idea of training Indians for scarce urban jobs and altered the curriculum of federal schools to reflect rural problems common to reservations. Collier, Ryan, and Beatty instituted policy changes that led to an emphasis on local day schools and public schools for Indian education.

After World War II, Indian education shifted more and more to the public schools. Administrative and policy changes, coupled with changes in public opinion, rising costs, and the increased availability of public schooling, led to a decline in boarding-school enrollments. Boarding schools increasingly served troubled students, although schools serving more remote Indian communities such as those in the Southwest or Alaska continued their vital function in junior and senior high school education. A handful of BIA boarding schools were still in operation in the early 1990s, including Chemawa in Salem, Oregon, and Sherman Institute in Riverside, California, and a number of schools have been turned over to local control to be run under tribal contracts.

Early Chilocco

Military regimentation, manual labor, and enforced uniformity; the investigations of the Meriam team; the administrative reforms of Rhoads, Ryan, and Collier—all are framed and reflected in the memories of alumni who attended Chilocco from 1920 to 1940. The student perspective does more than reflect the documentary record, however; it supplements and contradicts it. Daily student life was structured much more by students and school staff than by Circular Orders from Washington, and alumni reveal the limits of Central Office authority. For the history of the earliest years of the school, however, we must depend on the documentary record alone.[10]

Early reports of the commissioner of Indian Affairs refer to the school as Haworth Institute, Chilocco, Indian Territory.[11] The name was later changed to Chilocco Indian Industrial School, then Chilocco Indian Agricultural School (*Chilocco: School of Opportunity* 1938, 1). The name *Chilocco* has generated more etymological heat than light. The author of *Oklahoma Place Names* acknowledges "several explanations" but decides "the name is probably from the Creek *tci lako* meaning 'big deer,' a name often applied to the horse" (Gould 1933, 45). Superintendent Leon Wall wrote in 1967, "Chilocco's name is said to be the white man's mixture of two Indian words, the Cherokee Tsalagi, and the Choctaw's Chilukki, both of which mean Cave People" (Wall and Wall, 1979, 11a). Alumni commonly assert that *Chilocco* is either a misspelling of the Cherokee word for "Creek," or a misspelling of the Creek word for "Cherokee," depending on which side of the tribal fence the narrator sits.

Congress intended Chilocco to emphasize English and industrial training for tribes whose education had been least provided for before the 1880s (Kappler 1975, 198). In Indian Territory, that meant the recently and still hostile nomads of the southern and central plains. Major Haworth faced the considerable obstacles of recruitment and transportation. He had to persuade parents to give up their children to the care of the federal government and place them on a wagon train bound for Chilocco in the dead of winter. As the new year of 1884 was being celebrated, Haworth wrote of his hardships to Miss Emma De Knight of Pittsburgh, Pennsylvania (later Mrs. Emma D. Sleeth, of Arkansas City, Kansas), who became one of Chilocco's first teachers:

> I have just returned from the Cheyenne-Arapaho and Kiowa-Comanche countries, having arranged for about a hundred children who will reach here in about ten days, or as soon as the weather moderates a little so they can travel safely in wagons. I have had a cold, rough, stormy trip day and night, traveling through storms and freezing weather, crossing unbridged rivers and untenanted plains, but tonight I am seated by a comfortable fire, for which I am thankful. (*Chilocco: School of Opportunity* 1938, 1)

After successfully navigating the rough waters of student recruitment, Major

Table 2. Number of Chilocco Graduates, 1894–1909

Year	1894	1895	1896	1897	1898	1899	1900	'01	'02	'05	'06	'07	'08	'09
No.	15	7	9	12	5	—	4	9	16	10	7	9	7	8

Source: Compiled from statistics in Oklahoma Historical Society. File: Alumni Association 20 April 1911–15 February 1913.

Haworth arranged for the transportation of students across the prairies to the school. On 8 January 1884, Frank Maltby, clerk and industrial teacher, led a wagon train carrying seventy-nine children out of Anadarko, Oklahoma, for an arduous 175-mile trip to the school. More wagons and more children from the Cheyenne and Arapaho tribes joined the wagon train at Darlington Agency. More than one hundred children arrived in late January as Chilocco opened its doors to students from the Kiowa, Comanche, and Wichita Agency, and the Cheyenne and Arapaho Agency (Bradfield 1963, 1). Children from closer to the school, including thirteen Pawnees, increased enrollments (Wall and Wall 1979, 11a).[12] Haworth continued to resist enrolling students whose homes were close by. "The location of the school is, in some respects, an unfortunate one, being neither in nor yet out of the Indian country; is easy of access by the various tribes, whose frequent visits are calculated to interrupt the studies of the children and cause some of them to become dissatisfied." As a result, Kaw and Ponca boys were shipped off to the more distant Haskell Institute in Lawrence, Kansas.[13]

Emma Sleeth wrote several articles for the *Chilocco Weekly Journal* (which later became the *Indian School Journal*) in the early 1900s chronicling the first years of the school and the challenges its personnel faced, including student recruitment. Three employees and three students (Comanche, Caddo, and Kiowa boys) would leave by wagon in the early summer for the two-hundred-mile trip to visit the Cheyenne, Arapaho, Wichita, Kiowa, Caddo, and Comanche tribes. They took provisions for a week's travel and replenished their water along the way. The days were hot and the nights cool as they traveled, and their trip was often delayed by flooding at the Chikaskia and Cimarron river crossings. Their first stop was the Kiowa school in Anadarko, where they visited the tepees and preached to parents about the virtues of Chilocco Indian School. From there, they procured horses and traveled all over the Caddo and Wichita reservations, seeking willing students (Sleeth 1907).

Chilocco recruited 150 children from the Cheyenne, Arapaho, Wichita, Comanche, and Pawnee tribes in 1884. By 1893, enrollments increased to 230 students, and they continued to creep up: in 1894, 273 students (172 boys and 107

Table 3. Promotion of Pupils by Grade, 1916–1917

Divisions	Percentage promoted (of pupils examined)		Percentage promoted (of annual enrollment)	
	Male	Female	Male	Female
Primary				
1	37.5	55.5	33.3	62.5
2	44.4	58.3	50	53.8
3	66.6	60	62.5	60
Prevocational				
4	20	25	18	17
5	73.3	52.2	97	67.6
6	68.9	62.8	47.6	44.8
Vocational				
First	61	4	42.8	31.2
Second	80.4	78	75	76.1
Third	100	100	85.7	92.3
Fourth	100	100	88.8	100

Source: Report on Promotions of Pupils, 1916–17, F/Curriculum, OHS.

girls); in 1895, 352 students (207 boys and 145 girls). A decade after its founding, the school was organized into primary level grades one through four, and advanced level grades one through five. In 1894 the first graduating class of six boys and nine girls received their diplomas from Chilocco Indian School for completion of the eighth grade (*Chilocco: School of Opportunity* 1938, 6). Although Chilocco had an annual enrollment of two hundred to three hundred students in its earliest years and exceeded seven hundred by 1907, the number graduated each year (see table 2) remained relatively small (*Indian School Journal*, March 1907).

By 1905, Chilocco's physical plant had expanded to thirty-five buildings and the staff had grown to seventy employees. The federal government kept the school as up-to-date as possible, and installed electricity in that same year (Wall and Wall 1979, 11e). Superintendent McCowan began to plan how to fill the school with advanced students, hoping that Chilocco would not accept or retain students under twelve years of age.[14] By 1906 Chilocco enrolled seven hundred students recruited from forty tribes. In the early 1920s, enrollments reached eight hundred and varied from this level up to about twelve hundred throughout the decades of the 1930s, 1940s, and 1950s.[15]

By the 1916–17 school year, Chilocco was organized into three divisions— the primary division (grades one through three), the prevocational division (four through six), and the vocational division with four grades—ten grades in

Table 4. Chilocco Capacity, Enrollment, and Attendance, Various Years, 1891–1930

Year	Rate per annum ($)	Capacity	No. of Employees	No. of Pupils Enrolled	Average Attendance
1891	167	200	31	187	164
1892	167	350	35	212	188
1893	167	300	42	236	224
1894	167	350	44	279	250
1895	167	400	52	352	339
1897	167	450	63	434	347
1898	167	450	66	331	271
1918	167	500	—	654	528
1925	—	750	—	895	758
1930	—	850	—	1,082	872

Source: Compiled from statistics in Annual Reports of the Commissioner of Indian Affairs, 1891–1930. Variation in record keeping over the years resulted in gaps in this table.

all. Total enrollment for the year was 597, and the enrollment in June was 406. Of those 406, 308 were promoted to the next grade. Promotion percentages of pupils examined were lowest in grade one and gradually improved as children passed through the higher grades (see table 3).

The discrepancies between the percentage passed out of a grade of pupils examined (at the end of the school year) and the percentage promoted of pupils enrolled for the entire school year offer a clue to one of Chilocco's salient and persistent enrollment characteristics: enrollments at the end of the school year did not correspond very well, on a student-to-student basis, to enrollments at the beginning of the year. The school lost students all year, through illness, desertions, and transfers to other schools. In order to keep the average daily attendance at levels necessary to retain congressional funding, new students were constantly enrolled. Thus, an annual enrollment figure of 800 students might mask an average daily attendance figure of 640. It was not the *same* 640 students attending all year long (see table 4).

In accordance with Chilocco's vocational charter, students spent half the day in academic classes, half in vocational work/classes or on work details.[16] As prevailing policy and theories of elementary education changed, this plan was altered. In 1910, the Indian Education office in Washington directed its superintendents to abandon the split-day plan for younger students, who should devote their time to academics until they were older, when industrial work would be more meaningful. This removed younger students from the vocational track for

Table 5. Daily Routine at Chilocco Indian School, 1911

Sunday			
A.M.	8:00	Catholic services
	9:00	General inspection in quarters
	10:00	Sunday School (Non-Catholics)
P.M.	3:00	General undenominational service, visiting ministers.
	7:00	(1st/2d/3d Sundays) YMCA, YWCA Meetings. (4th/5th Sundays) general assembly
Monday		
A.M.	7:30–11:30	Industrial departments in session
through	8:30–11:30	Academic departments in session
Thursday		
P.M.	1:00– 5:00	Industrial departments in session
	1:15– 4:00	Academic departments in session
	7:00– 8:00	Study hour in classrooms or in quarters
Friday		
A.M.	7:30– 5:00	Same as Monday-Thursday
P.M.	7:00	Meetings of literary societies
Saturday		
A.M.	7:30–11:30	Industrial departments in session as on Monday-Thursday
P.M.	11:35– 5:15	One Saturday per month in town (one day for girls, one day for boys)

Source: Response to Circular #590, 22 December 1911, F/Curriculum 12 January 1904–30 June 1917. OHS.

several years but did not exempt them from the work details necessary to the up-keep of the school in the dining room, kitchen, sewing and mending rooms, dormitory, butcher shop, and bakery. Institutional needs dictated administrative efficiency, and reveille awoke Chilocco students at 5:30 A.M., the first of twenty-two bugle calls punctuating the daily schedule. Weary students were released after Assembly at 9:05 in the evening (see table 5).

Chilocco's academic program expanded from 1910 to 1920 while retaining the basic educational plan, which emphasized manual labor and work details.[17] In 1917, girls stitched long curtains and school dresses, wove rag rugs, and pieced quilts in the sewing rooms, while boys worked hard in the trades departments, and the carpentry department finished the new porch on Home 2 (*Indian School Journal,* March 1917). The school achieved accredited status under Oklahoma state school law in 1932 and continued to phase out the elementary grades (*Chilocco: School of Opportunity* 1938, 6). By the late 1930s, Chilocco offered junior and senior high school instruction only. After World War II, instruction was restricted to the senior high level, with the exception of the Special Navajo Program, a remedial instructional program for Navajo children at least twelve years old with little or no schooling experience.

Over the years, Chilocco gradually enrolled students from a wider and wider range of tribal backgrounds. In the late 1800s, tribes represented included, among others, Caddo, Delaware, Kaw, Miami, Omaha, Otoe, Ottawa, Pawnee, Peoria, Ponca, Pottawatomie, Sac and Fox, Seneca, Shawnee, Sioux, Wichita, Winnebago, and Wyandotte. Beginning in 1900, students were also recruited from the Chinook, Chippewa, Colville, Comanche, Crow, Eastern Cherokee, Oneida, Osage, Pima, Pueblo, and Stockbridge tribes, among others. In 1906, Chilocco enrolled over seventy Navajo students (*Indian School Journal,* March 1907). Large numbers of the so-called Five Civilized Tribes, relocated from the American South to eastern portions of Oklahoma (known as Indian Territory before Oklahoma statehood in 1906) did not appear at Chilocco until after 1910 (see table 6 for attendance at Chilocco by tribe from 1903 through 1925).

The sixteenth article of the (Cherokee) Treaty of 16 July 1866 authorized the United States to settle friendly Indians in the Cherokee Outlet, and Major Haworth had selected land there in 1883 to build Chilocco. [18] The initial reservation was insufficient for agricultural instruction, and Major Haworth recommended that it be enlarged. Emma Sleeth wrote that it was Major Haworth's idea to set apart thirteen sections of land to establish a little colony of Indian boys and girls from the school who might marry one another. Each couple would live on ten acres of land where school personnel could assist them to lead "a civilized life" (Sleeth 1906). President Chester Arthur expanded the school reservation by executive order in 1884 to 8,640 acres. [19] In 1967, Congress sold 2,688 acres of the Chilocco campus back to the Cherokee Nation at the original 1882 price of $3.75 an acre. When the school was closed in June of 1980, the campus was locked up and put under the care of resident caretakers. Bids by local tribes, including the Poncas, Kaws, and Otoes, to assume control of the campus buildings were unsuccessful. Various proposals for use of the physical plant, ranging from the establishment of a minimum security prison to an internment camp for Cuban refugees, came and went. In the late 1980s, Chilocco's acreage was leased to local farmers and the campus housed a substance abuse rehabilitation clinic, while the Cherokee tribal government petitioned for return of the land.

Many Chilocco alumni today agree with the land history reported in the 1938

Table 6. Attendance by Tribes, 1910–1925

Tribe	1903	Number of students per year 1910	1915	1920	1925	% of 1925 enrollment
Apache	22	14	17	4	3	—
Caddo	12	13	10	17	18	2
Cherokee[a]	167[b]	7	119	90	234	26
Chickasaw	—	0	26	19	29	3
Chippewa	68	28	13	0	0	—
Cheyenne/Arapaho	35	52	33	25	51	6
Choctaw[c]	—	0	41	104	136	15
Comanche	25	7	5	6	11	1
Creek[d]	—	0	43	59	105	12
Delaware	4	0	7	10	15	2
Kaw	18	0	11	1	22	3
Kickapoo	23	0	0	0	0	—
Kiowa	1	10	11	3	23	3
Osage	43	0	0	0	0	—
Otoe	75	8	12	22	28	3
Pawnee	18	40	23	21	35	4
Ponca	44	22	25	13	39	4
Potawatomi	54	28	13	14	10	1
Sac and Fox	16	9	7	10	24	3
Seminole	—	0	25	13	37	4
Seneca	10	3	14	9	7	1
Shawnee	49	13	5	12	19	2
Wichita	6	6	6	8	13	1
Southwest[e]	187	121	34	5	1	—
Northwest[f]	55	28	1	3	5	1
California[g]	11	8	2	3	1	—
Other[h]	53	37	29	31	30	3
Totals	996	455	532	502	896	100

Source: 1902–3 figures compiled from RG 75, E67, Record of Pupils, FRC. These figures probably represent total enrollment for the years 1902 and 1903, regardless of runaways, transfers, or other students who dropped out of school. Figures for later years approximate average daily attendance.

a. includes North Carolina
b. Eastern Cherokee only
c. includes Mississippi
d. includes Euchee
e. Hopi/Moqui, Mojave, Navajo, Papago, Pima, and Pueblo
f. Crow, Digger, Gros Ventre, Nez Perce, Shoshone, Siletz, Sioux
g. Klamath, Modoc, Modan, Pitt River, and Hoopa
h. Arickaree, Assiniboine, Clatsop, Iowa, Iroquois, Kickapoo, Menominee, Miami, Omaha, Oneida, Osage, Ottawa, Peoria, Quapaw, Stockbridge, Tonkawa, Walipia, Winnebago, and Wyandotte

school publication, *Chilocco: School of Opportunity*. In that view, the reservation was increased to 8,640 acres "by the generosity of the Cherokees who deeded a portion of their Outlet to the United States government. . . . Immediately, the President issued an order setting it aside for that purpose" (1938, 6). This may be an overly generous interpretation of the Cherokee tribe's generosity when Chilocco was founded. William Savage, Jr. (1972) sketches a more realistic scenario in his description of the relations between the Cherokee tribe, the federal government, and the Cherokee Strip Livestock Association, made up of non-Indian cattlemen from Kansas. The Livestock Association obtained a five-year lease on the Cherokee Outlet in 1883, and expansion of the Chilocco reservation to over eight thousand acres removed fifteen sections of land from their use. When Superintendent Minthorn complained in 1885 that cowboys were making intrusions on school lands, the federal government did not intervene directly but referred the problem to the chief of the Cherokee Nation, Dennis Wolfe Bushyhead, as a problem of his jurisdiction. The special agent for the outlet, in his 1886 annual report to Bushyhead, objected to the size of Chilocco's reservation because "as a training school one or two sections is enough for pasture and farm" (Savage 1972, 202). In 1885 at least, both the central office in Washington and the local agent recognized Cherokee jurisdiction over outlet lands.

Since 1885, the question of the original ownership of Chilocco lands has been argued incessantly. In 1947, Chilocco superintendent L. E. Correll, in correspondence with J. B. Milam, chief of the Cherokee Nation, expressed his opinion that the land in question had *never* belonged to the Cherokees, based on his own analysis of executive orders and congressional appropriation acts: "I believe it is fair to assume that the U.S. government reserved this land, which is to be perpetual, to be used as an Indian school, and that it was never given to the Cherokees and they in turn gave it to the government as a school. It was just reserved out of the federal domain to be used for the purpose that it is now used for."[20]

Superintendent Correll may well have been correct in his assessment of how unwillingly the Cherokees gave the land on which to construct the school, but his assertion of the federal, not Cherokee, original claim ignores the precedence of Cherokee jurisdiction assigned by the Interior Department itself in the review of claims by organizations such as the Cherokee Strip Livestock Association.

The first superintendent appointed at Chilocco was Jasper M. Hadley, followed by Dr. Henry J. Minthorn (*Chilocco: School of Opportunity* 1938). They, like Major Haworth, were Quakers. In the wake of revelations of abuses in the Indian Agency system after Grant's presidency, Quakers were appointed in increasing numbers, based on their reputation for honesty and integrity. Superintendent turnover was high in Chilocco's formative years: five superintendents in the first five years. Eight more superintendents served between 1889 and 1926. Strong leadership came to Chilocco in 1926 when L. E. Correll, one of the agricultural teachers, was appointed superintendent. Correll devoted thirty more years to Chilocco, serving as superintendent until his retirement in 1956. After Correll, no superintendent served longer than seven years. Six superintendents oversaw the school's operations from 1956 until closure in June of 1980.

Chilocco was established in 1884 as an agricultural school, but there was no organized agricultural curriculum. Agricultural education was an incidental by-product of the work students did to keep the school self-sufficient. In the 1901 Annual Report, Superintendent McCowan insisted that Chilocco should become a "genuine agricultural school for Indians":

> Not only has the education of the white boy been 'away from the farm and toward the factory' and the city, but the education of our Indian boys has been toward the city and the professions instead of to the higher, broader, and better life of the farm and country. Methods of teaching, even in our best Indian schools, have been of such nature as to disgust the Indian boy with the farm. Drudgery has been called farming, and chore boys have been dubbed farmers. The result has been a continual and constantly increasing exodus of our most promising boys from the rural homes they own to the professions they are as yet unfit to adorn, and to fields of football where they shine. Chilocco makes the farm the center of interest, and its industries, its economies, its science the subjects of thought and study.[21]

In 1906, all the children in the school were assigned their own garden plot, and the boys from the fifth grade up were assigned small fields. Students left the school building at four in the afternoon with rakes and hoes to tend their gardens. In 1907 a completely equipped creamery was built, fifty stands of bees were added to the poultry department and one hundred Shopshire sheep were purchased.[22] By 1908, Chilocco's industrial curriculum privileged agricultural instruction as its first priority. Pupils received practical instruction and made "original investigations and experiments. . . . [but] The classroom work was more or less retarded by the burning of the main school building."[23]

Chilocco's administrators were committed to building the flagship modern agricultural training institute in the federal school system, but a structured vocational educational program in agriculture was not established until 1923 (*Chilocco: School of Opportunity* 1938, 33). In the interim, agricultural instruction continued as "learn by doing." The plot system, begun in 1905, was revived in 1923. Boys contracted for a small acreage and farmed it under "expert instruction." The school furnished seed, horses, farm machinery, and other necessary equipment and instruction, and the boy received one fourth of the market value of his crop (*Indian School Journal,* July 1905). "He was encouraged to market his own product in order that he might gain that experience also" (*Chilocco: School of Opportunity* 1938, 6). In 1937, the government established a "cooperative project system" at Chilocco: "Each cooperative includes three or more projects in the different branches of agriculture, such as poultry, dairy and garden" (*Chilocco: School of Opportunity* 1938, 33). Boys worked together in small groups to gain experience in a wider range of agricultural vocations. They could choose among feed crops (wheat, corn, oats, barley, or rye) or livestock, dairy production, poultry production, vegetable gardening, or fruit production (*Chilocco: School of Opportunity* 1938, 37). Chilocco was noted nationwide for high quality livestock, particularly the Hereford cattle herd established in 1920 (Bradfield 1963, 83).

In September 1906, the federal government augmented agricultural instruction at Chilocco and established a two-year normal course to offer a new career opportunity to young Indian men and women: "these patient, cheerful workers," especially the women, "for teaching is essentially women's work." Indian students who had completed the eighth grade were eligible to enroll. The course outline offered all the ordinary normal school instruction available to whites plus advanced instruction in agriculture for the men, "thus especially qualifying them for teaching Indian children rightly. Our purpose is to prepare Indians to teach successfully in Indian schools." Women, of course, were trained to teach domestic science: "Educators are recognizing the fact that no woman can be called well educated until her hands are trained to obey her head in intelligent home making—and that home making is as much a need of our land as law making."[24]

Despite federal rhetoric, which claimed to train young Indian people unencumbered by tribal loyalties for a place in white mainstream society, schools

Table 7. Chilocco Graduates Employed in Indian Schools, 1906–1907

Mary Brown	Oraibi, Ariz. (Hopi)	
Henrietta Miller	Ft. Defiance, N.Mex. (Navajo)	Ass't. matron
Martha Matoxin	Ft. Defiance, N.Mex.	Ass't. matron
Minnie Barker	Whittiker's Orphan Home	Matron
Louis Roy	Flandreau School, S. Dak.	Printer/Ass't.
Leona Grayeyes	Ft. Sill School, Okla.	Disciplinarian
Lulu Wilson	Ft. Sill	
Adelaine Default	Ft. Sill	
Clara Star	Ft. Sill	
Josephine Parker	Kickapoo School	
Homer Hill	Whittiker's Orphan Home	Head Print Shop
Mike Lemeaux	Jicarilla, N.Mex. (Apache)	Teacher
Frank Marquis	Riverside, Okla.	Chief engineer
Minnie Skenendore	Potawatomi	
Betty Welch	Potawatomi	
Fleming Lavender	Albuquerque, N.Mex.	Harness maker

prepared Indian school students for employment—as support staff and vocational instructors, rarely as academic teachers—in Indian schools. Bureaucracy lived to perpetuate itself. Recruitment of employees from among the ranks of the converted, so to speak, might have been responsible in part for the conservative character of Indian schools over the years, lending reinforcement to a staff resistant to change, even though nonacademic staff might be largely Indian. Alumni who participated in this research recall with fondness school staff who were Chiloccoans themselves, and alumni who worked for the Indian Service, Education Division, tended to draw on their own experiences in a sincere effort to improve the schools and the quality of student life.[25] The six issues of the *Indian School Journal* in 1907 list sixteen Chilocco students who obtained employment at other Indian schools in the federal system in 1906 and 1907 (see table 7).

Like many Indian schools, Chilocco sent students and exhibits to world's fairs and expositions. Pratt began the tradition of aggressive public relations by sending Carlisle students to the 1883 Columbian Exposition in Chicago. In 1903, Superintendent McCowan of Chilocco helped plan the Indian exhibit for the anthropology department of the 1904 World's Fair Exposition in St. Louis, Missouri. He wrote to federal Indian agents, asking them to help locate traditional Indians to demonstrate arts and crafts. The caustic reply of John H. Seger, superintendent of the Colony Indian Training School in Oklahoma, was no doubt an accurate barometer of federal regard for the preservation of traditional Indian cultures:

As my work and experience among these Indians for thirty years has been with a view of getting them to forget their old ways and pursuits, and I have been so far successful . . . the old time occupation of these Indians have about passed away. When I first knew them they hunted the buffalo and lived by so doing. The work of the men did not go much farther than making bows and arrows and herding their ponies. The women tanned the robes, skinned the buffalo, built the lodges, leaving the men but little to do when in camp. So it is not strange that their time was put in, when in camp, smoking and playing 'Montey,' and I might add in pulling out their eyebrows. As I don't imagine these occupations would add much to the exhibit, I must frankly say you have struck the wrong man. . . . I received a letter today from another person asking me to contribute to the St. Louis Exposition. In this letter he says 'would like to have grasses of every kind and the wheat, oats, etc., and the grain when thrashed.' Now this man struck me with a full hand, and I can play to his ante, and if I don't win trump from the bottom of the deck on his deal and sweep the stakes, it will be because my experience in the Indian work has profited me nothing.[26]

Despite Superintendent McCowan's interests in traditional Indian arts and crafts Chilocco's exhibit at the exposition mirrored John Seger's priorities and showcased student skills in domestic and agricultural arts.[27]

Other administrators felt public promotion of Indian skills and abilities could go too far. The chief of the Education Division visited the school in 1914 and relegated to storage the beautiful table and chairs that Chilocco boys had so carefully crafted for the 1904 exposition. He sternly instructed the superintendent to keep things "intensely practical" and not train Indian students "to too high standards."[28]

R. H. Pratt's legacy of military discipline was bequeathed to Chilocco, and the student body was ranked in companies from private through major. Officers drilled every Monday night in the gymnasium; they drilled their companies every weekend and on dress parade Sundays. The federal government took pride in the spit-and-polish image of its boarding schools and welcomed visitors. Chilocco hosted its share of local, national, and foreign dignitaries over the years. The December 1906 issue of the *Indian School Journal* reported:

An Officer of the German Imperial Army visited Chilocco recently to study methods of discipline and military tactics as promulgated at this institution. . . . He was very much pleased with his visit, and like other foreigners, did not hesitate to say that he was greatly enlightened and surprised at the thorough manner in which Uncle Sam is training his Red children (1906, 58).

Harsher aspects of military discipline and punishment were gradually phased out of the boarding-school setting: "The school guardhouse has been torn down and now adorns the scrap-pile in the rear of the shop building. This institution is now without this least-to-be-desired building" (*Indian School Journal* January 1908). Each home, however, retained a small room called the lock-up, usually on the porch, where runaways and other miscreants could be isolated and placed on a bread-and-water diet. The lock-ups were a feature of Homes 1 and 2 (for boys) and Homes 3 and 4 (for girls) until the early 1930s.

Chilocco's first building, the "Light on the Prairie," housed students and employees, kitchen, dining room, hospital, classrooms, and employees' club. It came to be known as Home 2 and in the 1920s and 1930s housed the younger boys. Home 2 was demolished in the 1960s (Wall and Wall 1979, 11a). Additional homes were constructed and reconstructed over the years (fires were frequent, although official records only rarely mention student arson), and by the 1930s, alumni recall Homes 2, 1, and 6 as dormitories for boys (ranked youngest to oldest) and Homes 3, 4, and 5 as dormitories for girls (ranked youngest to oldest).[29]

World War I drained Chilocco of its men, as the older boys and male employees joined the armed services, and the younger boys were kept at home to help when older brothers were called to enlist. Chilocco sent over one hundred men to serve in the Great War (Speelman 1924).[30] Even with the reduction in strength of the agricultural force, the school obtained considerable revenue from farm production ($80,000) and their 1918 wheat harvest was the largest in the school's history. Federal supervisors reviewed the curriculum and judged the academic work poorly organized and the industrial training substandard. Immediate action was impossible, because Spanish influenza swept the country in 1919. The school was placed under strict quarantine from October to February and achieved the distinction of being the only large Indian school to escape an epidemic that year.[31]

The end of the year review in June of 1919 once again pronounced the boys' industrial instruction poor and observed that better wages were desperately needed within the Indian Service in order to attract a better grade of employee. The girls' industrial education, on the other hand, was judged very credible. In

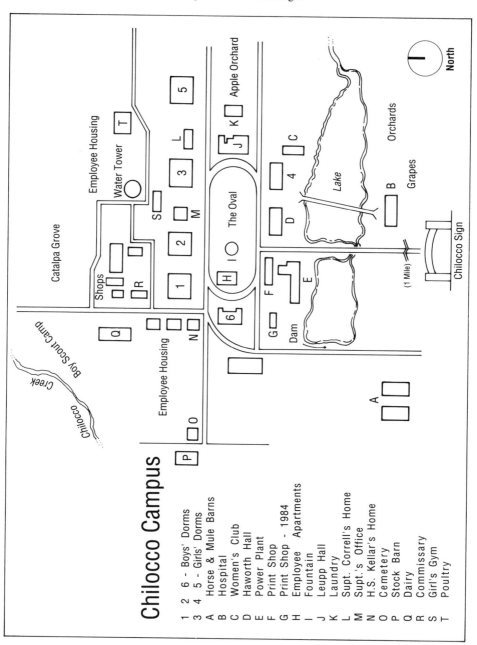

Chilocco Campus

1 2 6 - Boys' Dorms
3 4 5 - Girls' Dorms
A Horse & Mule Barns
B Hospital
C Women's Club
D Haworth Hall
E Power Plant
F Print Shop
G Print Shop - 1984
H Employee Apartments
I Fountain
J Leupp Hall
K Laundry
L Supt. Correll's Home
M Supt.'s Office
N H.S. Kellar's Home
O Cemetery
P Stock Barn
Q Dairy
R Commissary
S Girl's Gym
T Poultry

addition, Superintendent Oscar H. Lipps reported high morale and good discipline in spite of the rigors of the lengthy quarantine and praised Chilocco in a flight of partisan boosterism well suited to the optimism of a new decade: "The discipline of the school has been excellent throughout the year. I doubt if there is an educational institution anywhere that is freer from vice, evil habits and general misconduct than is the Chilocco school."[32]

The First Students

Dusty gray boxes in the federal archives tell us more than the statistics of home construction, student enrollment, and superintendent tenure during Chilocco's early years. Within Emma Sleeth's memoirs, official correspondence, letters from parents, agency reports, and the documentary flotsam saved by conscientious clerks, we catch glimpses of student life before 1920. Occasionally, each source surrenders a fragment of the students' voices.

Emma Sleeth recalled that in her first years of teaching, the children's meals were very meager, lacking even bread. The disciplinarian in charge of the dining room customarily closed his thanks with "Sanctify this food for the nourishment of our bodies." The children learned this grace by heart and one day a boy asked his teacher, "What for he always say, scantify this food for the nourishment of our bodies?" The scanty fare had predictable results, and the teachers were not surprised "very much if it were announced any morning that seventeen had taken . . . leave." Punishment in those days was solitary confinement in the "dark room," where the only light entered through a four-inch square in the door (Sleeth 1906). Emma Sleeth also recalled how one superintendent chose school staff members:

> And the mistakes we made in our early teaching of Indian children. The Indian Superintendent, Dr. W. J. Minthorn, had been a physician in the army, and was a man of indomitable will. In selecting employees for the school, all things being equal, he gave the preference to the Indian and seldom made an unwise selection (Sleeth 1906).

When his selections were not so wise, he dealt with the consequences firmly. Dr. Minthorn placed two Cheyenne students from an eastern school in positions of trust, then learned they were planning a mass runaway among the Cheyenne students. According to Mrs. Sleeth, he called the ringleaders to his office. Telling them to undress, he handed each one a blanket, transported them ten miles out into the prairie and left them. The remainder of those in the plot were sent to

Haskell "where they remained for several years and proved themselves very good students" (Sleeth 1906).

In the early 1900s, Chilocco recruited students for a five-year program. Because transportation was expensive and difficult—a rationale that suited federal goals of separating Indian children from "unsuitable" homes—students could not go home for five years, unless they ran away. Communication with their families was sporadic and slow, even though the school paid the postage to write home once a month. These letters were composed as a class exercise and read by the teachers.[33] As a result, parents in remote areas received little reliable information about the federal schools. Letters from parents in El Paso, Texas, and New Mexico (1903 to 1911) repeated the anxious rumors of boarding-school life that were filtering back home.

Parents in El Paso heard in 1905 that diptheria had struck the school and children had died; who were these children? A mother wrote to ask, is it true all government school children were to be sent home, or, if their parents could not afford their transportation, placed in poor houses? Her concern was sharpened by the report that the children were half-starved and naked, and she pleaded: "And I should like to know this if I send a dollar would you please have my babies picture taken if you will kindly do this let me know and I will send you the dollar to have their picture taken." Closer to home, the Pawnee agent passed along parents' concerns, prompted by close proximity to the school and the firsthand accounts of runaway children. On 22 December 1903, the agent reported that several boys said Mr. E. whipped them, kicked, and struck them while on the ground. "They claimed this was a common occurrence and gave other instances. Two employees of the Chilocco School stated to me that they knew of these things. One of them stated that he had seen Mr. M., on the playground, go to one of the boys, choke him and throw him to the ground."[34]

The Pawnee agent wrote again in 1904. Roam Chief [sic] had a letter from his son claiming an employee had hit him over the head and he was in the hospital. Also, Hiram Good Chief confirmed that he was told by the disciplinarian to "hit the road for home." Mr. Sanchez of Santa Cruz wrote, "What about the big boys getting the best food in the dining room and the little boys getting hardly any? Are the children's letters read before they leave the school?" Occasionally students' letters would be forwarded to the Indian agent in their home district, who could be relied upon to be less sympathetic than their parents. A 1905 letter from a North Dakota agency to a Chilocco student instructed him to stop "whining about little matters"; he had written home complaining of a broken collarbone and not enough to eat. A former student refused to return in 1907: "I could stay there [at Chilocco] if they furnished clothing and good food. I don't like to have bread and water three times a day, and beside work real hard, then get old clothes that been wear for three years at Chillocco [sic]. I rather go back to Cheyenne School."[35] It is impossible to prove or disprove these early charges, some ninety years later, but the conditions cited are documented for later years.

Not all complaints focused on the food or alleged physical abuse. One student wrote to his mother in 1911, "Mama beg papa to bring me home I do not like this darn place and bag [sic] papa to send me money to come home. . . . I will show you where they kicked me on the leg their are two nigers [sic] here." An alumna who went on to become a teacher felt her academic training at Chilocco was quite inadequate. A graduate of the class of 1894, she wrote straightforwardly to the superintendent in 1910 after receiving an invitation to commencement exercises.

> Yes, I graduated from Chilocco after completing about seventh grade work. There had to be a *first graduating* class, and, unfortunately mine was the one. . . . Chilocco has my gratitude for her training in the sewing-room, assistant matron's work and about three years of good, solid class-room work; and this out of eight years attendance. Five years of important foundation work were practically lost—due to incompetent primary teachers. . . . Misses Belle Roberts and Flora E. Harvey, the Arkansas City public schools, Carlisle, Chicago, Colorado Springs and Los Angeles summer schools and the Philadelphia Training School (for Kindergarten and Primary Teachers), deserve much credit for rendering me excellent instruction in Literary work. Am sorry I cannot credit Chilocco with my success—such as it is—but it is my policy to "Take the bull by the horns" and give credit where it is due. With best wishes for a successful commencement and pleasant vacations to all.[36]

Despite Chilocco's strict discipline and literary shortcomings, former students kept up a correspondence with school officials that reveals their attachment to and regard for the school. Students from the first decade of this century wrote to bring school staff up-to-date on their employment, marital and family status, to order fruit tree seedlings from the nursery, or just to express homesickness. A former student wrote in 1908, "I love Chilocco and like my trade and would like to go if you will let me come next summer."[37] C. M. wrote in

November of 1900, "We are all sorrow that we had to come home. . . . I wish I was there today. . . . We raised as nice corn in school as anybody did in our Country. And I am proud of it too. We would all like to goe back to Chilocco School," a sentiment echoed by I. F. in the same year: "I have regretted many a time for having had to leave Chilocco, but it has sure learned me a good lesson. . . . I am still working at my trade (harness maker)." The superintendent also heard from two girls working as assistant matrons in the Indian school at Lawton, Oklahoma in 1903: "The other day as I was reading the *Farmer and Stock Raiser,* it just made me wish I was back there again, I am such a funny girl anyway, I never do realize how well I like a place until I leave it. . . . Annie she cried and is feeling better, I did not cry so I feel worse than ever."[38]

A Hopi alumnus who must have been struggling to make the transition from Chilocco back home wrote from Keams Canyon Agency in 1910, where he was working as an interpreter. "I am trying my best to please my employer and I hope that he realizes it. I am trying to get some turkeys for my Thanksgiving dinner. I wish that I would be to Chilocco to get some of those nice things. How is everybody at Chilocco? I hope fine. Love to everybody, I remain, Yours truly."[39] The search for turkeys was easier than the dilemma facing Apache graduates. A former student wrote from Fort Sill in 1910 that he was working at his harness trade, thanks to Chilocco, but some of the Apaches were having a hard time following their trades because they were being held as prisoners of war.[40]

Some Indian students seemed determined to preserve the relationship with authority impressed upon them in their years at Chilocco. Superintendent Mc-Cowan received at least two letters in this vein in 1904, one from a woman requesting permission to date a "well brought-up" young man at her home agency, another from a former student seeking advice on whether or not to divorce her husband, also a Chilocco alumnus. In the latter case, the superintendent obliged, telling her she was better off without him; he was "more flighty and unsettled today than ever." Other alumni wrote to report their success and express their appreciation of Chilocco: "[I] will have to admit that Chilocco made a man out of me. I am still Barbering, Running a Shop of my own. . . . As for myself, I think Chilocco is the fines' school on Earth."[41]

Chilocco at once appeals to the nature
loving instincts of the Indian child. Here
he finds his heart's desire: open air,
freedom and the open road. It is an
institution of ideals, ideally located. It
stands for character and service, and aims
to train Indian boys and girls, in their
theory and practice, to become
independent, self-supporting citizens.
Superintendent Oscar H. Lipps, 1919

You got up early in the morning and
got dressed, went down in the
basement and had roll call, and
marched to the dining room. And then
from the dining room we went back to
our rooms and we went on our way.
There were schedules all *over* the
place. [Laughter] You had to have a
schedule or you never would know
where you belonged. It was very hard
when I left there because there were no
schedules, there were no bells ringing
and no whistles blowing, I didn't
know what to do. . . . That was one of the
big complaints that I heard from
kids that left Chilocco, especially if
they spent a lot of years there.
Juanita, Cherokee
Entered Chilocco in 1929, age 12

2

'The Fines' School on Earth'

Chilocco framed within its spacious acres a power struggle between white administrators and Indian students, a clash between policy makers' hopes and institutional reality. Superintendent Lipps's lyric "freedom and the open road" beckoned to runaways, judged deserters in monthly AWOL lists. The "institution of ideals" attracted students who valued its training and cherished the friends made there. Lipps hoped to produce "independent, self-supporting citizens," whereas some Chilocco alumni floundered in a social setting with no schedules, "no bells ringing and no whistles blowing." The contradictions that introduce this chapter were created and sustained within the institutional culture at Chilocco, a culture produced simultaneously (if not always cooperatively) through the interactions and oppositions of staff and students. Student experiences and feelings were not, as a rule, tributary to the stream of documents flowing between Chilocco and Washington, D.C. Much of student life was unobserved by and unknown to school staff or administrators.

Our knowledge of student life comes from the personal reminiscences of alumni and employees, whose narratives recall boarding-school culture and society. The Chilocco pictured within these pages approximates reality, an image shadowed by time and the idiosyncratic processes of memory. Nevertheless, prominent themes and mundane daily activities of the 1920s and 1930s emerge clearly when sixty accounts are compiled and compared. Application to school, arrival and induction, dormitory life, agricultural instruction, trades and vocations, home economics, student camaraderie, and rare private moments come into focus. Narrators vividly describe the first few days or weeks of their life at Chilocco: arriving by train and being hauled by wagon under the main entry

arch, a swift initiation in institutional rules and regulations, struggling to over-
come homesickness. They conjure clear images of their Homes, the matrons
and disciplinarians, and above all else, each other. The bonds and rifts among
the students crafted a patchwork of social interaction shaped by family, tribe,
hometown, age, gender, and personality. Students built a richly detailed school
culture within the bounds of federal control: their lives were severely regimented in many ways, astonishingly free in others. Student life changed slowly
from 1920 to 1940 as administrators implemented new policies and reforms in
the boarding schools; narratives and school documents reveal how those reforms were implemented, ignored, or sidestepped at the local level.

In the two decades after World War I, Chilocco grew in plant size, student
enrollment, and employee numbers. As boarding schools across the country
were growing in the 1920s, public scrutiny and criticism of the institutionaliza-
tion of Indian children were also mounting. A new administration in Washington, new leadership within the Indian Bureau, and the scathing critique of
boarding-school education published in the Meriam report in 1928 led to reev-
aluation and reform. The Meriam report marked a turning point in federal educational and social policy for Indians. The project began in 1926, when secretary of the Interior Hubert Work contracted the Institute for Government
Research (funded by private sources) to survey administrative problems in the
Indian Bureau.

Lewis Meriam directed the survey staff in seven months of intensive fieldwork and their report was published in 1928 as *The Problem of Indian Administration,* known since as the Meriam report. Henry Roe Cloud, noted Winnebago minister, teacher, and founder of the American Indian Institute (an accredited high school for Indian boys in Wichita, Kansas) served as Indian
advisor. The survey was to identify what was necessary "to adjust the Indians to
the prevailing civilization so that they may maintain themselves in the presence
of that civilization according to at least a minimum standard of health and decency" (Meriam 1928, viii). The institute compared federal services for Indian
peoples with services for the general population, which were assumed to be the
"practicable ideal" to which federal services should aspire (viii). The general
summary pulled no punches: "[The] overwhelming majority [of Indian people]
are poor, even extremely poor, and they are not adjusted to the economic and
social system of the dominant white civilization" (3).

The survey staff examined on- and off-reservation boarding schools and
found "itself obliged to say frankly and unequivocally that the provisions for

the care of Indian children in boarding schools are grossly inadequate" (Meriam 1928, 11). The government was feeding children on an allowance of eleven cents a day, when recognized nutrition standards for growing, healthy children recommended thirty-five cents. As the report noted, these children were not healthy, and health care was inadequate by any medical standard. The discipline of the schools was merely restrictive, not developmental, and did not encourage individual expression or responsibility. Finally, the positive role of these schools as industrial and agricultural training grounds was mitigated by a number of insufficiencies. The report suggested that the Indian Service should devote its energies to social and economic advancement so that Indians might be absorbed into the prevailing civilization, *or* that they might be fitted to live in its presence, on their own terms, at a minimum standard of health and decency. As radical as the idea of the federal government allowing Indians to live on their own terms seems even today, we should not overestimate the survey staff's cultural liberalism.

The survey staff assumed that within three generations Indians would be prepared for modern life and believed that the "Indian problem" would work itself out in thirty or forty years:

> The belief is that it is a sound policy of national economy to make generous expenditures in the next few decades with the object of winding up the national administration of Indian affairs. The people of the United States have the opportunity, if they will, to write the closing chapters of the history of the relationship of the national government and the Indians. (Meriam 1928, 51).

Educational reforms inspired by the Meriam report and mandated by commissioner of Indian Affairs Collier and directors of education Rhaods, Ryan, and Beatty had to be implemented by local school personnel. Chilocco is well suited for the study of the local impact of new federal policies because its work force was so stable. Policy implementation or avoidance is not obscured by a high turnover rate among administrators and staff. Superintendents Blair (1920–26) and Correll (1926–52) worked with a loyal "employee family" headed by three principals: Ray Heagy, W. Keith Kelley, and Ernest Mueller. Many employees and their families lived and worked at Chilocco throughout their tenure in the Indian Service, as the following list shows (Bradfield 1963, 11):

Rose Daugherty	38 years	Carrie Robinson	29 years
Henry Hollowell	37 years	Ensley Morris	26 years
Pearl Colglazier	36 years	Kay Ahrnken	25 years
Claude Hayman	36 years	Lizzie McCormick	25 years
Sam Lincoln	35 years	Frances Chapman	24 years
Emma Antone	30 years	West Toineeta	23 years
Ray Colglazier	30 years	Ray Heagy	20 years
Vivian Hogg Hayman	30 years	Argot Knudsen	18 years
Roy Trost	30 years	Ernest Mueller	11 years

Many of these employees appear in the alumni narratives of the next few chapters; at least four (Daugherty, Toineeta, Lincoln, and Chapman) were Indian, although that did not necessarily mean better relationships with students, as the men's reminiscences about the tough disciplinarian Sam Lincoln attest. Rose Daugherty set up a little basketball court in the basement of the small boys' dorm, and she is remembered affectionately by many. West Toineeta was supervisor of repair carpentry in the trades division, and Frances Chapman directed the print shop. Lizzie McCormick, non-Indian head matron of the girls' dormitories is a strongly prominent personality in the women's narratives, and several of the teachers (the Colglaziers, Emma Antone, Kay Ahrnken, the Haymans, Ensley Morris) are mentioned by alumni.

School personnel benefited from the stable leadership of one superintendent from 1926 to 1952, and from Meriam report reforms such as pay raises, upgraded living quarters, and more stringent hiring guidelines. In the 1930s, the retirement of certain employees gave Superintendent Correll the opportunity to hire employees responsive to new policies, which John Collier directed from the Central Office. The student body benefited from changing enrollment procedures and a shift from elementary grades to junior and senior high school education. Students were, more and more, coming to Chilocco as young adults (rather than as young children) with a maturity and desire for education that motivated their adaptation to institutional living.

In Anticipation

Children applied to Chilocco Indian School when they could not attend public schools, because of depression era hard times for large families, or to continue a family tradition. Educational choices were restricted in Oklahoma in those days. Many Indian children who attended Chilocco in the 1920s and 1930s came from isolated, rural communities where public schools were unavailable or unfriendly. Chilocco may have been the only option, especially for junior or senior high school. The Great Depression motivated boarding-school attendance for a majority of the alumni interviewed:

Noreen 1923/12 Potawatomi:
At that time, the three oldest girls went to Chilocco. My brother went to Haskell. It was a case of economics, actually. And of course in this little town that we lived in, Washunga, Oklahoma [which is no more], I don't even believe there was a school there, it was just a little teensy country town north of Kaw City, Oklahoma. * We only went [to Chilocco] because my folks couldn't afford to send us to public school. I think that was one of the criteria then, that you had to be in that sort of position to go to a government school. So, in a way, it's a good thing it was the way it was when *I* went, because I couldn't have afforded, my folks couldn't have afforded to keep me in clothing, like that.

Hubert 1940/18 Choctaw:
Well, we were living on the farm out in the country, it was kinda, a poor family trying to get an education, and Dad decided they had to send us to a boarding school, it'd be cheaper on them.

Irene 1929/15 Potawatomi:
I had never really been around Indians, maybe one family until [Chilocco]. I was one out of ten children, and of course in 1929 it was a bad year, I think that's the year the banks closed. Up until then we were doing alright and then it came that if, myself, and my sister younger than I, would go to Chilocco, they could manage [at home].

The 1929 economic collapse made life tough for intact, two-parent families; it was devastating for single parents trying to raise children and for families who had taken in orphaned relatives. Chilocco enrolled many children from single-parent or guardian homes.

Curtis 1927/9 Creek:
I don't think [my mother] *wanted* us to go, it was a question, she had three kids and she couldn't support us. They had us in a children's home in Wichita at that time, my brother and I, my sister was seven years younger than I, she was too young to go [to Chilocco] and that was all my mother

could handle, was the one child. And she didn't feel that that Children's Home was the proper place for us, so [she] sent us [to Chilocco].

The economy was not the only force pushing children toward boarding school. Parents or guardians turned to boarding schools for temporary relief in case of illness, invalidism, or unemployment.

Albert 1926/13 Cherokee:
In September 1926 why I boarded a Midland Valley train en route to Chilocco Indian School at Arkansas City. My sister and my brother and I, I think I was about twelve years old, and the reason we went up there, my mother was invalid that summer, and there was no one to care for us. So Chilocco was really a blessing for them, they got rid of us pesky kids. [Laughter]

Parents, guardians, and heads of families were not the only ones making application to boarding school. Intellectually curious children and adolescents wanted to go to school, especially high school, or they wanted to escape excessive discipline or responsibilities at home. Older sisters fed up with child care or older boys fed up with farm labor might apply without their parents' knowledge.

Ellen 1927/13 Creek:
TL: Did your parents want you to go to Chilocco so you could finish up your education?
No, not really. They didn't say anything but everytime they went to church somewhere, we'd go, and missed a whole lot of schooling. So my sister, my half-sister, and I decided we'd like to go [to Chilocco]. We didn't say nothing to my parents, and one day . . . we were in town so we went up to this lawyer's office, we didn't know where to go, you know. We went up there and asked him if he'd ask for application for us for Chilocco. . . . and our applications came back, so then we told my dad, we had an application to go to school. So when we went to town again he took us to the Indian Agency office and he filled 'em out for us and sent it back in. We were accepted. And we *went*.

Edward 1932/7th Cherokee, and *Rachel* 1929/4th Cherokee:
[Edward and Rachel married after graduation]

Edward: Well, my first impression was that I didn't want to go. But, my
mother had passed away. I remember getting in [to school] late in the evening . . . and they told us to go in and eat. It was a hot day, I thought it
was just foul smelling in the dining room, not at all appetizing.
Rachel: Now see, he went there with resentment. . . . He was critical
when he first went in. He didn't feel lucky like I did. My older brothers
had gone the year before I did but they ran off. I loved the school, and I
couldn't go to school at home. I was the oldest girl so I had to take care of
the younger ones. I *wanted* an education.

Once a family began a tradition of going to Chilocco or Haskell or another
Indian alma mater, younger siblings and younger generations looked forward to
their own school experiences. Of the fifty-one alumni interviewed, forty-one
had relatives who attended Chilocco: thirty-seven attended with contempor-
aries (siblings or cousins), nine were members of the second or third generation
at Chilocco, and three alumni sent their own children to the school.

Charlie 1934/14? Cherokee:
My father's family was about eight or ten and the grandparents died when
some of 'em were still young. They sent those younger brothers and sisters to Chilocco, and as we came along [the next generation] it was a sort
of a family tradition, everybody goes to high school up there. . . . Another thing, it came along about the depression time and in those days,
there wasn't any school buses and we lived twelve miles out. You either
had to find a ride, which in those days were scarce, or room and board in
town. So the logical thing was to go to Chilocco, since all the family had
been up there.

Even for the families and individuals who applied to Chilocco because of the
perceived benefits of education there, things did not always turn out as planned
or hoped.

Florence 1933/7th Choctaw, and *Maureen* 1931/14 Choctaw.
Florence: The reason we attended Chilocco . . . it was my mother's
thinking that we would have some educational advantages there that we
could no longer have at home.*

TL: How come your parents only sent the two of you [and not your two
younger sisters?]

Maureen: Well, I don't think that my mother was really too impressed with the way we turned out. We came home singing Indian songs, and doing little Indian dances and she said, I thought I sent you kids up there to be educated, and get civilized. 'Course we didn't grow up in an Indian environment anyway. [My parents] tried to make me stay home my senior year, but I didn't want to. So Florence went two years and I went three. I wanted to go back to my buddies.

Many schools in the Indian Service coerced families and kidnapped children to maintain student enrollment levels. The *Rules for Sending Children to Schools* issued by the Indian Bureau in 1917 outlawed some of the strategies used in earlier years to obtain students: "Hereafter no Indian child shall be sent from any Indian reservation to a school beyond the State or Territory in which said reservation is situated without the voluntary consent of the father or mother of such child," or the legal guardian. Guardian consent had to be made in the presence of the agent and verified by sending a certificate to the commissioner. The guidelines continued: "And it shall be unlawful for any Indian agent or other employee of the Government to induce, or seek to induce, by witholding rations or by other improper means, the parents or next of kin of any Indian to consent to the removal of any Indian child beyond the limits of the reservation."[1]

Involuntary recruitment by coercion or starvation was not necessary at Chilocco in the twentieth century. In the Indian Territory, education was by and large a desired commodity. The Cherokee, Creek, Choctaw, Chickasaw, and Seminole nations were removed to Indian Territory in the early 1800s, where they built their own schools and seminaries. Tribal education continued until the tumultuous years before 1906, when the state of Oklahoma was created. At the turn of the century, tribal governments were dissolved and their schools closed for lack of funds. By the early 1920s, Chilocco had more applications than it could handle. In 1922, the superintendent reported an enrollment of 75 above the school's capacity of 550; an additional 350 eligible applicants were denied admission because of lack of space.[2] Admission guidelines clearly delimited the scope of the Indian population that Chilocco was designed to serve. Students from Oklahoma, Kansas, Mississippi, and Iowa were admitted to Chilocco, whereas students from other areas, students over twenty-one, and those of less than one-quarter Indian blood had to obtain special permission from the Central Office. Policy restricted subsidized education for those of mixed blood,

Table 8. Restricted and Unrestricted Students Enrolled at Chilocco School, 1919–1920

| | Restricted | | Unrestricted |
	Full-bloods	One-halfblood or more	
Cherokee	58	21	7
Chickasaw	9	11	0
Choctaw	85	16	0
Creek	48	8	3
Seminole	13	1	0
Total	213	57	10

Source: RG 75 E4 B11/Records of the Superintendent: Correspondence F/Letters, 1919–20, FRC.

and the occasional students of less than one-quarter blood who were accepted had to pay tuition.[3]

Changing admission guidelines for *unrestricted* Indians complicated student recruitment in Oklahoma between 1910 and 1930. In the wake of the Dawes Act land allotment to individuals and the dissolution of tribal governments, two classes of Indian citizens were created in the state. Individuals classified as *restricted* maintained their legal status as wards of the federal government. They had limited control over their own financial affairs and were eligible for various benefits granted by treaty, such as education for their children. *Unrestricted* Indians were judged competent to handle their own affairs and were awarded legal independence from federal wardship.

The judgment of legal competency basic to unrestricted status was linked in the ideology of the times to racial classifications, that is, to the degree of Indian blood. Full-bloods were less likely to attain unrestricted status than mixed bloods, but the designations *restricted* and *unrestricted* were complicated by many factors beyond race (as a perceived or claimed designation). Level of education made a difference, as well as the racial status of one's spouse. In the conflicts over census taking to establish tribal rolls before allotment, some families resisted enrollment because they resisted the dissolution of communal landholdings. Others enrolled as racial entities, full-blood or mixed blood, that had more to do with their political opinions or desire to manage their own financial affairs than it did with their biological heritage. Guidelines for the enrollment of unrestricted children, that is, children of Indian blood who were not wards of the government, were published in 1920 as follows: "Only Indian children who are wards of the government may be enrolled at an Indian school supported by gratuity appropriations free of tuition. An unrestricted child is required to pay $200 a year, or $20 a month."[4] (see table 8 for the numbers of

57

Table 9. Percentage of student enrollment at Chilocco School by degree of Indian blood, 1924–1950

	4/4	3/4	(%) 1/2	1/4	<1/4	Total No. of Students
1924–25	54	9	22	11	4	954
1929–30	43	6	26	19	6	1,082
1934–35	31	17	26	25	1	754
1939–40	28	19	26	26	1	746
1944–45	32	20	28	19	1	418
1949–50	64	9	20	6	0.4	805

Source: RG 75 E 5a B38 F/201.17, FRC.

restricted and unrestricted students enrolled from the Five Civilized Tribes in 1919.)

Federal policy directed Chilocco to educate restricted Indians, full-blooded or close to it, who were felt to be most in need of a civilizing influence and training for agricultural or skilled labor in the rural environment. Accordingly, enrollment regulations specified, "The Chilocco school is maintained by the government for restricted Indian children, for those of one-half blood and more, and preference is given to full bloods who do not have good school facilities at home."[5] The number of full-blood students however, barely exceeded 50 percent in the mid 1920s, declined to 31 percent by 1940, and did not increase until the institution of the special Navajo program in the 1950s (see tables 9 and 10). The Central Office mandate for enrollment at Chilocco simply did not correspond to the demographic realities of eastern Oklahoma. The difficulties lay not only in the definitions of *restricted* versus *unrestricted,* or *full-blood* versus *mixed blood.*

Enrollment policy defined "school facilities at home" as a public school within two miles of the home. This arbitrary perimeter ignored or overlooked the racist realities of rural Oklahoma. In 1920 the commissioner of Indian Affairs questioned the enrollment of 424 Chilocco students who were judged to live within the two-mile radius of a public school. Superintendent Blair pointed out that his pupils were often older than the white students in their grades and were too timid or ashamed to go to class with them. He observed, "There is a sentiment in many localities in Oklahoma unfavorable to the enrollment of the Indian pupils in the same school with the Whites." It was difficult to secure attendance at home schools, and some students never went to school as youngsters but entered Chilocco at a late age in order to get industrial training not of-

Table 10. Enrollment at Chilocco School by degree of Indian blood for Five Tribes, 1926

	Full-blood	Mixed blood
Cherokee	102	157
Chickasaw	17	39
Choctaw	62	45
Creek	43	51
Seminole	14	9
Total	238	301
	24%	30% of total student enrollment

Source: RG 75 E4 BI6/Records of the Superintendent F/1925–26, FRC.

fered in public schools.[6] Chilocco administrators continued to enroll mixed blood students from Oklahoma communities despite the policies preferred by the Central Office in Washington.

During the 1920s, enrollment gradually shifted to older students as administrators sought to minimize Chilocco's role in the education of very small children. It was felt their educational needs were better met closer to home, although young orphans and children from broken homes were accepted until the late 1920s. Chilocco's industrial, agricultural, vocational, and domestic curriculum was intended for older children and young adults ready for employment and independence after graduation. Enrollment in grades seven through ten more than doubled in the five years from 1920 to 1925.[7] By 1922, students under the age of fourteen were encouraged to enroll in schools close to their home agency (with the exceptions noted above, made by petition to the commissioner in Washington), and about two-thirds of Chilocco's students were in grades seven and above. Guidelines for admission published in June of 1926 stated that Chilocco would "accept students here between the ages of 12 and 21, who have at least one quarter Indian blood and who are enrolled in an agency."[8] Students in the lower grades were often significantly overage and thus suited for vocational training: 18 of 39 children in the third grade were fifteen or older; 46 of 67 children in the fourth grade were fifteen or older; 41 of 75 children in the fifth grade were sixteen or older, and 32 of 67 children in the eighth grade were eighteen or older.[9] After the Meriam report, Chilocco phased out the lower grades, one year at a time. By the mid-thirties the school offered high school and post–high school instruction only (Bradfield 1963, 112).

By 1930, federal policymakers preferred that the public schools educate American Indian children. Despite this explicit policy preference, the Great

Depression placed special demands on the nation's educational system to which Indian schools were not immune. Director of Indian education Will Carson Ryan, Jr., had to postpone his vision of the demise of boarding schools. He wrote to L. E. Correll that high unemployment levels necessitated the removal of as many older students as possible from competition with adults in the labor force. Ryan maintained his belief in keeping young children at home, despite pressures to enroll them in boarding schools, and reiterated his commitment to vocational training for Indians:

> I believe we shall have to reverse our policy and admit practically all eligibles who apply and be more liberal in our interpretation of eligibles, even though it means overcrowding, in order that we may hold these youths out of the competition with labor in the present emergency. This is believed to be much better than taking in large numbers of small children—a policy that has been urged upon us recently because of unemployment and bad financial conditions generally. To take older boys and girls, who would otherwise be competing in the labor market, does not have the same disastrous social effects that taking little children does. . . . A more liberal policy of admitting older youth brings with it certain obligations that we must not overlook: (1) We must be surer than ever that we give these young men and young women training that will really fit them for their future needs as workers. . . . The risk of inculcating dependence—always a serious one in the Indian work—is especially bad under present conditions, and every experiment in developing responsibility for earning and spending wisely will be vigorously encouraged.[10]

Chilocco staff tried to attract students to the higher grades. By 1938, applicants had to be a graduate of the eighth grade or eligible for the ninth grade. Applicants below the ninth-grade level who were sixteen or older made application for the special vocational course. Generally, students at Chilocco could not be younger than thirteen or older than twenty-five (application of older students had to be approved by the commissioner of Indian Affairs). Finally, every application had to be approved by the appropriate agency superintendent and submitted with a physical certificate filled out by a doctor (*Chilocco: School of Opportunity* 1938, 21).

Federal administrators effected many changes in policy and practice in Indian education in the 1930s, but job training remained a constant. Chilocco's annual report of 1934 notes:

The object of Indian secondary schools is to offer training in occupations requiring specific skills which will be of use to Indian boys and girls in making a living, especially on their own reservations or in Indian villages or communities; to provide them with information and activities which will equip them to appreciate and perpetuate those elements of Indian culture which hold real values for the present and future generations. . . . in accordance with the commissioner's requirements that, "Indian schools be made more serviceable to Indian communities and reservation life."[11]

Chilocco was reaffirmed as an agricultural and "vocational training school for Indian youth of one-fourth or more Indian blood, who have completed eight grades or the equivalent, or who have the maturity and the ability to profit by the courses offered."[12]

Arrival and Induction

Arrival on campus and first impressions of the school are vivid and immediate Chilocco memories. The "mature and able" young people who arrived in the early fall were struck by the size of the campus, the crowd of hundreds of young Indians from dozens of tribes, and the speedy induction into military discipline. Intense homesickness ameliorated over time, but the first few weeks tested students' stamina, perseverance, and attachment to home and family. Most runaways made their break in September and October.

Barbara 1928/12 Cherokee/Pawnee:
Three of us went [to Chilocco] but we all ran off. [Laughter] I'm the only one that came back and stayed. . . . Even though I was from a large family our disciplining wasn't too good, we more or less did as we pleased, and I learned a lot about discipline after I got to Chilocco, because I was so homesick. . . . I was just so homesick, I guess everything was different, too. Also I hadn't been around Indians much, that was all new. * I was so homesick that, there was a big clock on the wall and I was looking at this clock and I'd say, how many minutes in an hour? [Laughter] And how many hours in a day? And how many days in a month? And how many months before I get to go home?

Maureen 1931/14 Choctaw:
I don't remember the first day, exactly. We went up on the train with a few more Indian students from Ardmore, Oklahoma. I remember them meeting us at the train station there, and taking us out to the school. Well, it

was all very strange because we hadn't been away from home before. I guess one of the earliest recalls I have was of the homesickness I had after I'd been there a few days. At the beginning of every school year they innoculate you, and they lined us up just like they do in the Army, I used to say, like cattle, and I remember I had five innoculations. * And I was so homesick, and sick, I just thought I would die. That's one of the earliest things I remember. And another early memory was of being finecombed, for lice. I had never had lice but I guess some of 'em did, they pulled long tables out in the basement, they put white sheets on 'em and they'd make us stand there. They had a little metal comb and it had short teeth, real fine teeth. I didn't have a permanent, but some of those Indian girls had that coarse black hair, big heads of hair standing out like that, I used to feel so sorry for them, but they'd find a few lice, at the beginning of every season. Thank God they did that, because if they hadn't we'd all had 'em.

Children reacted individualistically to the stress of separation from family and home. Those who came with siblings of the same sex seemed to fare best, but strict segregation by age and gender limited sibling support. Younger sisters entered different dorms, or Homes, than older sisters, and the literal No Man's Land surrounding the girls' dormitories separated brothers from sisters.

Noreen 1924/12 Potawatomi:
TL: So did you go down by train?

No, my father drove us. Sad day! [Laughter] All piled in the car, and Mom and Dad in the front seat, and it was . . . early fall, you know. 'Course we were already enrolled, all this stuff was taken care of ahead of time. But what a sad parting that was! To leave your mother and father, at that age, you know. And, drop off into a strange place, it looked so forbidding with all those brick buildings. Sad day.

TL: So did you and your sisters stay together, did they put you in the same Home?

Well, my sister[s] Clara and A. and I went to the smaller children's home for the first year, Home 3. So A., Clara, and I went at the same time but of course we were separated from A. in the second year when she transferred to Home 4, which was another tragedy, I thought, at the time. [Laughter] * You were just brought in and dropped there, and they didn't allow you any time with your parents or anything. You're in school and

that's it. And of course you could only keep the clothes you had on. * My
main trouble was sleeping . . . that's when I get the loneliest, you know.
The lights would go out, and quiet, you had to be real quiet. And then you
would think and you would just get so homesick, oh! dear! Homesick is
really sick. You can get really sick from it.

Albert 1926/13 Cherokee:
We got to Chilocco about six o'clock in the evening, my first time away
from home, and it was a brand-new experience for me . . . I recall . . . it
was dark when we got on Chilocco proper. . . . And they took us to what
I later learned was Home 4. I promised not to say anything hateful, but
[Laughter]. . . . the matron of Home 4, which was the older girls' home,
had us in there. My sister was only nine years old, and her first time away
from home, and she was crying, and she cried and cried and cried, and I
wasn't gonna leave. The matron tried to get me to leave, and I was the
only one there with my sister, and I felt protective. Well, finally I left; naturally I didn't stay all night [in the girls' dorm], but I went over to Home 2
[the boys' dorm]. . . . The first thing [in the morning] I did was to go
back over and try to find my sister, see whether they kidnapped her or
what. I wandered into Home 3 where she had been transferred, for the
small girls. And Miss Robinson met me at the door and I thought she was
gonna hang me because there was an imaginary line about halfway between Home 3 and Home 2, and boys don't cross, or girls don't cross. It
was highly segregated, and it was sort of like murder if you crossed over,
but anyway, boy she jumped on me, up and down, and thought I was Jack
the Ripper, I guess, [Laughter] trying to sneak in Home 3. She let me go,
at least, I went back, and that was my most vivid *first* memory.

The alumni who contributed to this story all attended Chilocco at least a year,
and after describing their initial homesickness, they discuss how they came to
grips with that homesickness and adjusted to the school.

Winona 1930/10th Cherokee:
I was a little bit frightened, because I'd never been away from home, and
well, just the *idea* of being with the Indians frightened me a little bit. But I
was very glad that I had my sister and brother and younger sister with me
there. . . . I didn't know what to expect, and . . . well, from the beginning, you know, the regimentation is another thing that we were quite re-

sentful of, [also] the clothing, government issues, *but* coming from a poor family, it was good that we had those clothes. . . . I was resentful of the regimentation, but it didn't hurt us, it didn't hurt us at all! [Laughter] It took awhile to get used to it, oh and we wanted very much to go back home, we didn't want to stay. And even wrote to my father and he said, well if he could at all make it possible, that by the second semester that we could go back home, but it only took us about three weeks to a month until we became acquainted with the different ones, and we adjusted quite easily.

An intense camaraderie, born of shared experiences, united students in affection and loyalty. The dominant social relations affecting student life centered in the peer group. Family relationships, important at first, were soon equaled by the close bonds of friendship that knitted the student body together in a complex web of support and mutual respect. Alumni say of their boarding school friendships, "We were a family." The importance of those bonds emerges from peoples' earliest recollections of Chilocco.

Irene 1929/15 Potawatomi:
My . . . sister [and I] went in and she was put in one Home and I was put in another one . . . the only time we saw one another, we'd cry. *

TL: Do you remember the first day, going in?
    That's just something you don't much forget [Laughter]. Well, just like I say, we had never been away from my parents and we were a big family and we were close, because of the large family. And fortunately I got into a room with some *lovely* girls, they were older than I was. See, I entered the tenth grade and one of 'em was in the eleventh grade, and then two seniors. This eleventh grader [it] was her first year but her sister and the other senior had already been there, so they could kind of help us, you know.

Verna 1916/16 Cherokee:
The first girl that I met was Mary . . . and let's see, the first day or so I was there, they put me up in the [large] dorm room . . . then the next day, why, Mary came up and asked Miss McCormick [the head matron] if I could come and room with [her]. So, I got adopted out. [Laughter] . . . Yeah, came down from a big old dorm down to three bed [room], I

couldn't imagine why in the world Mary came and asked for me to room with 'em. She said, "I just like you." Three days [she had known me], "I just like you."

The first impressions of alumni remembrance are vivid vignettes of life with dormitory personnel and other students, the drudgery of everyday work details, and the regimented schedule of daily life. In the next narrative excerpt, Curtis recalls his arrival at Home 2.

Curtis 1927/9 Creek:
Well, [my brother and I] went to Home 2, which was the old building, and where the young kids were. And the disciplinarian, they called 'em disciplinarians then, later they called 'em advisors, but the disciplinarian at Home 2 was a man named Lincoln, he was an Otoe, *great big* fat man, Oh Gad! he was a big guy. And of course everybody called him, behind his back that is, "Hippo." He was a big rough, tough man. And he took us into his office and explained the rules and regulations very succinctly: [Laughter] what you were expected to do and what you were expected not to do, and that was it. Then they put us in the dormitory, and we were practically on our own. They had a matron at the Home, and she was Indian. I can't remember her name now but she was a sweet gal.

Matrons and Disciplinarians

Matrons and disciplinarians organized Chilocco students through military protocol. Dormitory personnel appear prominently in alumni reminiscence, much more so than academic or vocational teachers. Despite the considerable influence of dorm staff on the students, the guidelines for their hiring were not very restrictive. The 1927 Civil Service Examination for Matrons specified that applicants for the position of matron had to meet the requirements in at least *one* of the following groups:

A. At least six months training in any three of the following categories: institutional work, child welfare, social service, home nursing or visiting nurse, home management or general housekeeping, domestic science, general cookery, family sewing, care of children, or teaching.

B. Six months successful experience as a matron in an institution.

C. Completion of one year's course of training in normal school.

D. Completion of one year's course of training as a nurse in nursing school.

E. Completion of one year's course of training in home economics.[13]

An applicant was "qualified" to supervise several hundred students based on six months experience in general housekeeping, home cooking, family sewing, and child care; in other words, with no special training at all other than caring for a small family.

Students had to make a difficult transition from family life to the military, mass discipline in the boarding school where the closest thing to parents were the matrons and the disciplinarians. Student perceptions of matrons and advisors ran the gamut from extremely negative ("I was as afraid of my matron as I would be of the devil today") to positive affirmations of friendship, or at least mutual respect. The reminiscences of female alumnae, followed by those of the men, highlight the variety and complexity of interpersonal relations and individual decision-making in the boarding-school environment.

Florence 1933/12? Choctaw:
I don't think that I would have *encouraged* really, a surrogate parent. Some of the kids needed that and that could have been helpful, but no, I don't think anybody who would have been capable of that would have ever been hired, as a matron. They just had to be the coldest. . . . I would think probably if they had a way to measure a mean streak, [Laughter] the meanest one got it! Now . . . some of the older girls did develop friendly relations, just good friends, with some of the teachers, a Home Ec teacher, for example, but I've never heard of anybody who became friends with one of the matrons.

Winona 1930/10th Cherokee:
The matron(s) *had* to be strict, they *had* to be strict, because there were some girls that . . . hadn't had a lot of training, and . . . some of 'em were just a little bit mean. They had to be real strict and as I think back now, really, nothing really hurt that they did but they were very, very strict on us. We just had to . . . stand direct . . . and we had to be inspected for our clothing and all like that because I'm sure there would have been people up there that wouldn't have kept themselves clean had they not been inspected. . . . But I think back now, and really there was not any of the things that really hurt us, and I believe that it made really a lot, (made) us more self-reliant people. * I don't remember that the matrons were people that you could, if you had really a problem, that you could have gone and talked with them, now there may have been some that did, but I never felt that I could have confided in them.

Vivian 1929/14 Choctaw:
But yet, you know, in those kind of places . . . they tried to take the place
of your home life but they can't . . . they can't touch everything, they
can't touch that personal, individual. My last year there, they began to
call us in, certain age groups, and our matron would read to us. She
wouldn't *talk* to us, about, you know, sex and things like that, that's the
first time that I ever heard that mentioned, and that was just about two,
three months before I left. You know all those years it should have been,
kind of mentioned, and discussed with the girls, but it wasn't. But there's
always something lacking in that kind of a, well it was just an institution,
[Laughter] that's what it is. . . . They just didn't have anyone we could
go to. We missed out on that part, you just had to learn from one another.
Which was a bad way, 'cause we learned by the grapevine. [Laughter]

The negative assessment of the matrons' characters and capabilities by the
preceding narrators are balanced by a kinder view. Just as there were girls who
could find no meeting ground with the dormitory staff, there were girls who
could sympathize, even ally themselves, with the matrons' positions. The girls
selected as matron's assistants or officers, however, did not often compromise
their loyalty to their peers. Flora had a good relationship with the head matron,
but it was not enough to persuade her to tell tales on her classmates.

Flora 1932/17 Creek:
When we first arrived, the matron showed us first to our rooms. Then that
first evening, the head matron, Miss McCormick, laid out all the rules. I
guess I adapted pretty well, by my second year I was a group leader, and
assistant to the Captain. I never told on a girl though. I left that up to
them, if they had done something wrong, and I never had any problems
with my group. I felt it was better to be put on your own initiative, your
own responsibility. If you were too stern, and there were too many reprisals, they wouldn't like you. So I did alright, Miss McCormick even
complimented me on it. . . . I got along with her fine. It was really an individual thing, it was easy to be good there, and it was easy to be bad, too.
Some girls didn't feel so free, or get along so well with the matrons, but
some of us did. You know, Miss McCormick asked me once, why didn't I
tell on the girls if they had done something wrong? And I told her, she
ought to talk to those girls individually, then they wouldn't be so scared of
her. If a girl was being punished, she could talk to Miss McCormick and

Miss McCormick would listen, but so many were just too scared of her. I told them, she's a nice lady, she's easy to talk to. . . . I think she was a very fair woman. If a girl had difficulty with her, a lot of times it was the girl's fault, she did something wrong that she knew she shouldn't do, or she somehow failed in her communication.

Alice, who was employed at Chilocco after her graduation [her husband, not a Chilocco alumnus, was an academic teacher] reiterates the value of loyalty. She refused to "carry tales" to the school administration throughout her years of employment.

Alice 1925/7th Cherokee:
But you know when you sit and listen to the girls tell their hard luck stories, and they're blue and down and out, well the thing that I didn't like about that, if they told you something in confidence, they asked you not to tell it, you was supposed to write it up anyway, and send it in. If they talked to us, just come in and wanted to talk to us, we was supposed to write that up, and send it in. Well, I'll tell you I didn't do it and I got more criticism on that. And they [the school administrators] would say, I know you counseled with a girl, I saw you in that room, but you know, I'd say, it wasn't important, it wasn't important. It just didn't strike my fancy to do things like that. Because I just couldn't tell, because they trusted me. I wasn't going to tell anything, and I was a grown woman then, but I still didn't believe in that. If it was an argument between two girls, I would write that up, but not just one girl, just feeling bad and low down and feeling like the world was against her, that's bad.

Miss McCormick, the head matron, stands out in many women's memories of dormitory life. The range and disparity within student responses to this one individual indicate the difficulty of making generalizations about key facets of boarding-school life.

Noreen 1923/12 Potawatomi:
The only time you saw your, talked with your matron was in a disciplinary area, you see, so you didn't *love* your matron [Laughter] too much. . . . They had a matron over where A. was, her name was McCormick but everybody called her "Broom," she was tall and 'bout that wide [holds her hands about eight inches apart] all the way up and down and very, *very* thin woman, and *very,* very strict. And she was always puttin' people in

48

the, we called it the guardhouse, it was actually just a room in the building but you were locked in and fed very meagerly for punishment. Luckily, I never had her.

Irene 1929/15 Potawatomi:
Have you heard the name Miss McCormick? She was my matron. [Laughter] And she, she was good, I, I appreciate what she done for me and I've heard a lot of people that went there, especially as she got older, that oh! go like this when they mention Miss McCormick, but it was a better school when Miss McCormick had her authority with it. So I appreciate that, I was glad it was, I was from a good family and, I was happy to be among good rules and I knew what it was to be disciplined.

Sally 1932?/12 Quapaw:
Well Miss McCormick did take an interest in me, and she did take an interest in knowing certain girls [Sally's husband, Bob: She was Catholic, too.] She was a Catholic and I was a Catholic. . . . But she did take an interest in some of the girls.

Cora 1929/12 Cherokee:
Everybody was real good to me, while I was there. And Miss McCormick, was my house [mother] over there at Home 5, and she was always good to me. * But you know, the funniest thing, I've thought about it so much. The day before I left she called me down to her office, through the intercom, and wanted to talk to me. So I went down there, and she told me her life history. . . . I won't tell it, because [it was] personal things. . . . She said, "Cora, I think you'll do alright, because you've always got along with the girls and everything," and she said, "[you] seem to enjoy life so much. And then she told me her life, and . . . I said, "If I'd a-knowed all of this beforehand I would have felt a lot different for you." "Yeah," she said, "but I was always afraid to get close, you know," but [she] said, "I wanted to tell you this before you left."

The central figure in the women's narratives, Miss McCormick, is matched in the men's narratives by Harry S. Kellar. Kellar is described in as equally varied terms as Miss McCormick.

Ira 1936/? Cherokee:
Old Man Kellar, he called me in one time, I'd been smoking, course I smoked from the time I was very small, and he gave me a good fatherly lecture and I always appreciated it. I let it go on through [Laughter] but, he meant well . . . but I never really had any difficulty with him because I had a hard time talking to adults or, to teachers or anything like that, express myself. I know one time this supervisor docked me two days on my plot because I'd gone to the wrong field, when I went to gather corn. I don't know now how much that cost me in money but I never gave him an excuse or anything like that, I just let him do the talking 'cause he was an adult, and I was a kid. * But all in all, I don't have any complaints. I think they were a little dense when it came to dealing with kids and their needs, either that or they were callous enough not to know.

John 1931/16 Chickasaw:
They used to call Kellar "Black Panther." He was always pretty fair. I mean if you had an argument, and presented it without any kind of animosity why then he would listen to you but if you went in there belligerent, you would remember it. [Laughter] So I always kept pretty calm, and one time . . . [I had] some demerits, give you a little red card with five demerits on it. . . . So I went in with mine one day and tried to talk about it. I explained the whole thing to him. . . . [I had been in the dorm and] . . . somebody come in and hollered at me, said the tank's running over. So I got clothes on and started out the door. . . . I got my shirt on and taken off out there, and [the matron] hollered, "Where you going?" Said, "I'm going out." That's all I told her, I kept on going. . . . The next day or two, Kellar called me in and tell me, how come I was so rude, or whatever it was I did. And so then I used what eloquence I had [to explain]. [Laughter] He said, "Oh, sometimes they don't know what they're talking about."

Other narrators portray Kellar as a rough and rugged ex-Army man who went out of his way to ferret out wrongdoing, often precipitating intentional rule breaking. He is described as a "snoop," taking his field glasses to the top of the watertower to spy on boys around the campus. A few alumni had extremely adversarial relationships with Kellar, and they remember neither fairness nor kindness. The men are not the only source of disparaging comments about Kellar.

Juanita 1929/12 Cherokee:
I couldn't stand that man [Kellar]. . . . I don't think he liked Indians, he used to sit up in the balcony [during the social dances in the auditorium], and blow that whistle . . . you know, you had to dance this far apart. Boy, he'd blow that whistle and you had to sit out the rest of the dance. If he thought you got too close. Or if your hand went a little too, your hand had to stay right here, like this. [Laughter] The end of each dance, those boys sometimes couldn't resist, they just kind of hugged you, you know, just not really a bear hug, and [Kellar] just couldn't stand it.

In recalling their home life at Chilocco, the men also remember the matron in Home 2 and an assistant disciplinarian, both of whom were Indian.

Curtis 1927/9 Creek:
[The matron in Home 2] she was a good cook when it came to rabbits and squirrel, and that type of thing, and of course she *loved* fried rabbit and fried squirrel! And we'd go out and bring in a whole mess of rabbit and squirrel, and then she would cook it, in her apartment there in Home 2 . . . feed us and then the rest she'd keep for herself.

Albert 1926/13 Cherokee:
Home 1 and 2 was boys, 3 and 4 was the girls. And Home 2 was the small boys' dormitory and that's where I was, but you got the little guys down there looked like they should be in kindergarten. I remember some of 'em didn't seem like they were even old enough to go to school. We had a real fine matron, we had a matron and a disciplinarian, I guess his name was Sam Lincoln, an old Otoe fella, and Mrs. Daugherty. . . . She took care of the laundry and the housekeeping, she was an overseer of the housekeeping duties. And she was really a fine, she was [a] *little* gal, but boy she could slap you down that hall! [Laughter] She was great, though. We bathed ever[y] Wednesday, and she had in the laundry room . . . everybody had a little box about this big and every Wednesday they had a new pair of underwear and a towel in there, see, but it [the room] was big enough to where she could put little homemade basketball goals up at each end, and we all had little basketball teams and we played basketball down there on Wednesday nights. She was, I won't say that she was motherly because you can't hardly mother three or four hundred boys at once but, she was kind, but she was firm. And she didn't take much guff. Why she'd crack them big old boys around and she had a firm hand but

everybody liked her. But Lincoln, he wasn't the most popular guy. He was an old full-blood and I guess he went to school, well I don't know how far educated he was, how far in school he went, but he used to get mixed up with his [words], he had a language problem. Such as . . . the building was heated with steam, and they had the steam pipes, they were insulated and covered. All the plumbing pipes went through what we called a muster room. . . . and they had roll call every morning. It was kind of like a play room, really. But the guys were hanging on those pipes and they were pulling the insulation off of 'em, so he [said], I'll always remember his statement, "You want to hang yourself, go out and hang on them trees!"

L. E. Correll

The quality and character of the superintendent, who wielded great authority and influence at a school Chilocco's size, made a real difference to students and staff. L. E. Correll was superintendent at Chilocco from 1926 until his retirement in 1952. He came to Chilocco as an agriculture teacher and remained dedicated to Chilocco's agricultural instruction. The participants in this research concurred unanimously in their positive assessment of Correll's leadership, a testimonial to his commitment to students and the school. Alumni references to Mr. Correll, either as short asides or more detailed accounts, all share a positive tone. He is described as Chilocco's "driving force," "wonderful," "a fine man, we called him 'Dad' Correll." No doubt his position as superintendent insulated him from some of the resentment students felt toward the matrons and disciplinarians who regulated their lives day-to-day; he could assume the stature of a benevolent but somewhat removed father figure. It doesn't seem likely that hierarchy alone, though, could have shaped such a positive assessment by students. Louis and Charlie recall Correll's recognition of individual students, his openness to student approaches, and his willingness to offer assistance when requested or needed.

Louis 1933/14 Cherokee:
And Mr. Correll was the superintendent at that time, and he was a person who took an interest in *all* the students. He made it a point to be personally acquainted with, I'd say the majority of the kids. Especially any student that was outstanding in any way, he made it a point to really know those students, and he did everything he could to help kids that wanted to go to college, to go on. I know he was a great help to me.

Charlie 1934/9th Cherokee:

Mr. Correll, the superintendent, I didn't appreciate it at the time, because I knew nothing about finance, budgets and all that stuff, but he had a personal interest in every student. And I've walked into his office when he had stuff scattered out all over the [desk]. At that time I didn't know what it was all about, but in later years, when I've had to do the same thing [as a school principal] [then I appreciated it]. But he never was so busy with his finance and budget, that he didn't put it aside and (talk to you). . . . And you know, that filters down through the rest of your employees too, when you have one like that at the head. If you have [one] at the head who is weak, and doesn't have that devotion, why, that feeling also infiltrates.

Correll was quite particular in his recruitment of staff who would follow his lead and contribute to the stability of the institution. He made every effort to employ married couples, finding positions for both spouses. Since employees lived on campus, he felt married couples brought a more permanent and home-like air to the school.

Laurie 1938/Employee, Home Economics instructor.

Yes, yes, we [lived in] houses on the campus, and then they had a women's club, and the men's club, and when I first went there, I stayed at the women's club, because [my husband] didn't come in until a year later. Mr. Correll brought him in. They liked to have couples. He said they were more stable and all, so he brought [my husband] in, too, and we were there fifteen years. So it was a wonderful experience, really.

Superintendent Correll believed strongly in the social and developmental advantages of athletics, and sports were an important part of student life at Chilocco. He took a personal interest in the individuals who excelled in sports, and Cecil, a Golden Gloves [amateur] boxer at Chilocco who went on to a professional career, recounts one of the trips the Chilocco boxing team made accompanied by Correll.

Cecil 1929/? Creek/Euchee:

I know that when we went to Boston, why Mr. Correll [and the coach] took us. [The coach] and Mr. Correll and J. M. and M. L. and I went to Boston. We drove up there. . . . It was [exciting], golly we went to all the historical places that you could see going up, and coming back. . . . Boy, it was something to walk down those streets, because we're walking

53

down the street, you know three in a row, walking down the street, and then people would see us coming, [Laughter] kind of give us the whole sidewalk.

The next two narrators offer another perspective on Correll's relationship with his students. Curtis and Edgar belonged to one of the gangs of young boys at Chilocco, and they had a lot of contact with the superintendent on a disciplinary basis. They recall Correll's approachability despite the distance imposed by his authority, his interest, and his fairness, particularly compared to the boys' advisory staff.

Curtis 1927/9 Creek:
Correll was a very fine, very fine man. I always thought he was one of the few people there that really had an interest in the kids. He knew what we were going through, and he had a lot of empathy. You could not get very close to him, because he kind of kept aloof but he *knew* what was going on, and if you were really in trouble, and he could help, he would, and did. He was very fair, some of 'em were *not* fair, the disciplinarians and the advisors. Kellar, he was an S.O.B. from the word go, but Correll was a good man.

Edgar 1929/10 Creek:
L. E. Correll was very distant because he was kind of, you know, someone that you didn't see very often. But L. E. Correll was a very warm person. He didn't enjoy a close relationship with students, because I think for the simple reason, like in the service, you don't fraternize. But later on, afterward, I also found that L. E. Correll was . . . a very magnanimous person . . . he loved Indians. . . . L. E. Correll was a very, very wonderful person. Nelson Rowe, of course, was the one really close to us, and Harry S. Kellar, we thought he was *meaner* [Laughter] than the devil himself.

Male students knew Correll much better than the girls, who did not have the same opportunities for acquaintance with the superintendent because they were closely confined and supervised by the matrons. There was some contact with the superintendent, and Marian begins her recollection of Correll with her feelings toward him as a student. He was instrumental in advising her on her further education and career choice. She goes on to describe her interaction with him as an employee; Marian taught at Chilocco for many years in the academic department.

Marian 1934/18 Creek:

I think he realized he was our last post of hope. I can't put that feeling in [words]. As a student, he always knew who I was, when there were nine hundred there, and I marveled at that. . . . Of course we were coming up in the time when a man was head of the house. I think that was *why* we *all* looked to Mr. Correll as a father. A male figurehead. He was all of it, even if he wasn't but five-four. But he was a man with giant shoes. And he, well, he just exemplified what you would want in a father. A caring father. A doing father. But the girls were hard-pressed for something. Then when I finished . . . my ninth year with the public schools, I realized there were many students, at Chilocco, that needed my help. So I filled out my application for the bureau schools and I was hired. . . . While I worked for [the bureau], my husband made his application for the bureau, and his first offer came from Mr. Correll. So he went to Chilocco . . . and at the end of his interview, Mr. Correll asked him if he were married, and he said yes. He said, "Can you tell me something about your wife," because it took a special kind of people to live in that type of environment, and everybody lived on the campus. You were the family, for the children. So he told Mr. Correll, he said, "Yes, I married one of your girls." And so [Mr. Correll] told my husband, "You go home and get your things." He said, "I will make a place for Marian." * [Superintendent Correll] lived on the northernmost end of the houses at Chilocco. Every morning, I mean, *every morning* he came down the back alley, he slapped everybody on the shoulder because he was walking. . . . They saw him *every day;* he wasn't gone for weeks and weeks to a training. He wasn't gone, when you called that office, he'll not be in today or he won't be this, I don't know if the man was ever sick. He was about his business. And the memory of him, can't help but bring tears to your eyes. Tears of appreciation. And tears for loss, of one human being that meant so much to so many kids.

Archival sources corroborate Correll's personal involvement with students. In the 1930s, Correll pressed the commissioner of Indian Affairs to partially compensate a Chilocco athlete injured in a tragic automobile accident. In January 1937, the van carrying the basketball team "ran into bad roads, mist and fog which soon turned to ice. Six and half miles south of Kingman they had to cross the Santa Fe tracks. Couldn't see train in the fog, and they were hit by the Santa Fe No. 49, running between Kingman and Ponca City." One student was killed instantly and an employee died soon after arrival at the hospital. Three boys were treated and released, while W. C. lost his left leg below the knee.[14] Correll requested an educational grant from the commissioner so that W. C. could attend Oklahoma A & M College. After two years of Correll's insistence, the Office of Indian Affairs finally provided "from three hundred to four hundred dollars per year for W.'s schooling."[15]

Narrative and documentary sources agree on Correll's commitment to the "Puritan ethic," and to the value of agricultural work in "individual character building" (Szasz 1977, 380). Alumni recall their perception of him as an approachable adult, sincerely interested in their future and willing to help. His presence at Chilocco for over three decades undeniably shaped the character and quality of the school, but even the superintendent could not make an institution into a home.

Home Life

Students arriving at Chilocco met the discrepancies between institutional life and family life at every turn. Military discipline entailed a high level of surveillance of students but constant adult supervision and control was impossible. The high ratio of students to adults and the comprehensive power wielded by those few adults compromised any flowering of surrogate parenting. In the dormitories, four adults might be responsible for over two hundred children. The loss of the parent/child relationship and the attenuated contact with school personnel reinforced bonds among the students, who forged new kinds of family ties within dorm rooms, work details, and gang territories. Dormitory home life—siblings and peers, living quarters and conditions, food and clothing, response to discipline—dominates narratives. Mealtime at Chilocco is a story unto itself.

The logistics of food preparation and service challenged the school budget as well as the disciplinarians. Lizzie McCormick, head of the girls' advisory department for many years, planned the meals. Whatever her qualifications as a matron, Miss McCormick was not an inspired menu planner. Bland and boring menus alternated between hash, beans, and stew, with few (and seldom fresh) fruits and vegetables. When Miss McCormick retired, superintendent Correll appointed Flora Maloy to direct the school kitchen and dining room. Meal quality improved dramatically, as the cooks used more of the fresh produce, dairy, and poultry products produced by the school.[16]

Students tackled the monumental task of preparing meals three times a day for over a thousand people. They labored over ninety-gallon copper and aluminum kettles, three large steam vats for pots and pans, four-by-nine-foot gas hot plates, and huge cast iron skillets. Labor-saving devices included electric potato peelers, food grinders, a food chopper and mixer, and giant can openers. Two cooks and two dining room matrons were assisted by sixty girls in the morning. The portions of food required for any one meal were staggering. Breakfast called for seventy-five pounds of oatmeal or cereal, or thirteen dozen packages of corn flakes. Dinner or supper where meat was served required 350 to 400 pounds of beef, 240 chickens, 175 one-pound cans of salmon, or 25 ten- to twelve-pound hams. Eggs were not served frequently, but when they were the cooks needed 85 dozen. In one meal, students could consume 60 gallons of milk, 180 two-pound bread loaves, 6 to 8 bushels of apples, and 200 pounds of jello. In one week, the kitchen went through 16 cases of eggs, 5,000 pounds of flour, 1,000 to 2,000 pounds of sugar, 150 pounds of salt, 1 barrel of pickles, and 400 pounds of fat (*Indian School Magazine* 1932, 19).

In the dining room, military discipline could not replace direct adult supervision, and the chaos at the table shocked new students. The administration resolved the problem of being "shut out,"[17] described in the following narratives, by integrating boys and girls at the dining room tables in the early 1930s. Noreen recalls that every meal began by the students singing grace.

Grace before Meals

MORNING GRACE:

For sleep and comfort through the night,
For strength and joy with morning light,
For food and friends and gracious care,
And all that makes the day so fair,
We thank Thee, Lord, and humbly pray,
That love may guide our steps today.

NOON GRACE:

Noon has come with peace and cheer,
In the home we love so dear,
Swift and bright the days go by
While our pleasant tasks we ply.
And for all Thy bounty's store,
Lord, we thank Thee ever more.

EVENING GRACE:
Father, evening shades are falling;
Busy, joyous day is done;
Thanks and love we bring recalling
All Thy care from sun to sun.
And when days no more are given
Pray we may be Thine in Heaven.
—*Chilocco: School of Opportunity,* 1938

Noreen 1923/12 Potawatomi:
Boys on one side, girls on the other, matrons sittin' in the middle, at a high desk, to watch. The older girls went clear to the back of their girls' section and . . . if anybody was absent then they'd move us younger girls up into these places so that *all* the tables wouldn't get messed up, I guess! [Laughter] Which was kind of nice in a way, 'cause once in awhile I'd get to see my older sister that way. . . . You kind of sang the grace and then everybody sat down at once and started right in. [Laughter] The food was horrible . . . it was *terrible*! Yeah, hardtack, you know, and stuff like that. But we wouldn't always have hardtack, sometimes we'd have bread. Course Chilocco had its own bakery . . . and it wasn't too bad. It was tasteless, but it was at least bread. And we'd make sandwiches, out of *beans* and, beans [Laughter]. * You had to eat fast because [the matron] *tapped* that bell, you started to eat and when she tapped that bell you had to quit regardless. And then the boys marched out first, all the girls watching 'em and if you found a guy you really liked, you might wink or wave [Laughter] you know, so nobody'd see you doing it. . . . But, that was the ritual, and then you marched out according to your company. * Now and then a little mouse in your milk pitcher, a little dead mouse. And in the hardtack, if you'd crack 'em open, you know how that hardtack is you might find some extra protein there, because there'd be a few little worms in there. [Laughter] Oh we had to be so careful, I wasn't so squeamish then as I am now. But, even those sights would make you slightly ill. . . . We'd have a kind of a stew, once in awhile, I suppose cooked vegetables, potatoes and carrots, onions. The boys I suppose must have been raising those vegetables and things. But never a fresh vegetable, never a fresh fruit, always lots of dried apples, apricots, and raisins, and made into pies that didn't have anything to keep 'em together. Still be dry, tough piecrust but that would just happen once a month, you'd have pie.

Almost every Sunday you'd have what they called cake which was really bread, we used to make cheese sandwiches out of it, 'cause you'd have cocoa, Sunday evening you had cocoa and this cake they called it, sliced cheese. But we used to make sandwiches out of the cake because it was more like just bread. The cocoa always tasted good, it would never be sweet, and it'd be very diluted, so you got some milk that way.

Francis 1931/16 Cherokee:
And the kids had no manners at all, on their eating, it was shocking. You would get "shut out," they'd grab it all up and trade, sometimes they'd keep it all, especially dessert. I like to starved to death. There were two brothers there, H. E. and C. E. They got to feeling sorry for me so they would go by the bakery and steal me some bread, then go steal honey from the beehives, and feed me hot bread and honey. I would also go to the dairy barn to get milk, get up around four in the morning and go help the dairy boys with their chores, so they'd give me all I wanted. After awhile, they split us up in the dining hall and put us in with the girls.

Students found ways, by hook or by crook, to eat reasonably well despite the shocking manners of their peers at an institution dedicated to the civilization of its inhabitants.

Curtis 1927/9 Creek:
When I first went to school there, I was horrified at the way they ate. They sat you down at a table about six or eight to a table . . . and they put the food on and then they blew a whistle, or rang a bell or something. . . . Rang a bell, I guess that was it, they rang a bell, and you started, then you were supposed to eat. If you weren't *fast* . . . about the first three days I almost starved to death, because I'd sit there and they'd ring this bell and by the time I looked up, the food was all gone, they'd just reach out and grabbed it. One guy'd grab a bowl of the oatmeal, and the other guy would grab something else, and somebody else would grab something else, and then they would split it up amongst themselves, and trade off, and if you didn't grab something, you were just out of luck, and you didn't eat! After about three days of that, why then I learned very quickly that if you wanted to eat there, you had to be fast. Then later, they changed that system, whereby you ate family style and . . . they had waiters on the tables. . . . Those fellas all went in early, before the meal, they ate *first* and . . . so I quickly realized that, if I wanted to eat regularly

and not have to grab for everything I got, my best bet was to get to be a waiter
. . . that was just an extracurricular duty, and for that you got to eat!

Edgar 1929/10 Creek:
And we used to sell our cakes, this was real common practice, sell our cakes
and pies. I owe you so many cakes and so many pies, I bet you and I didn't
have any way of paying you so I'll give you a cake, maybe two cakes, or I'll
give you two pies. So . . . on Sundays, you got pie, boy, these were bets you
paid off [Laughter] . . . you didn't welsh on any of these.[18]

Serious complaints about the food at Chilocco diminished when Flora Maloy
introduced a varied and nutritious dietary plan. The school bakery worked to
capacity, baking bread, cakes, pies, and rolls, and the kitchen staff used fresh
produce from the farm, dairy, and orchards.

Maureen 1931/14 Choctaw:
When I first went there, I don't remember too much about breakfast, I
think we had oatmeal, which I didn't eat because I've never liked oatmeal. And we had something with syrup, which I didn't eat. And if we
had beans . . . tonight we had beans, what was left over tomorrow at
lunch. And then we had mutton stew or hash the next night and then we
followed with lunch the next day. That was the first year. I don't remember whether Flora Maloy came the year I was a junior or senior,
but after she came the meals were really good, balanced, variety. She
was way overdue, or somebody in her capacity. I admired that lady
very much.

In describing dormitory life, Chilocco alumni remember the lack of privacy,
inspections by the matrons and student officers, the emphasis on cleanliness
and orderliness, close friendships, and solidarity in the face of administrative
authority. Girls lived in Homes 3, 4, and 5 in ascending order of age and grade,
under constant supervision. They could play only in their yards and could not
roam Chilocco's large campus as the boys did. A line invisible to the eye, but
not the mind, divided the campus between the girls' dorms and the boys' dorms,
each off-limits to members of the opposite sex.

Florence 1933/12? Choctaw:
I remember that . . . *one* Saturday a month was Trunk Day. We were permitted to go into the basement, the room where our luggage was stored,
and be there for a limited amount of time, and you could handle your

things. Well, it wasn't [just] things like your civilian clothes that were packed there. . . . Just maybe like something you'd make in school, maybe a picture you'd drawn you'd wish you could send [home], well, half the time you wouldn't have a stamp, you didn't have an envelope. It wasn't handy but you'd keep the things you treasured in there. . . . You didn't have a *drawer,* you didn't have a room, you didn't have a shelf, all you had that was actually private was [only] accessible then for maybe a short period once a month. * We slept in what we called barns. The bigger girls, lot of times, just had two to a room, three to a room maybe, but our so-called barns were a ward of maybe eight or twelve beds, and one of the rules that was most strictly enforced was that you were *not* to be in anybody's bed but your own, fearful of masturbation, I assume, or something. 'Course bedtime was very early, in the wintertime, you weren't really sleepy and we used to pull the blankets over to the side and push a couple of beds together, and tell ghost stories and so on and so forth. [Laughter] And of course if you got caught, and we *did* get caught at times, that meant that you were going to spend Saturday or all your free time on your hands and knees, scooting up and down those halls, shining them, shining the floor. I was as afraid of the matron as I would be of the devil himself today. But what reminded me of this rule about the beds, it was cold there, and the first year I was there, I had made friends with a Yuma girl. . . . On the occasion of the first snow, it was cold, and the snow, where I thought it was pretty, it scared her, she was literally, really frightened, and shaking. Well, with our lack of language, all I knew to do, when Susie whimpered and cried and shook, was to hug her, which she understood. I think I could communicate to some degree at least, that snow is a natural phenomenon, it's going to stop, you know. Anyway . . . I remember the both of us being caught and being called into the office, and *lectured,* and all the things we were lectured about we didn't have in mind, you know at all, but it was one of those things that just make you think that there was a lot more so-called discipline than there needed to be! [Laughter]

Home 1, Home 2, and Home 6 housed the boys at Chilocco. Home 2 was the oldest building on campus, the "Light on the Prairie" constructed in 1884. It was home for the youngest boys in the 1920s and 1930s. Home 1 housed the older boys; the senior boys lived in the newer Home 6.

Curtis 1927/9 Creek:
They had different size dormitories in [Home 2]. The largest one, of course, was for the youngest kids, and that's the one that we went into. I can't remember exactly but I would guess there must've been forty or fifty beds in there. * Then they had smaller dorms where they had fifteen, twenty in one of the dorms which I went into later, and then they had smaller ones there that had as little as seven or eight. Of course the older you got and the more responsible you became in their eyes, the better accommodations you got. And they had one room where there were two guys in it, and they were head honchos, for the students. * You had a footlocker and you kept your personal belongings in that and of course you had to keep it locked but that didn't deter anyone. They'd knock the locks off, and if you had anything of any value, it didn't stay long, somebody would get it.

Charlie 1934/9th Cherokee:
They'd come by and inspect your room every day. And . . . that was part of your training, keep that room shining. They came by and inspected every day, and if it didn't meet specifications, why Saturday afternoon when everybody else was off, you found yourself working somewhere, so it didn't take long for us to learn that room had to be spic and span. * I think after I left there they got to where they didn't have any discipline, that's when it started downhill. I went back there a year before the place was closed, and my heart was broken to see the lack of cleanliness, orderliness. The hallways when I was there was spit and polish, you could see yourself. The hallways in the dormitories when I went back there, just before it closed, filthy, down in the corners don't look like they'd been cleaned out. Writing on the wall, filth, broken mirrors, broken windows, I couldn't believe it.

Many alumni today share Charlie's dismay at Chilocco's deterioration in its final decade. The contrast with the spotless, immaculate school of their youth may reinforce the nostalgic glow of childhood memories. In any case, Chilocco's verisimilitude of home life depended on student labor and production in the fields, shops, laundry, and kitchen. Labor and life were strictly sex-segregated, and it was truly the case that neither a man's nor woman's work was ever done.

We offer all the courses necessary to make our race independent and worthwhile. Our broad acres produce valuable crops. What is left of our prairies graze pure-bred cattle. In our shops we learn the industries of the white man whose civilization we have adopted for our own . . . The Indian wigwam, the Conquistadors and most of the prairies are gone. The little creek still runs, and our school will go on for many years a light and a guide to the Indian youth of Oklahoma.

Chilocco graduate, 1927 *Chiloccoan*

3

'I Could Always Plow a Pretty Straight Line'

Vocational education was part of a broad social movement at the turn of the twentieth century to refashion the home, school, and workplace. Activists and social scientists like Jane Addams and John Dewey saw in vocational education an opportunity to fit industry to the needs of the workers. Industrialists and corporate planners saw an opportunity to construct workers according to a blueprint of production requirements (Kantor and Tyack 1982, 28–30). Modern educational historians have viewed vocational education as part of an upper-class movement for social control and social order in a corporate state (Kantor and Tyack 1982, 3–4; see also Willis 1977). They contend that vocational education was designed to produce docile, efficient workers. Vocational education in Indian schools is a case study supporting the educational historians' arguments.

Educators with preconceived notions of the capabilities and needs of Native Americans have for centuries promoted a particular *type* of education variously called manual labor, industrial, agricultural, or vocational training. Indian school "industrial" education did not mean training for urban, mass-production, factory-style industry, but small-scale, individual craftsmanship in harness making, blacksmithing, printing, carpentry, masonry, and other trades. The conception of industrial education for Indians ran counter to developments in mainstream America. Cremin (1980) focuses on the textile and shoe industries in his discussion of the opposite trend in American society, away from craftsmanship and apprenticeship to mass on-line production. He notes that this transformation was well under way by the 1860s, nineteen years before the first off-reservation boarding school for Indians was built.

Federal Indian education maintained a rural orientation long after the white

American work force had shifted into employment in large factories. By 1919 in states east of the Mississippi River, nearly three-quarters of all workers labored in factories with less than a thousand employees, and 30 percent worked in factories employing a thousand or more (Kantor and Tyack 1982, 17). As late as the 1940s, Indian schools stressed mechanical and construction trades suitable for farm life, small-town living and local service industries. The idea of an "appropriate" education for Indians fit educators' preconceived notions of racial minorities' "appropriate" place in American society, as manual laborers supporting America's agrarian economic sector. This educational philosophy emphasized the nuclear family as the basic economic unit and eschewed higher academic or professional training for Indians (or enfranchised blacks; see Adams 1977, Anderson 1978 and 1982, and Armstrong 1883). Industry meant instruction in the rudiments of civilized living, especially the hard labor necessary to serve the most civilized elite, and anticipated the integration of native people into Euro-American economic and political systems. Training in manual skills, agriculture, crafts, and industries constituted the synonymous processes of civilization and conversion that had begun in early European missions. Catholic historian Van Well (1942) portrays Southwestern Spanish missions as large industrial and agricultural training institutes, whose function was almost purely educational, in a broad sense.

Chilocco in the 1920s and 1930s was the flagship federal school for agricultural instruction and it epitomized "appropriate" industrial training for Indians. Throughout the 1920s, Chilocco students spent half their day in academic classes and the other half on work details, in vocational or home economics classes, or in trades labor. If a student went to class on Monday morning, he or she would work that afternoon and the next morning. Academic classes resumed Tuesday afternoon and continued through Wednesday morning, and so on through the week (the schedule reversed in alternate weeks). During this decade the school maintained a junior and senior high school program with academic courses in English, math, science, and social studies (Chilocco graduated the first senior class in 1926); vocations in agriculture; nearly a dozen trades for the boys; and home economics instruction for the girls. The half-day policy was scrapped in 1929 because of criticism of how the drudgery of work details dominated student time. The new three-quarter-day plan allocated 50 percent time to academic courses; 25 percent time to art, music, physical education, and extracurricular activities; and 25 percent time to vocational work. The three-quarter-day plan was implemented first in the lower grades, whereas agricultural students continued to spend half their time on the farm, and postgraduates devoted up to 75 percent of their time to their trade (Bradfield 1963, 113). In addition, four small vocational classes (average enrollment of fifteen) were reserved for overage pupils or those "unable to make satisfactory progress," who found academic work "tedious or difficult." These students, designated as slow learners, were placed in the "opportunity" class, where they spent one-quarter of their time in academic work limited to the fundamentals in arithmetic, English, and social science. The rest of the day they worked.[1]

Despite policy pronouncements, Chilocco alumni do not report any substantial reduction in students' work responsibilities. In all instances, memories of work details far outstrip academic recollections in number and detail. Narrators indicate that the "productive" labor necessary to maintain Chilocco in the 1930s was more extensive than federal policy dictated. Congressional appropriation did not keep pace with inflation or policy needs, and school superintendents could not relinquish student labor on work details as readily as some might have wished.

The work detail seems too literal a translation of Bourdieu's "pedagogic work (PW), a process of inculcation which must last long enough to produce a durable training, i.e. a habitus" (1977, 31). The durable training that the federal government had in mind stressed speed, efficiency, and a willingness to follow orders. Chilocco's Annual Report of 1934 sets forth the goals of the trades and industrial department:

When an Indian boy arrives at one of the government schools he has been accustomed to doing the things which he likes to do, he has had plenty of time to work as slowly as he chose, and to follow the dictates of his own fancy. Vocational education of the modern type will teach the Indian youth the value of time, it will eliminate the fault that many have contracted, that of "puttering around" a job, he will be taught to follow instructions carefully, and finally, he will realize for himself that speed and accuracy are essential for vocational success.

Vocational training of the type offered at Indian Boarding Schools should prepare Indian youth for effective citizenship more efficiently than any other method known. Indian youth is naturally shy and timid and needs to come in contact with tradesmen, tools, materials, and processes . . . in order to make the adjustments necessary for social efficiency.[2]

A Man Needs a Trade

Chilocco boys could pursue printing, commercial baking, butchering, construction and repair, masonry, painting, electrical wiring, shoe and harness making and repair, power plant maintenance and plumbing, or general mechanics. These choices were dictated by the logic of "appropriate" education defined by the dominant society and by the economic necessities of maintaining a large institution. James Haworth had foreseen in 1884 the productive possibilities of Chilocco's fields and shops. "Under the management of the right man, and properly sustained by the Government and agents from whose agencies the children are sent, it will not only be successful but in a few years help very materially in its own support."[3] The amount of material produced by student labor was astonishing: twelve boys in the bakery each week produced 2,000 loaves, 2,000 buns, 900 cinnamon rolls, 220 pies, 900 cookies, 900 slices of gingerbread and cake, and 1,800 pieces of cornbread.[4] The laundry annualy processed 475,000 towels; 98,000 sheets; 35,000 shirts and tens of thousands of nightgowns, pillowcases, bloomers, and long underwear.[5]

W. N. Hailmann, Haworth's successor as superintendent of Indian Schools, praised the industrial schools' training in 1894 because it "affords an opportunity to inculcate respect and even love for work . . . [and] it relieves the monotony of the literary schoolroom exercises. . . . In many cases, however, the farm and workshop are carried on more as a matter of business, that is, for the pecuniary results of the labor rather than as a matter of education."[6] Congressional appropriations never met Chilocco's financial needs, and the school had to depend on student labor and sales of surplus production.

The survey staff of the Meriam report compared the per capita rates established by Congress to support federal Indian boarding schools with per capita rates of state and private boarding schools, and the federal schools suffered in the comparison. For years the Indian Service maintained their per capita rate of school support at $167 per year (see table 4, chapter 1). Indexed to the rate of inflation from 1900 to 1926, the per capita cost by 1926 should have been $375, when in fact it was near two hundred dollars. The only state Indian school with per capita rates available in 1927 cost $610 per student per year, and the lowest cost private boarding schools charged about $700 a year, which did not include transportation or clothing. Per capita allocations for Chilocco for 1929 were projected at $225 per student.[7]

Every trade taught at Chilocco contributed in some way to the maintenance of the institution. Much of the work subsumed under "trades training" could fairly be called drudge work, with little or no educational value. Despite this reality, federal educators maintained that Indian schools prepared Indian youth for effective leadership and a productive role in the American work force. Chilocco's superintendent offered the following rationale for vocational education in the Annual Report of 1934:

> Very soon the Indian child grows up to become a man in all respects except his means of earning a living in a society where the language of the dollar is better understood than any other. Vocational training will fit him to earn a satisfactory living with all of the accrued benefits to society, neither does such education hinder the Indian boy or girl from pursuing his education farther if the time and the means are available.
>
> Indian youth is very similar to the youth of any other race so far as the human qualities are concerned, but on account of his home environment he is handicapped in making adjustments to our modern society. . . . [These] children are left with no parental examples to follow in choosing a vocation and with little essential information with reference to what occupation would be best for him to choose.

In lieu of parental guidance, upperclass students received advanced training in the trades and industrial department. In the lower grades boys were rotated through the trades departments, so they could choose their area of specialized training as they matured. Curtis and Francis describe the trades at Chilocco and the sampling process.

Curtis 1927/9 Creek:
They paid you a stipend for working during the summer months. . . . I got 25 cents a day for cutting grass all day long. At that time I worked in the butcher shop, and a man named Hunt ran that, very nice man, was very good to me. And part of his duties were to take care of the campus and the lawns and so forth, and that was part of my job. I had the old reel type push mowers and I'd mow grass all day long, it was a never-ending job. * When I was nine they assigned me to the butcher shop, and I learned to cut meat. Mainly I went out to the employees' homes every morning and took their orders for meat, and they bought their meat through the butcher shop. Everything was self-sustaining there. . . . They had to pay for it but it was relatively inexpensive. * I worked in that butcher shop two or three years at least, and then when I got big enough I went into painting. . . . I took that as a trade, and that was more or less

because I was not big enough yet to go into carpentry, which I wanted to be in. So I was in that about a year, and then I was old enough to take carpentry, and I went into the carpenter shop. . . . But all the kids contributed in one way or another, they all took some kind of a trade.

Francis 1931/16 Cherokee:

I worked for six weeks in the butcher shop. I didn't like it so I went to the superintendent and told him I didn't like all those sheep and hogs. So then I was put over in the horse barn. We had to get up early and feed the horses, clean the stalls. It didn't take too long and I'd had enough of that, I was there for six weeks and asked for reassignment to the shoe and harness shop. I should have stuck with that. Later on I bought a shoe shop in town. I had that a year and made good money. Anyway, after I was in the shoe and harness shop for six months, I was walking over to the dining hall one day and met these two carpenters, each with a double handful of doughnuts. They said they would get something like that everytime they did a little work over there. So I went to the superintendent again, and said this job (shoe and harness) is too confining, I'd like to do carpenter work, repair work. Mr. Toineeta, West Toineeta was our overseer on construction, I mean, repair. Learn repair, he said, anybody can build something new. He talked real broken English. So, we sanded store fixtures, out of the show room, and fixed chairs; those wild Indians were always breaking up chairs and tables. [Laughter] And we fixed doors, and windows. About that time, they had what they called Special Vocation Program, where you would quit school, the academic part, and only take vocation. I had drafting class, arithmetic, and spelling, and then we'd go back to work; we put in 4,800 hours. I did that and spent three summers there. I decided I needed a little iron work so I went to work as a blacksmith for six weeks. I learned how to bend iron and make welds with a forge. There was no electric welders at that time. Then I went back to the carpenter shop, and I stayed there for four years, aside from my time on the rockpile.

Although the dirty work was delegated to the young boys, the older boys in the trades assumed a great deal of responsibility for directing the younger students. Federal policy makers achieved their goal of producing self-sufficient, self-directed workers, but not quite in the way they may have planned. Students learned from each other as much, if not more, than they learned from the appointed trades instructors. The older students developed leadership and work skills in the niches of opportunity provided within the trades.

Coleman 1937/14 Delaware:
The first year I worked at the print shop, we did nothing but clean those little mats that they use for type. We used erasers, he'd bring out a whole boxful of erasers and we'd clean the black off of 'em. And that was *that* and oil down the, wipe the oil off the press, that was the only thing he'd allow us to do. [Laughter] And we wanted to learn to print and all, so the second year we got to work on the presses and all of those things, so I was going through some of my stuff about a year ago and I found one of those cards I printed, way back in those days. Old English type printing.

Charlie 1934/9th Cherokee:
On the days that we were working [in the bakery] instead of going to school, in the morning, one of us would get up at three o'clock and go down, mix up about four hundred pound of flour, mix the dough for the bread that day, put it in a trough, and let it be rising. When we all got there at eight o'clock it was ready to work up and make into bread. And then we made all the cakes, pies, cookies, rolls, what have you, during the day. We fed those thousand students bread and pastries. And we learned a lot of skills, too, that I used a lot of mine, later. Like when I was going to college, I . . . did some baking, helped supplement my income, and I worked two years in between college. . . . By the time they were seniors, why, they could pretty well supervise, lead the younger ones. And I presume that was the way in all the shops; the younger ones learn from the older ones, in each shop or department . . . whether it be carpenter or baker, or candlestick maker. [Laughter]

In retrospect, Charlie gives Chilocco credit for the good use he made of his trades training in later life. Alumni value the school as the place they "learned to work." They believe the attitudes and skills associated with working hard, and working well, in whatever field, did carry over strongly into adult life.[8] Although the majority of alumni look back favorably on the skills they learned at Chilocco, few continued their trade career as an adult. Of the twenty-one male alumni interviewed, five continued their trade. Of those five, four were employed by the school and they spent the majority, if not the entirety, of their working life at Chilocco itself.

Regardless of policy shifts in Washington, appropriate education for Indian

71

children was invariably construed as vocational. When newly appointed commissioner of Indian Affairs John Collier instituted post–Meriam report reforms and required that "Indian schools be made more serviceable to Indian communities and reservation life," Chilocco administrators responded by working out "courses which are primarily for vocational training, supplemented by the necessary basic school subjects."[9] The more things changed, the more they stayed the same. By 1936 the academic department was renamed the "Related Department" to conform with policy dictates that academic instruction be "(1) related to vocational work, (2) [with] courses of practical importance." In the Annual Report of 1936, several pages after a glowing description of the new and improved Related Department, the chair of Trades and Industrial Education made his contribution to realistic reporting: "The work set up by the Related Department did not coordinate" and was "of little help" to trades students.[10]

Down on the Farm

In 1922, supervisor Spalsbury wrote to commissioner Peairs: "This school is so favorably located, so well equipped, and so efficiently manned in its agriculture department that it should be made the leading agricultural school of the service. To accomplish this, it should be authorized to give the complete four years senior vocational agricultural course."[11]

We need look no farther than the name, Chilocco Indian Agricultural School, to answer how agricultural instruction figured in the school's appropriate education for native people. Chilocco was founded to educate native people in the Indian Territory/Oklahoma. These groups were targeted in the late 1800s for the allotment of tribal lands in severalty, to break up the communal land base of tribal societies. The communally held trust lands of the reservations fractured into a crazy quilt of individually owned family farms and small rural communities. Independent of tribal identity, nuclear families could be fit (but not necessarily assimilated) into the larger fabric of American life. This model of civilized living for American Indians was outdated compared to white society of the 1920s and 1930s. Mainstream society had already shifted from the agrarian lifestyle of a previous century to urban centers with a vigorous industrial economic base, but schools for Indians were clearly not intended to produce the same kind of citizens as schools for whites.

Remember Superintendent McCowan's complaint in 1904 about the exodus of "our most promising boys from the rural homes they own to the professions they are as yet unfit to adorn, and to fields of football where they shine."[12] Indian boys *were* judged fit to adorn fields of sorghum and cane, and agricultural instruction remained the backbone of Chilocco's offerings through the second World War. In the 1950s and 1960s, agricultural training was relegated to the past. In its place came a renewed emphasis on trades training in fields such as electrical engineering and auto mechanics. In any case, Chilocco in the 1920s and 1930s was an agricultural school, renowned for its fine livestock (beef cattle, dairy cattle, Morgan horses, poultry) and up-to-date instruction enriched by a close association with Oklahoma Agricultural and Mechanical College faculty and researchers.

L. E. Correll arrived at Chilocco in 1918 as the agriculture teacher, and he developed a comprehensive agricultural training program, which he implemented as superintendent in 1926. The basic idea of his Boy Farm Plan was to turn over acreage to the supervision and care of individual students. The students learned directly the responsibilities of personal ownership and hard work and also enjoyed the fruits of their labors. Theoretically, the first step of the plan was a close look into the history of each boy who expressed an interest in farming. In practice, Correll was so desperate for farm workers he accepted everyone who applied and drafted a few more.

Correll's concern over the fate of the agricultural program crested in 1938, when only 10 boys out of 104 new students really wanted to take agriculture and had a chance of making it on their own (or family-owned) land: "This information is a little alarming to me, since I am extremely anxious, as you know, to develop and maintain a real agricultural school." He told the commissioner that only 20 percent of Chilocco's total enrollment [of boys] wished to take agriculture and that the boys applying to enter in order to study trades "probably . . . have made a wise decision in that they will have no possible chance of taking up farming after graduation."[13] In the 1937–38 school year there were 109 boys enrolled in the aggie classes and over 200 enrolled in trades, and Superintendent Correll felt this trend was sure to continue. He summed up the situation as he tried to balance Central Office enrollment directives with Chilocco's agricultural charter: How can we get boys with land of their own interested in agriculture if the education field agents hold as their first priority the enrollment of orphans or those from broken homes, who do not have the land resources available? Correll wanted to recruit young farmers but recognized this would conflict with regulations prohibiting solicited enrollment: "I hate to see our aggie work reduced because of lack of interest in agriculture on the part of students being enrolled. . . . I am still convinced there are plenty of boys in the state of

Oklahoma who need this agricultural instruction who will go back on the farm to farm. It is just a matter of getting them signed up for our school.''[14]

The subsistence homestead program was Chilocco's innovative answer to the problem of graduating agricultural students with no land to farm. In 1936, the government established fifteen homesteads on school property, bought the necessary farm equipment, and selected suitable Indians to lease and farm the homesteads. The homestead program enjoyed limited success but petered out after the 1940s. Most of the homesteaders could not make a living on their small-lease farms and were forced to take jobs in nearby towns, where they re-settled.[15]

In theory at least, Correll intended to rigorously screen boys interested in agriculture. He investigated the amount of land owned by the boy [or his father], his health and his preferences, and solicited the judgment of school personnel as to whether he might be the ''farming'' type. Primary consideration was given to boys in the upper grades and then to the older boys in lower grades (such as nineteen- to twenty-year-olds in the fifth and sixth grades). Each boy accepted into the program was allocated a plot of sixty-five to seventy acres. The plot boys worked thirty plots under the supervision of two practical farmers, who organized the horse and mule teams, allocated and greased the machinery, and supervised the farm work. The boys worked together in summer as a threshing team; if a boy needed help with his plot at other times, he had to pay other boys for their labor. The boys were encouraged to participate in every aspect of marketing their crop. After harvest and sale they received one-fourth of the value of their grain crop or livestock raised for slaughter.[16] None of the narrators who participated in the plot system made a career of farming.

Albert 1926/13 Cherokee:
I'll never know whether I volunteered or was assigned the Dairy Barn, that was another rude awakening! [Laughter] I found out later that that was probably the *least* desired assignment as far as vocational was concerned. Really it wasn't that bad. . . . it was a lot of fun, but it was a lot of hard work. . . . We milked forty-five cows, I believe, twice a day. We also fed 'em, put up feed and mended the fences, separated the cream, they had automatic milkers incidentally, and I guess the prize job down there was being a milker. . . . They put us in a dormitory of our own, and the night watchman would wake us up at 3:30 in the morning and we'd milk the cows. And being vindictive, the only pleasure I got out of that was the fact that we were through milking, had the milk separated, and

74

cooled and in cans by about five-thirty, I suppose, they served breakfast at six. . . . We had two beautiful Percheron horses. . . . We hitched 'em to an old buckboard, and that was what we hauled the milk to school in, and that was a prize job was getting to drive these Percheron horses up to the Mess Hall . . . the clippity-clop of the horses echoed all over the campus in the morning, it was so quiet and still, plus the fact that we had those five-gallon, galvanized iron milk cans bouncing back and forth there. As we turned the corner from the Dairy Barn heading onto the road going to the Mess Hall, there was a bent post. It must have been a 45-degree metal post, and we found out if we could drive the team straight ahead, and let the rear wheel hit this metal post, why it would throw the back end of the buckboard clear over across the highway [Laughter], and cause the cans to rattle that much more, and we imagined we'd wake more people up. * Then the last year I had a plot. . . . They give you sixty acres and you plant wheat, corn, and oats, and you have to stay up there all year then, and then you get the proceeds, you get one-fourth of the profit . . . of this crop. So I stayed up that year and I worked all year and all summer and I got *seventy-five* bucks! . . . We had a huge horse barn and we'd harness the horses, and then we'd have to follow 'em, drive 'em by foot clear out, way out, oh, maybe three or four miles, and hook up to our plow, and we'd plow. Talk about a demeaning job!

Edgar 1929/10 Creek:
We had a real big horse barn, mule barn, and I worked with mules, I had four old mules. I got in on the tail end of the plot and of course as you worked your way up, you get better mules, you know. Mine looked like a staircase, [Laughter] one little old bitty short one and a big old tall lanky one and they pulled the same way, one would be stopped and the other'd be going. When I'd get one stopped moving, the other one would start. But I got to love mules, because they have a lot over your horses . . . they would never drink too much water, you couldn't overwork them, they wouldn't overeat. They just have more sense than a horse. And when they got ready to quit, they *quit.* And you could build a fire, you could do anything else underneath 'em, that was it. We had a whistle that blew in the morning and blew at noon. . . . I could always plow a pretty straight line, I'd take my old mules, and I'd line, right between 'em you know, the four of 'em with some old tree or something distant and head in that general direction. . . . We had some old tractors, we didn't use 'em very much.

75

When that noon whistle would blow or the evening whistle would blow, the mules would stop wherever [Laughter] you were, whether you were all the way around or not. *That* is where they stopped. They started braying, and one of the hardest things to do . . . in the harvest was to get these mules to go beyond the whistle.

Ira 1936/? Cherokee:

Well I got conned into going to work in that general agriculture, diversified farming. They needed hands. I wanted to work in the blacksmith shop and too, they had a rotation system. You worked awhile . . . well let's see, I worked a day at the poultry, the dairy barn, the blacksmith. It may have been longer than that but anyway you would rotate around. It was interesting, but I wasn't quite heavy enough to do that kind of work, with a four-horse team. When I tried to harness the horse, they had [the harness] suspended on a rope, take the rope loose down here to let it down. Well, my feet would come off the floor. [Laughter] So I had a system, I would wrap one leg around the stanchion. I don't think they used a lot of wisdom, in counseling and so forth. Other things I rather would have done than work on the farm. . . . A fellow named Seafeldt, he came over to the dormitory one time . . . and he talked for seemed like hours, I thought he'd never finish, then he got me committed to the farm. . . . I worked with the assistant instructor in agriculture my first day. We had a four-horse team, those big Percherons, with a Fresno, and that Fresno picks up dirt and then you tip it, where you want it. And I couldn't tip that thing. Well, then he gave me the reins, and I couldn't turn those horses. I'd pull the rein and they'd just go on like they had their minds [set]. [Laughter] But I was always impressed with him, from that first day, because, you know, he was a gentle person. Quiet. But all in all, it was a good experience, all the way through, I appreciate it. The one thing, if you didn't learn anything else, was to learn to work. I don't remember learning anything in school [academic classes]. Except not to write on walls. [Laughter]

The grain and hay, dairy products, vegetable and orchard produce, eggs, poultry, and livestock raised by the students were prepared in the dining hall or sold to supplement appropriations.[17] Agricultural revenues kept the school

Table 11. Farm Production Report, 1924 Season

Grain and Hay	$25,087.95
Vegetables	434.76
Fruit	4,002.88
Dairy products	4,517.60
Meat products	11,658.75
Poultry products	2,765.30
Total	$48,467.54

Source: Blair to Commissioner, 27 April 1925, RG 75 E1 B4 F/1, FRC; Correll to Commissioner, 13 April 1927, ibid., F/4.

open. Superintendent Blair protested the commissioner's proposed budget cut of $10,000 for 1926 by noting that as it was, Chilocco's appropriation was $20,000 less than for schools of nearly equal size, and that they would need to raise $30,000 to $35,000 in farm sales to make up the deficit. This deficit was estimated before adding in the cost of expanding their course of offerings through the eleventh and twelfth grades. The deficit in some years was much larger than $35,000, especially if construction costs for badly needed new buildings and dormitory sleeping porches were figured in. Congress allotted $235,745 to Chilocco in 1927, whereas the estimated budget need was $309,999.[18] See table 11 for the value of farm production for the 1924 season at Chilocco.

Since the school depended so heavily on farm revenues, Chilocco had to maintain an adequate force of agricultural workers/students over the summer months when farm work was the most demanding. It was a never-ending struggle to keep enough boys over the summer to handle all the work, especially in harvest time from late August to early September. Superintendent Correll had the problem foremost in his mind as he recruited students from various agencies. In August of 1926 he wrote to the superintendent of the Cherokee Agency:

> Could you send us any students? We would be happy with boys or girls in the 5th, 6th and 7th grades. Also, older students if they are in the lower grades, work in the summer is quite heavy and we want a few students from your jurisdiction to have summer help. If you have some good boys, 14 and up who can't pay their own way we will send them travel vouchers if they enroll for four years.[19]

The need for student labor in the summertime also minimized the outing system at Chilocco, contrary to the practice at other off-reservation boarding schools of the time:

Due to the fact that the students at Chilocco are practically all from Oklahoma, and nearly all wish to go home during the summer months, funds being placed for this purpose by their parents, very little has been done at Chilocco in the past along the line of developing the outing system. Those boys and girls who have remained at the school have all been needed to accomplish the very large agricultural operations: in fact it has always been difficult for us to induce enough to remain to handle our work.[20]

Summer labor was not the only factor limiting an effective outing system. In 1884, Chilocco's very first year, Haworth faced unfriendly neighbors as he tried to implement the outing: "The people of the West are rather reluctant to take Indian children into their families. During the past harvest I was at Chilocco and accompanied Supt. Hadley . . . to visit several farmers, to try to arrange for work for Indian boys; in some cases we were rebuffed quite harshly."[21] In the summer of 1924 Chilocco placed thirty boys (paid three dollars a day) with local farmers for harvesting and threshing season, but this was not its usual policy.

The best laid plans of federal policymakers were thwarted by the realism and self-direction of Indian parents and children. The Chilocco model of education for Indians, like the Hampton model of education for blacks, was racially defined. It was the product of a complex interplay of ideologies: the Puritan work ethic, the myth of Europeans lifting savage nomads up the ladder of civilization toward sedentary agriculturalism (the most advanced and productive use of land), the Christian glorification of manual labor to train primitive minds toward an understanding of God, and a national agenda of allotment to free up Indian lands for white settlement. In 1818, Congress investigated how best to produce the desired object of the civilization of America's native people and recommended that the government establish schools, distilling centuries of ideology into one concise statement.

Put into the hands of their children the primer and the hoe, and they will naturally, in time, take hold of the plow; and as their minds become enlightened and expand, the Bible will be their book, and they will grow up in habits of morality and industry, leave the chase to those of minds less cultured, and become useful members of society.[22]

By the 1920s and 1930s, Chilocco's rural, agricultural education was socially and economically outdated. Correll was scrambling to recruit, enlist, or shanghai boys who had the good sense (or lack of land) to desire better academic training and/or meaningful trades instruction. Parents simply wanted to have their children home whenever possible, which meant the summer months. Chilocco kept some students over the summer through economic strategy: students could not go home unless their parents sent enough money to cover their transportation costs home in May and back to school in the fall. Most families were able and eager to pay for transportation, and their children spent summers at home.[23] Other students were happy to work over the summer, pursuing an economic strategy of their own. The proportion of sales receipts that the plot boys earned (*seventy-five* bucks!) was a persuasive incentive, and the boys had definite purchases in mind while they worked.

Curtis 1927/9 Creek:
But if you had enough money . . . you could go to town, buy your own clothes, and wear 'em whenever you wanted to. . . . Tailor-made trousers were the "in" thing, at Chilocco at that [time]. There were two things as far as wearing apparel was concerned that the guys bought themselves: tailor-made slacks were one of the things and I can't remember what tailor-made slacks cost at that time but it seems to me that it was around seven dollars. There was a tailor in town that would make you [trousers] and they all had to have twenty-two-inch bottoms, they called 'em bell-bottoms. . . . That was the in thing, if you had a pair of twenty-two-inch tailor-made bell-bottom trousers, that was the ultimate at Chilocco. [Laughter] The *next* thing that probably was secondary, and this was not for dress up, this was for everyday wear, were bib overalls, the pinstripe bib overalls, kind of bluish and gray . . . and *that* was the in work clothes, [Laughter] and if you had the money, you bought a pair of those. It seems to me that I made enough money one summer that I bought a pair of those. . . . I couldn't afford the bell-bottom trousers, but I did have those bib overalls. Another thing that was [in], you bought a pair of sneakers if you had the money. Sneakers were another thing, you got rid of the bullhides,[24] those things were terrible!

Chilocco students asserted themselves and their freedom in subtle and obvious ways. In their eyes, the difference between government-issue denim and store-bought twenty-two-inch bell-bottom trousers spanned the gulf between authoritarianism and independence. As the next chapter shows, clothes made the man or woman at Chilocco. Students who could avoid or subvert the uniform won a victory in the boarding-school theater of operations.

The purpose of the home economics course
through its various branches, is to teach family
relationships in such a manner that homes
become happy places in which all members
share the joys and responsibilities that are
involved. To further this purpose, girls are
taught the proper methods of doing work
in a home, a liking for home life, ability
to analyze and solve household problems,
to form judgements of qualities, conditions
and situations that lead to good selections
of the essentials of correct living.
Chilocco: School of Opportunity, 1938

The purpose of these schools was:
To break down our family ties.
To steal our children's hearts and minds.
To train our children to a life of servitude and trade.
Boarding School Exhibit
Yakima Indian National Cultural Center
Toppenish, Washington

4

'You're a Woman, You're Going to Be a Wife'

Chilocco's domestic training for girls was even less attuned to reality than its agricultural/vocational training for boys. In part, it was in step with the unreality of the times, as patriarchal American society envisioned women's place in the home. Indian women's place reflected the double burden of gender and race. Their domesticity training prepared them not to labor in their homes but as employees of white women or the boarding schools that trained them. Limited Indian school vocational training in "appropriate" fields such as teaching, nursing, business, or cosmetology lagged several decades behind educational opportunities for white women in the same fields. We can better understand the disparity between educational policies and practices for white and Indian women if we attend to the special circumstances of Indian girls in the boarding schools.

Federal policies of domestic education and federal practices of intense surveillance, control, regimentation, and restriction of Indian girls in these schools warrant close examination. Why did the girls have to labor so long and hard? Why did they have to wear the uniform? Why was every moment of their waking and sleeping hours monitored so carefully? Why were they strictly forbidden to step outside their own yards? Analysis of the roots of domestic education for all American women makes clear the underlying federal agenda, which was to train Indian girls in subservience and submission to authority. Surely this agenda underlay the manual labor requirements of the boys as well, but that instruction was at least minimally linked with employment in life after school.

The degree of surveillance and knowledge of Indian students that federal policymakers demanded of school personnel dwarfed any possible requirements of straightforward education. The Indian Service demanded such minute documentation of Indian personal lives and backgrounds, it is remarkable school staff had any time to educate. In 1917, commissioner of Indian Affairs Cato Sells requested the following information on all students proposed for graduation that year from federal schools: name, age, sex, tribe, degree of Indian blood, health condition, course of study and how long, how his or her personal funds had been handled, biographical sketch, statement of industry—reliability—apparent business qualifications, and general character and habits, recommendation as to competency, *plus* a statement from the student's reservation superintendent as to all their property holdings.[1]

Beyond domesticity as subservience training for all women, the acute, piercing focus on Indian girls' attire, comportment, posture, and hairstyles betrays a deep-seated, racially defined perception of Indian peoples' corporal physical bodies as "uncivilized." Late nineteenth- and early twentieth-century racist ideology linked physical and mental competencies and capabilities to heredity. It is not surprising, then, that an education appropriate to Indians' perceived lower intellectual capacities would stress so vigorously the concomitant need to develop physical skills and habits. In the years after Pratt enrolled the first Kiowa and Cheyenne POWs at Hampton Institute, Booker T. Washington was appointed the Indian boys' "housefather." Steeped in Samuel Armstrong's racial "scale of civilization," Washington immediately commented on these young savages' physical ineptitude:

> The untutored Indian is anything but a graceful walker. Take off his moccasins and put shoes on him, and he does not know how to use his feet. When the boys and girls are first brought here it is curious to see in what a bungling way they go up and down stairs, throwing their feet in all sorts of directions as if they had no control over them.[2]

Domestic Education

After the Civil War, federal and public schools turned to popular manuals such as Catharine Beecher's *A Treatise on Domestic Economy* (1846) as they created departments of "domestic science."[3] Beecher spoke clearly to women: every civilized society requires a system of laws to sustain social relations, and it is a fact of nature that those social relations entail duties of subordination. In her view, freedom in a democratic state meant that every individual was free to choose for her or himself their superior, to whom they owed obedience (1846, 25–26). A promotional brochure printed at Chilocco in 1938 repeated this message in the student code of conduct: "I believe that intelligent obedience is necessary to leadership. Therefore, I will have respect for authority" (*Chilocco: School of Opportunity* 1938, 8). Respect was naturally engendered by productive manual labor, an assumption that also underlay practices in French prisons[4] (Foucault 1979) and schools for American blacks (Anderson 1978, Hultgren and Molin 1989).

John Stuart Mill also recognized the relationship between domesticity and subservience in his criticism of white women's "superficial" education, "calculated to render women fit for submission, vicarious experiences and a service ethic of largely ineffective philanthropy" (Millett 1970, 70). We can see similarities in the links between domesticity and subservience training for all women, but certainly the experiences of white and nonwhite women were quite different. Feminist authors point out that the cult of domesticity enshrined white women's fragility and invalidism and demanded that *someone* be strong enough to work. Dr. Sylvanus Stall addressed the National Congress of Mothers in 1893 and contorted the cultural evolution stance of racist ideology to suit the challenges of finding good domestic help.

> At war, at work, or at play, the white man is superior to the savage, and his culture has continually improved his condition. But with woman the rule is reversed. Her squaw sister will endure effort, exposure and hardship which would kill the white woman (Ehrenreich and English 1978, 114).

Habituation to simple labor clearly superseded any truly vocational goals (training for employment) for Indian girls. In the 1920s, even school officials recognized the gap between vocationalism and mindless labor in their distinction between "vocational" and "prevocational." Most vocational girls worked in the sewing room and the laundry; a few were detailed to the kitchen, dining room, and the dormitories. The drudgery in kitchen and dining room was assigned to the prevocational girls, who could someday look forward to moving up in the ranks, promoted from scrubbing pots to darning socks by the bushelbasketful.[5] Students spent half of each day on vocational, or work, details, sewing hundreds of shirts, darning thousands of socks, polishing miles of corridor. In reality, little distinguished prevocational from vocational, itself a misnomer, because the girls' productive labor was more important to sustain the institution than as training for employment. Training for the girls in home economics was

Table 12. Sewing Room Production, 1924

From a total of 24,902 yards of material including muslin, sateen, gingham, toweling, flannel, linen ticking, denim and hickory were produced:

- 505 aprons (printer, bakery, kitchen, carpenters, and so on)
- 85 brassieres
- 608 pillow cases
- 755 night gowns
- 632 shirts, blouses and nightshirts
- 3,071 sheets
- 436 underskirts
- 1,430 dresses
- 75 skirts

Plus quantities of towels, table covers, linens, 2 piano covers, scarves, and other items

Source: RG 75 E1 B4/Records of the Superintendent: Correspondence with the Commissioner, F/1925, FRC.

divided into the categories of food (menu planning, nutrition, gardening, canning, food preparation, serving, table manners, entertaining) and clothing (fabric selection, clothing construction, embroidery, patchwork, mending and darning, home decoration) with peripheral attention to child care and home nursing. In the early 1920s, Superintendent Blair outlined the organization of the girls' vocational department as follows:

> Half of the vocational girls are detailed to the sewing room. Of the remaining half, five-eighths are assigned to the laundry, the balance divided among kitchen, dining room and homes. Not more than one-fourth of the kitchen detail is vocational so that at all times there are enough prevocational girls to keep the work going. As a result, we have a large detail of vocational and a small detail of prevocational girls in the sewing room and laundry. If extra workers are required in the kitchen, they are drawn from the sewing room. Prevocational girls entering Chilocco are always assigned to the kitchen/dining room if they are large enough. A double detail of kitchen/dining room girls work before breakfast, after breakfast and after supper.[6]

The designation *vocational department* validated the labor of the girls as they cooked, served, cleaned, sewed, and mended to keep the institution self-sufficient. Just as the boys shouldered the burden of the school farm, the girls fed and clothed eight hundred to a thousand students. See table 12 for a partial listing of the items made by the girls in the sewing rooms from January to December of 1924.

Florence 1933/7th Choctaw:
As far as the work though, I remember learning to darn socks, on a light-bulb, [Laughter] which I've never done since. A later semester, when the *patching* came along and . . . I got to use the machine . . . that was an interesting part. So I liked that part of it, and I remember very vividly . . . working in the dining room; we carried trays around. I don't think we got to serve food, I think we just did the pick-up, you know, the clean-up afterwards at that age. *

TL: Was there any trades training for the girls?

Not anything, I don't think, that was expected to really develop into a trade. . . . I don't think there was such a thing as First Aid or anything that was going to even develop an interest in nursing or something. No, I think at that time it was just, you're a woman, you're going to be a wife, you know. Learn to patch, and sew, and darn. * I got pretty adept at making pillow cases, but we really did things that were used there. I think I spent half a semester hemming dish towels and I graduated to pillow cases. I don't think I ever got beyond pillow cases! [Laughter] But I still like to sew, and I did get some good foundation, but I liked to sew when I went.

Cora 1929/12 Cherokee:
The first year I was there, I worked in the mending room. We worked a half a day and went to school a half a day. . . . we mended sheets and anything. They'd just pile you a great big pile of clothes up beside of you and you'd work them up during the hours that you were there. You had so much to do, and that's what you done. So then, the next year, why I worked in the laundry, I worked on the mangle, running sheets and dresses. They was two great big long mangles [for steam pressing] with . . . three girls that worked on each side. And that's what we done. And then the next year I took Physical Education, to major in it, so I worked over in the gym, the next two years.

A few schools placed Indian women in domestic service, but documentation of this placement is incomplete. In his history of the Phoenix Indian School, Trennert (1988) documents how the school provided domestic help to the white households of Phoenix over the years. Chilocco placed some girls in summer domestic service in the early 1900s but never mobilized this placement on a widespread or permanent basis for the same reasons it was difficult to implement outing for the boys.

The only employment available in domestic service for many young Indian women graduating from boarding schools was in the boarding schools themselves. In 1917, the Matrons' Reports on the skills and aptitudes of the senior girls graduating from Chilocco ranked their competencies in sewing, washing, ironing, housekeeping, and responsibility, all with an eye towards their suitability as assistant matrons.[7] Only a fraction of female graduates could expect employment within the Indian Service. An economic rationale of placing Indian women in domestic employment does not account for the centrality of domesticity training in their education.

An ideological rationale more fully accounts for domesticity training: it was training in dispossession under the guise of domesticity, developing a habitus shaped by the messages of subservience and one's proper place.[8] Domesticity training for Indian women suited the goals of the federal government above and beyond training for subservience. It fit integrally into governmental plans for a fundamental alteration of Indian peoples' relationship to land (see Adams 1988). In the 1800s, U.S. policymakers promoted an agrarian lifestyle for Indian people, as a step up the cultural evolutionary ladder from barbarism to civilization. Passage of the Dawes Allotment Act in 1887 empowered Congress and the Bureau of Indian Affairs to break up communal, tribal lands—reservations—and allot parcels to individuals. Policymakers viewed allotment as a humane mechanism to dissolve tribal identity and to forge new citizens. Millions of acres passed out of Indian hands in the wake of the Dawes Act. The outright loss of "surplus" lands was compounded by the eventual loss of many allotments when trust protection expired. The federal government exercised its power to take Indian lands under the guise of elevating Indian's lives as independent, civilized agriculturalists.

In 1917, commissioner of Indian Affairs Cato Sells issued a "Declaration of Policy in the Administration of Indian Affairs," announcing the government's intention to discontinue guardianship of competent Indians and end their status as wards of the Bureau of Indian Affairs.[9] He felt Indian school graduates could be judged "competent" in the legal sense, a judgment crucial to the successful allotment of land. Dispossession of communal tribal lands, coupled with the creation of small "Indian homesteads," supported the rationale of domestic education for Indian women.

The struggle to reform and reshape the Indian home targeted the education of young women. They would serve as the matrons of allotment households, promoting a Christian, civilized lifestyle and supporting their husbands in the difficult transition from hunter, or pastoralist, to farmer. Women's capacity to bear this burden was taken for granted by the Victorian vision of Woman as Mother, influencing society and shaping the future through her nurture of her children (Richards 1900). An epigraph by Helen Hunt prefaced a description of "Home Economics Class Instruction" at Chilocco: "A woman who creates and sustains a home, and under whose hand children grow up to be strong and pure men and women, is a Creator, second only to God" (*Chilocco: School of Opportunity* 1938, 31). To create this Godly creature, Indian schools had to convince or force Indian girls to renounce the teachings of their own mothers and accept the dictates of the federal curriculum and the Allotment Act. Estelle Reel, superintendent of Indian Schools from 1898 to 1910, encouraged the matrons to assure Indian girls being trained in housekeeping that "because our grandmothers did things in a certain way is no reason why we should do the same."[10]

School training in acquiescence to federal authority was more important than the details of needlework, laundry, or food preparation. Chilocco's "Requirements for Graduation" in 1938 emphasized the acquisition of proper codes of behavior above academic or vocational skills. Students had to demonstrate vocational achievement, complete all projects, remove all *F*'s and *I*'s from their academic record, and then:

> Inasmuch as a purpose of the school is to train Indian youth for citizenship, THE STUDENT WHOSE RECORD IS NOT SATISFACTORY AS TO PERSONAL CONDUCT WILL NOT BE RECOMMENDED FOR GRADUATION (Emphasis in the original, *Chilocco: School of Opportunity* 1938, 47).

This was a wonderfully flexible system for the exercise of power. Students who fulfilled all the requirements except "personal conduct" might not achieve the distinction of "graduating" from the school. Correspondingly, hard work and a good attitude were rewarded. Students with commendable conduct and "satisfactory skills in a chosen profession" could earn a "special vocational certificate" without completing the "related [academic] requirements."

As I uncover what I believe to be the core goal of federal domesticity training—the development of subservience among Indian women rather than realistic training for employment—I do not deny the uses many Chilocco alumnae have found for that training or the value they assign it today. I intend to show there was more going on in the boarding schools than just teaching Indian girls how to make a bed or sew a straight seam. I am not saying that straight seams are a bad thing in themselves.

Winona 1930/10th Cherokee:
We were also a little bit resentful because we felt that the home economics course was the only course that was open to us. And we didn't like that, but I'll say, I've used it. [Laughter] I've certainly used it. In the foods class, we learned how to prepare food, and we also learned nutrition, also how to serve it. Which was very, very good, because the home that we had come from we really didn't learn the right way to serve at a table when you had company. . . . My mother was a very ambitious sort of person and wanted us all to be educated and to learn, but we were able to learn things up there that we would not have learned in grade school, in public school. As far as the home economics, it was a good course, a *real* good course in Home Economics. . . . Also, we . . . had a little course, I believe it was called housewifery, and we had a little bit of interior decorating in the course . . . and it's something that I have really used, really enjoyed a lot. Well listen, I tell you, I do my own sewing even yet, and I was very conscious when I married about the food that I gave my family . . . and tried to be meticulous about how it was served, too. And so all of the things that I learned there, and even the interior decorating, I found that it was something that I have always been able to use in my own home.

As part of on-the-job training in domestic skills, girls were assigned to two practice cottages, which were constructed in the early 1930s. Junior and senior girls spent six or nine weeks in the cottages, where they practiced home life, each girl adopting the role of mother, father, daughter, or son. They rotated roles throughout their assignment to the cottage, so each week a girl assumed different tasks and responsibilities. The idea for the practice cottages had been encouraged as early as 1906, when superintendent of Indian Schools Estelle Reel visited a similar arrangement at Tuskegee Institute, dedicated to the domestic instruction of young African-American women. Tuskegee's senior girls lived, five at a time, in the cottage. They marketed, planned menus, cooked meals, and kept the home "in good order" on $4.50 a week. Estelle Reel felt "this putting them upon their own responsibility is a step in advance of what we have undertaken in the majority of the Indian schools. . . . I am explaining [the plan] at each school I visit."[11] Chilocco's students, unmindful of federal intentions, welcomed the practice cottages' six-week fantasy of family home life, a respite from institutional dormitories.

Irene 1929/15 Potawatomi:
They built two houses just exactly alike and this one was for we girls to learn how to keep house: cook, serve a dinner, clean up the kitchen, make beds, and the teacher lived over there in this other house. . . . To me it was a *wonderful* way to teach you. I learned so much out of that, that right today, I know . . . I've always known about nutrition because of what I was taught at Chilocco. I was taught how to *serve* that meal, properly: I was there three years, see, and I had home ec all three years. So that was great, for girls. . . . Now the fact that we had government clothes, I guess we made a few clothes for our own. But I learned a lot, I've sewed all my life. Winona's a *good* seamstress, she even made a coat suit, the suit was *beautiful,* and she probably makes her coats, too.

Juanita 1929/12 Cherokee:
And we also had a practice cottage . . . [where] we stayed for six weeks. Let's see, there were four of us at a time, you had a mother, a father, a little boy and a little girl. And during all of that time, you would switch roles. And we had a garden and one had to carry out the garbage and one washed dishes, one make beds, you know, it was a play house, it was fun, we liked it.

Mary 1937/9th Cherokee:
We took, of course, foods and sewing and arts and crafts: we had that in the morning. And specialties, I don't know what she called her class now, but grooming and manners, and a lot of that stuff. And you know what? This is something I remember from way back when I was a student. There was a man in our neighborhood, said one time, he said, course all the kids would come home in the summer and there would be activities, and he said, that you can pick 'em [Chilocco students] out of a crowd. They stood out in a crowd, so you see, you got so much more than what you get out of a textbook.

Thrift and economy motivated a great deal of federal practice in boarding schools, although thrift was occasionally at odds with policy goals. Government issue clothing cost more than requiring students to wear their own clothes, but G.I. uniforms won out in the interests of regimentation and control. Domestic instruction fit policy goals of appropriate feminine education, but school budgets did not cover instructional costs. Students were caught in the middle. Chilocco girls had to buy the material required for the extensive project work in home economics sewing classes, as well as for their graduation and prom dresses. Several alumnae relate the pressures of being forced to write home for money or material when they knew their families were barely getting by in the depression years.

Sarah 1926/12 Shawnee:
I was getting up in those grades where they [required] a lot of things for home economics that I didn't have, material and so forth. I felt like I couldn't go on under those circumstances. I up and left school. * I couldn't see no possibility of my graduating, having the things that was required for graduation, such as your formals. . . . And then we had projects in our home ec classes, domestic art, that we had to make, I just never had the material that we were required to use to make those [things].

Women who did graduate value the skills learned in home economics training at Chilocco as a stepping-stone to, but not full preparation for, employment.

Ellen 1927/13 Creek:
I think that Home Ec did [good], especially the sewing class. You know that's the way I make my spending money. I sew all the time, and I worked in sewing factories like [when] I lived in Los Angeles, and I worked in those factories and that helped me a whole lot. Course I didn't know how to use the industrial machines then but I learned. * So there's where my spending money comes from, and I always said, what if I hadn't ever learned those kind of things? . . . Course they taught us child care classes . . . and I have twelve children.

The Battleground of the Body

To construct the ideal Indian Woman, educators had to teach Indian girls new identities, new skills and practices, new norms of appearance, and new physical mannerisms. Dormitory personnel, matrons and disciplinarians, academic teachers and trades instructors all enforced the rigid code of appearance for Chilocco students. Ellen (Creek, 1927, age 13) recalls the impact of that scrutiny:

I remember [two of the teachers], they were on the side of our matron when it came to strictness. In Mrs. S's class, sometimes the girls would keep their red sweaters on because it was cold. She wouldn't say anything, she would just stand there and look at them. They'd like to try and ignore her, avert their eyes, look at the ground. Finally she'd say, "Well, when these grandmas take their sweaters off, we can start class." That's what she did, she'd call us grandmas. I can still remember seeing [one of the boys] on his way to class in the morning, trying to button his shirt collar, button his cuffs, tie his shoes. Because she was his first class. All the boys would really button up, then after class they would unbutton their collars, roll up their cuffs, even roll up their pants if they thought they could get away with it.

Surveillance of female students penetrated well beyond their classroom appearance. One alumna recalls the "blue bag" full of rags issued to girls during their menstrual periods. A matron dispensed the bags, and in the process kept track of each girl's cycle. Hospital records from 1926 corroborate this record keeping in the list of students hospitalized or treated: dysmennorhea was one of the categories of cases catalogued each month.[12] Records and reminiscences attest that authority's gaze focused more intensely on the girls' appearance than that of the boys. Boys were allowed more latitude in dress on campus and on their work details.[13] Official correspondence and inspection reviews mention girls' clothing more frequently and in more detail. The girls had to pass inspections to determine whether they had donned all the required undergarments. Clothing was a clearly marked terrain of power in the boarding school, especially in the girls' dormitories.

The boys wore World War I uniforms, with high collars and wrap leggings, to drill every morning and dress parade on Sundays. Work clothes, overalls and dungarees, were provided for farm and trade work and classroom wear. The girls were issued school dresses in a check or gingham pattern and blue chambray work dresses. The government provided everything, and the girls were required to wear everything provided. That included black cotton stockings, heavy bloomers, and long underwear in winter. Gray (later red) sweaters were all that warded off winter's cold, even when the wind swept down from the northern plains. Boys, especially the farm workers, had to dress warmly and they were issued heavy denim or wool jackets.

Shoes were made at state prison workshops and repaired at the school's shoe and harness shop. The girls especially dreaded the heavy, unfashionably high-

91

top "bullhides," and when allowances were made in the late 1920s, they made every attempt to provide their own shoes of the required style, a low-cut black oxford. In April of 1926, new uniforms were issued to the girls: black skirts with white middy blouses, a tie, and stylish cape. The girls wore these special outfits to town on Town Day and to church on Sunday.[14] The new uniforms were made by the clothing classes and the girls' old uniforms were recycled for classroom wear. Black sateen bloomers were provided as gym suits. The ubiquitous bloomers were issued to all the girls, black sateen for the older girls and gingham or hickory for the younger.[15] The boys could wear sneakers if they purchased them, but the girls were not allowed such leeway. One alumna recalls her father mailed her black oxfords adorned with a small patch of gray; the matron refused to let her wear them. Another alumna's shoes were judged unfit because of two eyelets instead of the regulation four.

Bureaucratic correspondence in the 1920s illustrates the discourse on girls' clothing and appearance. In 1923, the superintendent wrote to Washington to protest inspecting field supervisor Spalsbury's remarks that Chilocco girls had an "uncouth appearance" and that their hairdressing styles should be improved. The superintendent noted that nearly half of the girls had arrived that fall with short hair.[16] He regretted to see the older girls' hair "bobbed in the latest fashion [as] Indians' hair is very straight and some of our girls look rather unattractive." He questioned the policy of total uniformity of appearance, and assured the Head Office, "Most of the girls at Chilocco I think give considerable attention to their personal appearance, and the matrons give the matter of supervising them along this line considerable attention."[17] The superintendent's weak plea for "some individuality" was not repeated often in his correspondence with Washington.

In 1925, supervisor Spalsbury suggested the Indian Service discontinue the olive drab uniform for students (since they were not likely to require the camouflage, in her words, unless the service had plans for military action) and replace it with a neat gray trimmed in black braid. The superintendent was noncommittal on this point, no doubt aware the service was not so free with funds or uniforms, but he responded at length to the supervisor's comments on the girls' shoes. Spalsbury felt the high-cut, heavy bullhides issued to all students ought to be relegated to the "realms of the departed": "They simply are not worn by well dressed girls or women any more . . . why should we impose them on our Indian girls (and not our own daughters)?" The superintendent's reply to this enlightened concept of applying the standards of white society to Indian stu-

92

dents was "I do not believe in adopting fads too quickly."[18] He was willing to agree that change in uniform dress was warranted, because "Any legitimate means of overcoming the mental apathy of the average Indian pupil, which is undoubtedly the greatest obstacle to his intellectual advancement, is worthy of serious consideration."[19]

The superintendent explicitly tied the "mental apathy" of Indian students to their physical, corporal bodies: spruce up the uniform and you will stimulate the mind. The accommodation of racially inferior intellects to retarded physical development was remarked upon earlier by Booker T. Washington. Estelle Reel spelled it out in excruciating detail in an interview at the turn of the century:

> Allowing for exceptional cases, the Indian child is of lower physical organization than the white child of corresponding age. His forearms are smaller and his fingers and hands less flexible; the very structure of his bones and muscles will not permit so wide a variety of manual movements as are customary among Caucasian children, and his very instincts and modes of thought are adjusted to this imperfect manual development. . . . In short, the Indian instincts and nerves and muscles and bones are adjusted one to another, and all to the habits of the race for uncounted generations, and his offspring cannot be taught like the children of the white man until they are taught to do like them.[20]

Reel developed a standard curriculum for the federal schools that privileged manual training, teaching to *do*. She stressed the moral development inherent in manual development but never as strongly for boys as for girls, the future uplifters of Indian home life. Reel's encouragement of native cultural crafts, especially basket making and Navajo rug weaving, was one interesting offshoot of her educational philosophy:

> All civilized nations have obtained their culture through the work of the hand assisting the development of the brain. Basketry, weaving, netting, and sewing were the steps in culture taken by primitive people. A knowledge of sewing means a support for many. Skill in the art of using the needle is important to every woman and girl as an aid to domestic neatness and economy and as a help to profitable occupation.[21]

Civilized women, particularly boarding school matrons and teachers, had to take the lead in inculcating the correct handling of a needle and thread. "Never permit sewing without a thimble. Do not let children make knots in thread. See to it that all sit in an erect position, never resting any part of the arm on the desk."[22]

Female students were drilled in the correct motion of the arm in taking stitches, as well as in marching, breathing, calisthenics, and games; all were necessary for "requisite muscular exercise." Reel rarely mentioned all the mental and moral benefits accruing from manual labor when she referred to boys' vocational training. In the same report where she spelled out correct sewing form and posture she simply mentioned shoemaking was good training for boys "that they may be able to do this for themselves . . . and, if any desire, to follow the trade."[23]

Whether or not school employees consciously recognized the link between enforced uniformity, regimentation of the body, and subservience training, some students did recognize it. Florence (Choctaw, 1933, 9th grade) makes the connection explicit in her remarks:

> One thing I think that figures in prominently into this lack of warmth I'm talking about, is the loss of individuality, that comes from that damn G.I. issue striped denim drawers, gray sweaters. If we were going to have sweaters, why did they all have to be *gray*? In that cold climate, you know? . . . That was just some of the kind of things that, well, it was just, I guess some kind of a feeling, at least on the people who controlled the purse . . . to encourage submission. I don't know what else you'd call it.[24]

Feminist critique of the Victorian cult of domesticity and theories of power relations contextualize the practices of surveillance, domination, and subservience training common to federal off-reservation boarding schools early in the twentieth century. The framework of critical theory connects school regimentation, domestic training, and work details; federal Indian policy of land allotment; racially delimited notions of mental and physical capabilities; and historical and social forces within American society that mitigated against Indian assimilation. What this framework does not directly illuminate is how students responded and resisted. Critical theory contextualizes the institution within the society that produced it, but it has not, as yet, contextualized the Indian student in her struggle for survival within the institution.[25]

Alumni Voices and Student Life

Narrative evidence from Chilocco alumni reveals that federal practice did not successfully accomplish subservience training and that Indian students successfully resisted policy and practice. The external perspective of analysis and the internal perspective of alumni converge at the image of the regimented female body. Both views see this image as the crucial embodiment of the net of power relations binding students and staff. From an alumni view, the story of student creativity is encapsulated in what I call "the bloomer story," a tale of ladies' underwear. The bloomer stories that appear in the next few pages enrich our understanding of student activity and control in the boarding school. Juxtaposed with the analytic framework provided earlier, the bloomer story illuminates the student side of the delicate balance of forces that opposed and interacted within the school setting. As we shall see, the bloomer story weaves together the elements of government issue uniformity versus the individuality of home clothes; adult supervision/inspection versus student sleight of hand; and the limited socializing allowed to students across the gender barrier. We can begin with home clothes.

When students arrived at Chilocco in the 1920s and 1930s, boys stored their own clothes in footlockers by their beds, and the girls' home clothes were locked in trunk rooms, open only a few hours each month. Girls wore their own dresses to the Saturday night dances, which alternated weekly with movie showings. The strictly chaperoned dances were one of the few times when girls and boys mingled.

Vivian 1929/12 Choctaw:
And [at the dance] you had to be held a certain way, the boys weren't allowed to put their hands high on you, or, you know, low on you because you would be punished for that, when you got back to the building. Oh, it was something else. [Laughter]

The omnipresent eye of authority had to mitigate the seeming freedom of home clothes, especially in what authority perceived to be one of the most dangerous moments of school life: the sexually charged mingling of adolescent boys and girls. Rules dictated that the bulky, shapeless bloomers must be worn under home clothes, and matrons inspected the girls as they left the dorms for the dance.

Barbara 1928/12 Cherokee:
And I remember this old matron, one time, said something about us arousing the boys' passions, [Laughter] that's the reason we had to wear these bloomers . . . and I didn't know, I hardly knew what that meant, you know. Really, it seems strange this day and age, but the farthest thing

from our minds was sex, I guess. And yet, the matrons seemed to be concerned.

Educators attempted complete surveillance of and control over female Indian bodies within the schools, but students successfully exercised their own power in their resistance. The battleground of the body was strewn with the corpses of those bloomers, as the following stories attest.

In the 1980s, male and female Chilocco alumni narrated contemporary renditions of the bloomer story. The story is told and retold, a staple of the frequent alumni association meetings held throughout Oklahoma. Narrators stress the solidarity of peer groups who shared risks and protected one another. The following versions of the bloomer story elaborate student cooperation, ingenuity, and flamboyant display of individual identity. The first version was narrated by a male alumnus, the second by a woman.

Coleman 1937/14 Delaware/Isleta:
My sister came up the next year after I was there, she tells a story . . . those girls had what they called G.I. bloomers, and [their matron] there in Home 3, she was a real strict disciplinarian. . . . [She] would require those girls to wear their bloomers to the dance. She had inspection, as they went out they had to pull their dress up to show that they had their bloomers on. And so, then they just march on out. Well, almost all those girls had their own panties, and it just irked them to wear those bloomers. So they came up with a deal where they would take their bloomers off and hide 'em behind the hedge there, and then when they'd come back [to the dorm], why they'd get their bloomers, and go on in. . . . A *whole* bunch of the girls were doing that, but *we* didn't know about it, the boys didn't know about it. So those boys that had to work at the bakery had to go to work at five o'clock in the morning. The night attendant would always wake 'em up so they would go to work. One time, Saturday night, they had a dance. And these girls pulled their little trick. Then it started raining, they took the school bus down there and brought the girls back so they wouldn't get wet. They just ran the school bus up, girls would get in, and it would take 'em right on up to the dorm. And just in a row, they'd go right on into their room. It was raining pretty hard. When those girls got up the next morning, the boys that had gone to the bakery had found some of those pants, those bloomers and they stacked 'em all out front, on the hedge, on the edge of the trees and it was just out there so pretty with all

96

The plow and sheaf of wheat in the center of the Chilocco-School seal indicate that it is primarily an agricultural school. Surrounding this motif are the words CHILOCCO INDIAN AGRICULTURAL SCHOOL. The book symbolizes the academic department, and at the base of the design appears the date of the school's founding, 1884. Around the perimeter of the seal representing various activities and departments of the school: a brush for the paint shop; a cog wheel for the engineering shop; scissors for domestic art; a horse for animal husbandry; a roller for the print shop; a shoe lath for the shoe shop; a football for athletics; Indian clubs for the physical education department; an anvil for the auto-mechanics and blacksmith shops; a nurse's cap for the hospital; a cow for the dairy department; a rolling pin for the domestic science department; a trowel for the masonry department; and a square for the carpenter shop. The seal was designed by students A. C. McIntosh, and Harvey and William Bedoka.
From *The Chiloccoan*, 1930.

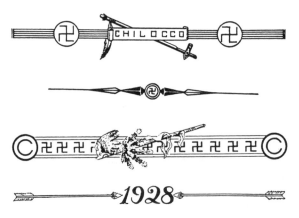

The swastika was used as a symbol for Chilocco School
until World War II. These logos served as page headings
in the annual yearbooks from 1928 to 1930.

The entryway arch was students' introduction to Chilocco. The school driveway
stretches one mile due west to the school campus. This photo appears on the last page
of *The Chiloccoan* (1938) owned by alumnus Curtis Carr. Partly visible is the
penciled inscription "Always open to you, And always welcome."

Chilocco's first building, the Light on the Prairie. By 1930, when this photo was taken, it was called Home 2 and it housed the younger boys. Photo courtesy of Mrs. Christine Scroggins.

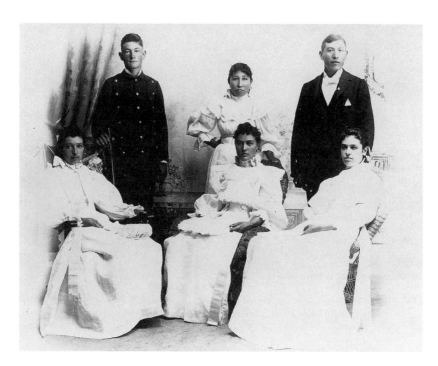

The graduating class of 1895. Students in the back row are unidentified. Front row, left to right: Effie Long, Josie Wright, and Esther Johnson. Photo courtesy of Eastern Washington State Historical Society, Spokane, Washington (Estelle Reel Collection #85).

Chilocco girls in school dresses, 1914. Left to right: Lillie Wilson and Stella DeCora.
Photo courtesy of Mr. Freeman Zunigha.

Oklahoma State Champion Baseball team from Chilocco (1916 or 1917). Photo courtesy of Mr. Freeman Zunigha.

Chilocco band in front of Leupp Hall in the early 1920s. Photo courtesy of Mr. Freeman Zunigha.

Horse barn and teams ready to start the day, early 1920s. Photo courtesy of Mr. Freeman Zunigha.

Group photograph of Chilocco school children, 1929. The panoramic process used to make the photograph moved so slowly that the boy in the bib overalls, Edgar Scroggins, on the extreme left was able to run behind the crowd and appear again on the right side of the photograph. Photo courtesy of Mrs. Christine Scroggins.

Senior girls in 1931. Photo courtesy of Mrs. Christine Scroggins.

Same senior girls, 1931, with Elizabeth (Lizzie) McCormick, Head Matron. Photo courtesy of Mrs. Christine Scroggins.

Senior home economics graduates in 1931, wearing their prom dresses. The girls sewed these dresses as part of their senior year home ec project. Photo courtesy of Mrs. Christine Scroggins.

those girls' names on 'em. [Laughter] They had to write their names across the seat. We teased those girls for so long after that.

Marian 1934/18 Creek:
I remember, though, we got smart, about the time we were seniors. We had those old black satin bloomers, so we cut the leg off of one, we had elastic up here and we had elastic down there [at the top and bottom of the cut off bloomer leg]. [During inspection] we had to pull up our dress and show we had those bloomers on. O.K., we got outside, we pulled that leg off, and we put it in the bushes. [Laughter] The wind came up—and we had our names in those legs, and you see, the first bunch back to the dorm would clean the bushes, and take the legs upstairs. And then after lights out, they'd slip down and deliver your leg to you. Oh God, my leg wasn't there. I waited all night for the leg, and the leg never did come, and the next morning going to breakfast, there it was, laying right on (the superintendent's) walk. I got that old leg and put it in my pocket and I tell you it was bulging out like this.

Settings and details of the bloomer story shift and transform according to narrator and venue of performance. Girls outwitted the matron on the way to the dance, before playing basketball, on the way to classes, or on the way to church. Winter versions of the story feature the shapeless woolen long underwear legs as the distasteful item of required apparel. The variety of permutations and the relish with which they are told signal the special status of the story among alumni today. Nearly all versions entail the girls' ruse being uncovered, by the wind or a matron's sharp eye, but alumni tell the story as part of *their* Chilocco experience, an experience that cumulatively covers nearly twenty years. Some Chilocco girls at some point in time undeniably pulled a fast one on their matron or basketball coach or commanding officer, but the bloomer story today is more myth than personal anecdote. It sums up critical realities, tensions, and meanings that permeated student life at Chilocco.

The story reveals the complex network of bonds and divisions that simultaneously bound and segmented the large student population. Girls united in groups formed by dorm-room association, shared hometowns, native language ties, company or work detail assignments, or similar personality. Loyalty to the group reigned supreme in the student code of ethical behavior, and groups also worked to cooperate—signaling the approach of a matron after lights out—or compete, as Companies vied to win the special dinner prepared for the best dress parade drill. Boys' gangs ruled Chilocco's 8,000-plus acres of fields and groves as tribal heritage brought boys together and mixed blood versus full-blood sorted them out. The bloomer story reveals the solidarity within groups, as girls cooperated to outwit the matrons. It also illustrates another important practice, *trixing,* which both crossed and highlighted group boundaries. Coleman recalls how the boys teased the girls about their errant bloomers. Trixing was student slang for elaborate joking and prank playing within and between groups and gangs and between students and staff.

The bloomer story has a symbolic resonance for alumni because it marks a milestone in their memories, of student triumph over a uniform(ed) existence. Whether full bloomer or only leg, the story drapes cloth scraps across the campus for all to see, incontrovertible evidence of the revolt organized within nameless, numbered Homes. It was not a hidden insurrection, carried out by boys in dark of night hidden from adults' view. This plan was executed under the noses of the matrons by the strictly guarded girls. The bloomers were not anonymous emblems either; they bore the full and public script of their owners' names. A blowing rain from the north washed away the facelessness of institutional life for a moment and left in its place a gray sateen proclamation of independent individuality, resting on the threshold of the superintendent's door.

There is nothing inherently "Indian" about the bloomer story; the isolated narrative does not reveal its origin in any striking way. Its status as a symbolic marker of Indian identity for Chilocco alumni today arises from the conditions of its creation and the contemporary contexts of its narration. Chilocco Indian Agricultural School was not an educational institution created by or created to serve (in a productive sense) Indian people. Like other federal and mission boarding schools, it was created to destroy Indian tribal communities and erase individual Indian identity. It was created by, controlled by, and directed by non-Indian people. It was, however, an institution inhabited by Indian students, who created its everyday life. Every student knew Chilocco was an *Indian* school. They also knew, or soon learned, that as Indian students they were subordinate to non-Indian authority. The petty, tyrannical details of a regimented life were linked at every turn to their identity as Indians. It follows logically that the details of their resistance to regimentation are also now linked inextricably with their identity as Indians, specifically, as alumni of an Indian school. Personal reminiscences and shared stories, such as the bloomer story, are powerful symbols of identity today not because of some Indian cultural content (in some

98

externally defined ethnographic sense), but because they are the chronicles of Indian experiences told by Indian people.

In the quest to individualize the tribal consciousness, federal Indian schools pressed Indian students into a strictly homogenous mold of uniform dress and appearance and limited educational opportunity. The seeming contradiction is no real paradox: federal boarding schools did not train Indian youth for assimilation into the American melting pot, but trained them in the work discipline of the Protestant ethic, to accept their proper place in society as a marginal class. Indians were not being welcomed into American society. They were being systematically divested of their lands and other bases of an independent life.

As tribal sovereignty was attacked on the political front, personal individuality was attacked in the dormitory and classroom. The schools attempted to divest Indian children of independence in an institutional setting. Proper training for young Indian women, and the emphasis on proper clothes for boarding-school girls, were exemplars of the federal practice of organizing the obedient individual whereas policy aimed to disorganize the sovereign tribe. Federal vocational and domestic education for Indian women was an exercise in power, a reconstruction of her very body, appearance, manners, skills, and habits. Federal educators hoped to manufacture civilized and obedient souls in civilized and obedient bodies, uniformly garbed in olive drab or snappy gray.

The federal government has not completely alienated Indian people from the land, or Indian woman from herself, but the forces and ideologies powering past attempts are still present in contemporary American life. The government's failure to achieve these goals is due in great part to Indian peoples' commitment to the idea of themselves. As individuals and as community members, Indian people cling stubbornly to making their own decisions, according to their own values. In the process, they have created spaces of resistance within the often oppressive conditions of education, evangelism, employment, and federal paternalism.

We'd have a lot of fun, but all the fun we had to have was *very quiet* [this is whispered]. . . . *If* we made *any* noise *what*soever, the matron was down there, "Everybody out in the hall and *stand*!" There was one little girl there, I remember so much about that, just like yesterday. Her name was R. I., and she couldn't speak English, or so we *thought,* she never said a word. And a girl named J. was our officer in our dormitory and we had to stand out in the hall *so* much you know, little kids are full of vim and vigor and they want to have fun and play. . . . One time we were standing out in the hall, never had heard one single word out of this girl and didn't think that she even understood English, and she says "Damn you, J.!" [Laughter] Our officer, you know, for making us stand in the hall!

Noreen, 1923/12 Potawatomi

5

'You Dizzy Bastard, Get in Step!'

The bugle sounded twenty-two times a day at Chilocco: reveille, assembly, mess call, school call, call to quarters.[1] Students practiced close-order drill every morning, and military companies of boys or girls competed in Sunday dress parades. Dormitory matrons in white gloves checked over door frames and under bedsteads for dust while uniformed students stood sharply at attention, dreading demerits and hoping they wouldn't be on their hands and knees Saturday afternoon polishing the hallways. Military regimentation dominated boarding-school life, and it dominates boarding-school reminiscences. Alumni recall the details of regimentation and punishment as well as the details of their resistance. The imposition of military authority at Chilocco was complicated by student officers: school matrons and disciplinarians appointed older students to command the companies and theoretically, to help enforce the rules. In reality, officers' paramount loyalty was to their peers. Students learned to test, stretch, and manipulate the boundaries of authority and its surveillance, establishing pockets of privacy in dorm room and catalpa grove, communicating in slang, enforcing an honor code of responsible behavior, and participating in a hierarchy of ranked resistance, from minor (smuggling bean sandwiches to the dorm rooms) to significant (making home brew) to the ultimate protest, running away.

Curtis 1927/9 Creek:
It was just like in the Army. We had old World War I uniforms, wrap leggings, and high-button collars, and if you can imagine a nine-year-old kid carrying a big Enfield rifle [Laughter] in close order drill, that was all part of it.

Albert 1926/13 Cherokee:
[The little boys were] in what we call the Ironhead Platoon. [Laughter]
They lined 'em up by size, regardless of age, and they had these little
guys, we called 'em Ironheads. Some of 'em were so young, they were
five or six years old, and their patience then isn't that great, so that's why
we called 'em Ironheads. * They had World War I, I think they were
Spanish-American War rifles. . . . We had all kind of guns.[2] [Of] course
there was no ammunition, but we'd tear 'em apart and clean 'em up and
everything else. We started drilling at five o'clock in the morning, one
hour before breakfast. And then in the spring why we'd have a competition drilling, we were semimilitary really, I mean we drilled with rifles.
And a little sidelight to that, I later joined the Marine Corps and did
twenty-eight years with the Marine Corps, and you hear people talk about
how tough boot camp was, that was a *breeze* [Laughter] after Chilocco!"[3]

Edgar 1929/10 Creek:
Chilocco had a military system, we had bugles, got up with bugles and
went to bed with bugles . . . went to Leupp Hall, the dining room, with
bugles. You marched, you had your little company, and they were graded
according to size, and age. You had your officers, which were other students, that were your company commanders. They were pretty much I
guess like the army. They called you everything, cuss you out, and kick at
you and holler at you. I think that's where I got my name, Dizzy. I remember, many times my company commander saying "You dizzy bastard, get
in step!" [Laughter] And it kind of stuck with me.

Noreen 1923/12 Potawatomi:
Run sort of like a military institution, actually. You *marched* everywhere!
You marched to *school,* you marched to the dinners: breakfast, lunch and
dinner. You marched to church, everywhere you went. No, now I think
the boys didn't always have to go that way, but anytime a girl went anywhere, she went in company formation, she *marched*! * I was Company
C because it was the smallest company [that is, made up of the smallest
girls] and I was at the tail end of *it,* myself and a girl called J. When line-
up time came, you lined up, kids were growing and so about once a
month, I'm sure it was once a month, we lined up so that we'd [go from
tall to short]. We always [were at the end], well sometimes we'd even be

dismissed. "J. and Noreen may go to their room" because they *knew* we were going to be at the end of the line.

Connie 1922/13 Cherokee:
We were organized into companies according to our age and size. I was the captain of the youngest girls' company, and I tell you, we never expected to win anything in the drill competitions they had, because those little girls could hardly keep up. You would see one take another one by the hand and just all string along.

Francis 1931/16 Cherokee:
As soon as you got out of bed, you stripped it and usually flipped your mattress, stretched that sheet, and put your blanket so: them officers would come through and check it. If they had a quarter they'd throw it down, see if it bounced. If it wasn't tight enough to bounce, why they'd tear it up and make you fix it again. Yes, it was army discipline. And it paid off pretty good, it give 'em control. If they hadn't, there would have been riots up there and everything else—they had some wild Indians. Literally, I mean, sure enough. [Laughter]

Juanita 1929/12 Cherokee:
And you've heard of course of the white glove inspection. We left our drawers open every day, our doors, closets open, the shoes lined up, all hangers going the same way, the bottom drawer pulled out all the way, everything folded, all the way up. And no dust. The sheets on the bed had to be as straight under the mattress as they were on top. [Laughter] They didn't always get down and look under there but you never knew when they would.

Maureen 1931/14 Choctaw:
Sunday morning we always had white glove inspection . . . they'd dust under the mattress, you know. I think we'd had a dance the night before and somebody gave me some chewing gum, and I had stuck it on the foot of my bed. In all the cleaning and polishing that room up that morning, I missed seeing this plug of gum. [Laughter] So they came through for inspection, and there's that plug of gum so I was busted to the rear ranks. I lost my commission.

A wave of reforms swept Indian educational policy in Washington, D.C., after the Meriam report was published in 1928, and the ripples affected boarding-school practice. Will Carson Ryan, Jr., a professional educator who chaired the Meriam committee's educational investigation, was appointed director of education in the Indian Bureau under John Collier. Ryan instigated many reforms and the military system of the boarding schools was an immediate target. Close-order drills and harsh punishments were discarded in efforts to humanize the schools.

Louis 1933/14 Cherokee:
The thing I think that impressed me more than anything else, was the fact that we had to march everywhere we went that first couple of years that I was there. But after that, it changed, they changed administration [in Washington] and they got a little bit lenient. They still were very strict. And by the time I was a senior you could go over to the dormitory, the girls' dormitory if you signed up, go over there in the evening. And you could go and sit in the lobby and talk with your girlfriend or, most of the time they would have a little, sort of a social on Saturday night, then the girls would invite [you].

Robert 1933/15 Creek:
The boys would line up at noon, to go to the dining hall and they had mail call, they'd call out and throw you a letter if you got one. But they didn't march, they just kind of went in a gang to the dining hall. They had gotten away from the marching part, but they still had to go in a group to the dining hall, and same way going to the school building. Kind of like a gang, just a group of guys. The girls were still marching in double file.

Charlie 1934/9th Cherokee:
TL: When you started, did they still have the military system?
    No, no, they didn't have, they had done away with that; *however,* whenever it was time to go to the dining room, they blew a whistle. We fell in and walked as a group over there. There was that much of it still lingering. We still had taps and you had to be in bed at ten o'clock. They came around and checked, bed check. If you weren't in bed, you paid for it later, shining halls or some extracurricular labor. [Laughter]

June 1942/17 Cherokee:
TL: Did you still have student officers as part of that military system?

No, we had what we called group leaders, instead of officers; they were sort of like a matron's assistant. They would check your rooms during mealtime, things like that, get the girls up in the mornings. We had a study hour in the evenings; we had to keep quiet then, no giggling allowed. Then there was lights out, and bed check. There no longer were the steel doors at the end of each hallway, but they did lock the dorm doors at night. * The lock-ups were gone, there was nothing like that. Discipline was mostly based on restrictions of privileges. You were grounded from social events, something like that.

Students as Officers

Whether they were called officers or group leaders, older students were an integral part of the authority structure at Chilocco. Recruited or appointed by the matrons and disciplinarians, officers walked a fine line between their supervisors and their peers. Being set apart as an officer was enough to alienate some other students.

Mason 1928/11 Cherokee:
We had drills, and companies, and in training they used to assign goons, as we called 'em [Laughter] in the building. Well they'd train them there before they'd assign 'em to be in charge of the marching, or so forth. They had the previous training before you got out to drill, so [they could] be corrective of the formations and so forth.

Winona 1930/10th Cherokee:
(The officers would) just see that the girls stayed in line, and . . . if they talked or laughed or did anything wrong, in going to the meals . . . they watched the girls. They were supposed to report them, if anything out of the ordinary happened.

Barbara 1928/12 Cherokee/Pawnee:
They were the pets, the officers were. So you couldn't get away with anything, because they weren't on your side at all. They were officers [Laughter].

Former officers take a different view. They unanimously stress loyalty to the peer group over alliance with the authority structure. Officers juggled the responsibilities school staff delegated to them and the social reciprocity students demanded of them.

Maureen 1931/14 Choctaw:

At Home 5, we were divided into three companies by height, and I was made captain of the B Company: I was the middle group.

TL: What were the officers' duties?

Nothing much except to give the orders to march, halt, fall in line [Laughter] and I guess we were supposed to tattle if we saw anything wrong, but we didn't . . . that wasn't any way to gain friends and influence people. [Laughter]

Flora 1932/17 Creek:

By my second year I was a group leader and assistant to the captain. I never told on a girl, though: I left that up to them, if they had done something wrong, and I never had any problems with my group. I felt it was better to be put on your own initiative, your own responsibility. If you were too stern, and there were too many reprisals, they wouldn't like you. So I did all right, [the matron] even complimented me on it.

Discipline and Punish

Chilocco personnel monitored and punished students by assigning demerits, which had to be worked off. Students on disciplinary work details kept the dorms spotless, scrubbing toilets, washing basement floors, and waxing long wooden hallways. Students who accumulated demerits also lost privileges and could not attend athletic or social events. Serious offenses such as drinking, stealing, or going AWOL earned incarceration (for both sexes) or hard labor (for the boys only). Both offenses and punishments reflected the federal obsession with disciplining the body in order to discipline the mind. Students risked demerits if they turned their heads when they were supposed to have eyes forward. Companies stood for hours without moving if things got too boisterous in the mess hall. Imagine what a shocking rebellion it was when a young girl climbed an apple tree.

Juanita 1929/12 Cherokee:

Oh [you worked off demerits] on your hands and knees, with our old wool sweaters. They made excellent polishing cloths; [Laughter] you could see yourself in the floors at Chilocco. And you carried something with you, and as you walked you thought "Oh, I wish I could fly!" and you dusted your tracks out as you went along. . . . Usually those demerits were worked off on your hands and knees. Just polishing something that is slicker than ice already, but you just keep doing it. Like one hour for ev-

106

ery demerit. . . . And those demerits, when you look back, they weren't given for anything except mischief. Like turning your head like this: you had to look straight ahead. Or talking in line was absolutely forbidden. Or sassing an officer. [A girl] climbed a tree one day and they couldn't get her down, things like that, that weren't really mean.

Noreen 1923/12 Potowatomi:
And if anybody was bad in the mess hall, the whole school, the whole room, the whole three companies in each building had to stand for an hour, without *moving*. . . . If they'd have on that certain dress that was striped, you'd stand there and I was always in the back row looking straight forward, you could see all these stripes. Many of the girls would faint and have to be carried out. Revived and brought back to stand in line again. That was about the worst punishment you could get, I thought, standing for an *hour* without *moving*. You weren't supposed to even move your eyes, or head, in any other direction. [Laughter] Oh dear!

Today many alumni value, in nostalgic retrospect, the discipline they survived at Chilocco. They compare their own experiences to the 1960s when the school "fell apart," in their words, wracked by congressional investigations of child abuse, drug use, and violence. Positive evaluations of earlier discipline are tempered, however, by recollections of punishments deemed excessive for "crimes" that were no more than youthful high spirits.

Barbara 1928/12 Cherokee/Pawnee:
I was locked up, I was locked up on my birthday. . . . I don't know what happened, some little something. We were all in the basement in a line, and I bolted and ran for some reason, probably wanted to go home. I bolted and ran and they ran after me and caught me and they put me in what they called the lock-up, which was a thing on the back porch of Home 3 . . . with a bed in it and I stayed there two or three days. And I would kick the slats, and they came and took my shoes away from me. [Laughter] I was just being real defiant because I was so homesick, or something, I don't know. But they locked me up and kept me there. So I could have been called incorrigible, too. [Laughter] But they didn't, and after that I was the top of propriety. [Laughter]

Edgar 1929/10 Cherokee:
Christmas, oh it was really something. The employees would wait the tables, they'd have the band, the orchestra there and they'd be playing Christmas carols. I mean we really had a meal. . . . I remember one Christmas, we had gone hunting, a couple of us, working up an appetite, and we purposefully missed breakfast, so we could just gorge ourselves. . . . And I remember we were just down there, by the Sheep shed or somewhere, when the doggone last call . . . [was sounded] for dinner. Ta-ta-ta-ta-ta-ta-da . . . you know, and this was the last call. And that was it [if you missed last call] you might as well turn around and go home [because they wouldn't let you in]. Well we ran . . . and we thought, well it's Christmas, maybe someone [will let us in] . . . not a one. I went on back, and we had a big old vegetable garden, down by the creek below the stock barns. . . . I went down there and I remember pulling up a couple of those big old turnips, building myself a fire, cooking those turnips on the fire and eating those turnips. I could taste the salt because my tears were going down into every bite of the turnip. . . . That sounds kind of cruel, I guess it was. . . . The discipline was such that . . . there were no exceptions. Maybe that makes a better person out of you; at least you learn there's a lesson in all of this, a *hard* lesson.

As harsh as these punishments seem, Noreen reminds us that more subtle actions also made a lasting impression on young children.

Noreen 1923/12 Potowatomi:
[The head matron] was always putting people in, we called it the guardhouse, it was actually just a room in the building but you were locked in and fed very meagerly for punishment. *
TL: What would they do to punish people, aside from [that]?
  They never beat you or struck you or anything like that, they were not allowed to do that. But, you know, Indians, being of such a sensitive nature, if somebody would even *look* accusingly at you or with a little bit of hatred, you just shrank into nothing: you couldn't bear it. So they didn't have to resort to any kind of violence, because we were so afraid of them and didn't want to be . . . pointed out, [or] draw attention to ourselves, and so you were pretty good.

Incarceration in the lock-up was discontinued in the 1930s and supplanted by restriction of privileges.

Nora 1943/10th Cherokee:

We just had what they called punish list, and you were punished according to the crime. If you were caught out of your room after hours at night; or on Sundays, when they had the white glove inspection; if you messed up that was punishable by missing the Saturday night event. We had a movie one Saturday night and the next Saturday night it was the dance. If you messed up on your housecleaning, then you missed one of those, the Saturday night privilege. If you done some little misdemeanor, you were seen walking where you shouldn't have been walking, on the grass instead of the sidewalk, then you missed Lawn Social.

Boys who broke the rules also earned special work details in the dormitories and restriction of social privileges. School records substantiate alumni memories of more extreme punitive measures: the rock pile and the beltline. In 1907, school authorities informed a student's father that his son had "disgraced himself" by getting drunk in town: "He has been on the rock pile ever since and spends his nights in confinement. He will not be set free for about two weeks yet."[4] The majority of boys at Chilocco may not have worked on the rock pile or run the beltline, but many men remember them very distinctly.

Coleman 1937/14 Delaware:

Oh, I remember some of those times that I fouled up . . . we'd have to wax the floor. First we had to strip the floor, we had those linoleums on there, and then we would scrub the floor. Then we'd have to take that soap off of it with clear water, then from there we'd have to let it dry a little while, then we had to wax it. They had those wax mops, and they had a mop with a cinderblock on it and it was wrapped in a torn up blanket. We'd have to pull those up and down the hallways to make 'em shine. Boy, those had to be shining. And you could go up to one end and look down, see where you missed, so you really didn't have to have somebody come and tell you.

Robert 1933/15 Creek:

[You] couldn't go to dances, you couldn't go to movies, you couldn't go to town. You couldn't go on athletic trips. If you didn't clean your room properly or if you were late to class, or cut class, why they would demerit you, put you on the restricted list and you were not allowed to participate in social activities. That might have been the wrong thing to do because the social activity might have been what the guy needed. [Laughter] I don't know. It's hard to say, but you have to do something, I guess. . . . They (also) had a rock pile there, and I remember a funny thing. There was a man there, his name was Lincoln. He was a night watchman. There was another man, he was just a young fellow, graduated I think in 1929 and then stayed on there as an employee. His name was Jeff Mouse. On Saturday afternoon when everyone else was gone to town, or doing something they wanted to do, free time, Jeff Mouse was the guy that was in charge of this rock pile. Boys that were on restriction had to report to Jeff Mouse. And *work,* for two hours or three hours or whatever their punishment was. It was down below the campus there, toward the creek. They had this thing, put big rocks in it and it'd grind 'em up and make little ones. . . . Someway this Lincoln got involved in it, he was a full-blood Otoe, I believe. In fact I think he had been a student years before, at Chilocco. He was the night watchman. He made an announcement at some formation, called off two or three names, and said "Report to Jeff Rock at the mousecrusher." Everybody talked about that for years, thought it was so funny, he got his words mixed up. 'Report to Jeff Rock at the mousecrusher.' Ever since then they called Jeff Mouse, Jeff Rock. [Laughter][5]

Although Coleman and Robert recall work details, restriction of privileges, and a lighthearted account of the rock pile, the next three narrators propose a grittier reality of student punishment.

Curtis 1927/9 Creek:
In the beginning when they had the military training-type thing, Saturday was inspection day and then they had a parade, and close-order drill and drill competitions and so forth. And they had a demerit system, if you got so many demerits during the week why then you had to walk those demerits off just like you do at West Point or army or whatever. And if you had done something *extremely* out of line, you worked on the rock pile on Saturday, Saturday morning was rock pile morning. They had a big rock crusher down there, and you went down there and took a sledge hammer and made little ones out of big ones so they could get 'em down to the size to get 'em in the rock crusher, and that was brutal work, it was like being in prison. At the age I was you didn't work on the rock pile, at nine, ten, and eleven, but I think, time you got around thirteen or fourteen then you were big enough to work on the rock pile. . . . You could do a lot of little

things and get a whole pile of demerits and you ended up on the rock pile
but *normally,* oh if they caught you stealing, or anything like that, that
was a rock pile offense, or if you got drunk, that was a rock pile offense. I
guess a lot depended on how they felt about you at that particular time.
[Laughter] If you were always in trouble, you got it! And if the disciplinarian was in a bad mood you caught rock pile. * If you got into so
many demerits they would also make you run a beltline. You'd line up, a
whole big line of guys on either side and they'd take off their belts, and
you had to run through the line, and they'd belt you with a belt as you go
through. That was another form of punishment for demerits and that
could get, for some of the smaller kids, that was kind of brutal. * They
[also] had a jail, in Home 1 and Home 2, both, they had iron bars on the
window and big steel doors. Flat steel doors with crosshatch, and if you
got in real trouble, like you got raving drunk . . . they'd lock you up in
there and put you on bread and water for a few days. Sober you up.

Edgar 1929/10 Creek:
If you ran off, they went after you and brought you back. We also had a
guardhouse where you were put in the guardhouse. That was pretty much
being discarded by the early thirties. They had the rock pile [if] you got
demerits, what they called red card; [if] you did something where they
caught you stealing or breaking in the commissary, the poultry yard, or
bakery or whatever you did wrong, you would be given demerits, and you
had to work those off on weekends at the rock pile. Where you make little
rocks out of big ones. I spent most of my weekends working on the rock
pile. [Laughter] I usually didn't have a free weekend.

Francis 1931/16 Cherokee:
We were talking about the rock pile, I used to play hooky from school and
you'd get a demerit every time you missed school. You get ten demerits,
you had to work Saturday afternoon, or all day Saturday, on the rock pile.
That's where I spent all my spare time, on the rock pile. [Laughter] It
wasn't hard to get a demerit, spit on the floor and get a demerit. They
[had] military, what do you call it? Discipline? And some of them officers
was pretty rough.
TL: They had that beltline then, didn't they? That sounds pretty rugged to
me.

III

Well, if you was slow, it was. [Laughter] There could be a bunch of them, and if you crowd 'em, they couldn't hit you very often. Just run like hell and, you kind of learned tricks. And they'd make you stand, too. If the whole dormitory did something, they'd march you down there and you had to stand in the basement for thirty minutes, an hour, two hours, without moving. Some of 'em would pass out, just keel over, faint. [They] just let 'em lay there, 'til the hour was up, or the two hours, whatever.

Violence Begets Violence

Violence was real at Chilocco. Physical violence against the bodies of children was the exception, not the rule, but it was the exception that proved the rule. The physical violence of the rock pile and the beltline was the capstone of a systematic violence to spirit and mind, reinforced by hours spent standing at attention, scrubbing on hands and knees, avoiding the matron's gaze, keeping still, keeping quiet. Federal educators envisioned the boarding school as a training ground, a controlled environment where behavior and belief would be shaped by example and instruction. Perhaps that vision came to fruition in unexpected ways, as students learned to use violence among themselves.

Ira 1936/? Cherokee:
I remember . . . one time when I was in Home 1. Had a room, there was two of us, and had a nice big closet. I went in to get my clothes to work at the Dairy Barn . . . and here was a lock on my closet door. Well, I went to the shop and got a pair of lock cutters and went back and cut that lock, and I like to got strung up. These guys had put their home brew stuff in there, all their makings, and I cut that lock . . . and I went on back to the Dairy Barn. Boy, the next day, couple of those big guys got me cornered on the steps and I thought they was going to slit my throat or something. [Laughter] Someone had taken that stuff out, after I had cut the lock. But they would take it, and make the stuff up and put it down in the silo in that ensilage, it gives off tremendous heat, and boy, that was like a factory-made business. What they'd done, they'd made arrangements with [my] roommate but he hadn't said anything to me about it. I was the one that got in trouble.

Violence determined rank and order within male student society, as gangs defended their territories and protected their own. Fighting to settle differences was common, and an accepted method of working things out. Not surprisingly, the boxers were foremost among Chilocco's athletic teams. They won Golden Glove status and traveled to fights in Chicago and Madison Square Gardens. In the early 1930s, *Ring* magazine rated Chilocco's boxing team the foremost amateur team in the nation.[6] Among the boys at Chilocco, as in the ring at the Garden, height and weight were advantages that usually came with age. The older students were at once the protectors and the exploiters of the young.

Ira 1936/? Cherokee:
There was a group I hung out [*away*] from [Laughter] and I usually managed to stick around closer to friendly, older, bigger guys. I had some problems, I guess I thought I was supposed to take it and seemed like it was pretty easy for guys to pick on me. I know quite often going to the mess hall, there'd be one on each side giving charlie horses, and they'd have me crying by the time I got there. Well, old B. H. was a big old muscle guy like Atlas. He'd say I'm going for him, and he'd grab me and he'd hold me up on his hand over his head like this. . . . See, I didn't weigh a hundred pounds until I was a junior, and all those guys, they looked like they was grown.

Edgar 1929/10 Creek:
We used to, on our way back [from town], we walked many times, it's seven miles to walk back to school. And we would stop by; in the summertime we'd take our bathing suits along. We'd always take a dime, have a dime to go swimming. People had their vegetable markets out there in front, you'd drop your bathing suit over a basket of apples, and pick up an apple, anyway, whatever you could steal, and then by the time we got down to the bridge, Arkansas City bridge, we'd go underneath and eat. Show off some of the stuff we'd stolen. We used to steal for the older students, and they'd tell us what to steal, what size socks [Laughter] and gloves, you know, put in an order for 'em.

Regardless of age, the boys at Chilocco conducted business among themselves according to a strict code of honor that valued bravery, discretion, and loyalty. "Telling tales," or "snitching," was a major sin, and honesty and fair dealing were the highest virtues. Edgar explicated these standards of expected behavior: "Kids had to fight, but they were always fair fights. I could truthfully say that I never saw any student use a club or a knife or stomp or anything like that." In the next excerpt, he expands on Chilocco's honor code.

Edgar 1929/10 Creek:

We had a bully, you know everybody's got their bullies. And I imagine Curtis remembers him, his name was Willy. Willy was part Cherokee, and I think he was part Gypsy [Laughter] or something, but . . . he had a beautiful built body on him, muscular, and most of us, we weighed around a hundred, hundred and five, six, eight pounds, he weighed a hundred and thirty-five, forty. He also was two or three years older than us, and when you've got somebody that's twelve, and another's that fifteen or sixteen . . . *big* difference. Hell, he beat the hell out of us. We stole for him, just like whatever he told us to do, why we did it. And he was a bully. And later on I found he was a coward, which is typical of all bullies. But, I remember one time we were playing marbles, and Willy . . . if you beat him at anything, he got mad. . . . Well on one occasion . . . I think I got one of his favorite marbles, and we used to play for keeps, you know. And he just reached over and hauled off and hit me right on the mouth. And knocked me down. I said, "Willy, you can't do that." I said, "I'll fight." [If things had been] otherwise I wouldn't have [fought] 'cause I knew it was fatal. So I started taking my jacket off, and Willy says, "Well, by God, you're not going to fight me, are you?" I said, "I'll fight you." Everyone thought, well what the hell, close your eyes, because it's gonna be murder. [Laughter]

We were at the back of Home 2, and they had some steps coming out and J. M. was setting up there. J. M. was a couple or three years older than me and never had any fondness for me, one way or another. He . . . never hated me, wasn't an enemy but he was no friend. He said, "Hell, Dizzy, you ain't got no business fighting (Willy), I'll fight him." And he just came down off the steps, and he really worked old Willy over . . . and that was the downfall of Willy . . . but that tells you something about J. M. No one else would dare attack old Willy, but he just, I guess didn't want to see some[body] murdered there.

Boys' gangs at Chilocco protected their own from other students, and exceptional individuals like J. M. sometimes stepped in to balance unfair advantage. Students also sorted out blame and reward among themselves when Chilocco's monolithic disciplinary system did not distinguish guilty from innocent. When "crimes" were committed and the responsible individuals could not be identified or apprehended, entire companies, floors, or dormitories shared punishment. By the same token, those guilty of escapades sometimes escaped detection. In both cases, students apportioned responsibility and exacted punishment. In Chester's narrative we see how one such inequality was rectified.

Chester 1946/? Cherokee:
We got into the employees' beehives one night . . . we got four buckets of that honey, and took it back, and of course we shared it with everybody. Everybody had honey all over Home 1, the little boys' building, and then they got stung on the tongue, because there'd be a bee in the comb. . . . It really made a mess, their tongue swole up and their lips, and all that, they had to go to the hospital at night. And so they came checking on us. There was four of us, and the [other three] they all lived down close to where the mess was on the first floor and I lived up on the second floor. [So] they didn't catch me, but they might as well have because, the [other boys] had to go down to the plumber, I think, they had to go down and clean his shop every evening. And so, they held it over my head. Boy I had to go make their beds in the morning, [Laughter] or they were going to tell on me. That was the worst [trouble] I ever got into.

Accomodation and Resistance

Different tribes, families, personalities, and experiences shaped Chilocco students, and it's not surprising that they responded so variously to military discipline. Some of the boys went out of their way to break the rules, just to sharpen their wits. They slipped out of dormitories after bedcheck, stole chickens and eggs and bread and whatever else was handy for private feasts in the catalpa grove. They made home brew, drank bootleg whiskey, shoplifted in town, and played pranks on one another and on their disciplinarians/advisors. Some of the girls tried to make home brew, but their resources were more limited than the boys. Both sexes turned to the final rebellion against Chilocco, running away. Covert resistance was more typical than the radical acts of bootlegging or going AWOL. It was not such an agressive rebellion against authority. Girls huddled in the dorm rooms after lights out, telling ghost stories and piling into bed at the hint of the matron's presence. Officers declined to inform on the ranks when minor rules were broken. Boys and girls passed notes in class, or communicated with winks, waves, and sign language. Boys shared one fifty-cent piece so a whole gang could go to town on Town Day. Girls conspired to outwit the matrons, to avoid wearing the bulky regulation bloomers to the dances.

At one end of the continuum were students who felt comfortable with Chilocco's discipline, who were happy to follow the rules, who felt part of a large, well-controlled, and well-mannered family. These students adapted, and adapted happily, to their life in boarding school.

Mary 1937/9th Cherokee:
Well, that [discipline] never did bother [me]. You know, it depends on how you were raised, we were sort of sheltered, and it was fine, I sort of liked it, I didn't resent it. I never thought I was missing much. [Laughter]

Flora 1932/17 Creek:
Later on, the discipline at the school got too lax altogether. . . . They had no control then, but in our day I think it was much better to have the discipline. It never was hard on me, I didn't mind it. I had come from a family like that, we were used to having discipline, and that wasn't all bad.

Irene 1929/15 Potawatomi:
TL: That was still the military system?
   Yes, that was ordered. I could understand that, why we did that, because it certainly kept peace and order. Some people didn't like the discipline of the school, they just couldn't take it. But to me, it went along nice with me because I was so disciplined [at home], that I was a pretty beat-down fifteen-year-old girl. [Laughter]

Maureen 1931/14 Choctaw:
TL: Did you ever feel resentful of the regimentation there?
   No, I didn't really because I had been reared very strictly at home anyway. That was one reason why I would rather be at Chilocco than be at home. So I just accepted it, tried to make the best of it. The ones who rebelled were the ones who had the hardest time.

Family background significantly influenced individual responses to Chilocco's discipline. These narrators equated the discipline they encountered at Chilocco with the discipline they already knew within their families. A common theme of alumni reminiscence is the feeling that one became accustomed to the school gradually (just as one gradually overcame homesickness) and then could appreciate it better. Alumni also comment on recognizing the good in later years, a perspective unique to the act of reminiscence itself.

Winona 1930/10th Cherokee:
And I was resentful of the regimentation [at first] but it didn't hurt us, it didn't hurt us at all! [Laughter]

Barbara 1928/12 Cherokee/Pawnee:
One of the punishments was standing at attention for an hour. It was very good for my posture [Laughter] in later years. . . . See that's what I mean about all this discipline that you realize later was good for you.

Cora 1929/12 Cherokee:
Well they had rules, but I can understand now, why. I wasn't rebellious against the rules, because that was what we had. And to me, I thought it was an opportunity, that we had something to appreciate. And *more* now, I do appreciate it. Because I know, to go to school, how much it costs, and to be educated. And everybody was real good to me while I was there.

The next three women all have a very positive view of Chilocco today. Juanita, the final narrator, epitomizes that view, but note her final few comments.

Alice 1925/7th Cherokee:
It didn't kill any of us, we got up and done all that [drilling], it was hard. My sister gets so mad when she thinks of how we had to drill and how we had to do, but I said, oh yes, it was good for us, it was really.

Norma 1925/12 Ponca:
Chilocco, even though they had all the strict, strict ways and all the strictness, that was the happiest time I ever had . . . I loved that. We had practically a military school, you know. * I really did enjoy that place, it was a beautiful place.

Juanita 1929/12 Cherokee:
(I was in) Company I, the Itch Company, [Laughter] and I was the smallest one there. I wasn't the youngest but when I was twelve years old I only weighed forty pounds. . . . We stood at attention many, many, many times; you've heard of four hours at a time without moving. If you moved, you got a demerit, or more, whatever the officer wanted to give. . . . We had competitive drill out in the Oval, it was pretty. And I

don't resent it, I mean, I think it's *great,* anything about Chilocco. But a lot of people I've talked [to] since, they didn't think it was [good] but I did, I didn't find anything wrong with it. * Yes, we had lots of fun there, outwitting the system, that was where it was a real challenge. You drew straws to see who was going to be lookout, and things like that.

Throughout her interview, Juanita maintained an overwhelmingly positive evaluation of Chilocco and everything associated with it. She would do anything to avoid uttering a word of criticism. And yet, we can see a clue in her narrative that there were social forces at work at Chilocco that tended to push the most "accommodating" students toward covert resistance as a symbol of peer group loyalty. "Outwitting the system" was a skill developed through student collaboration and practiced with pride. It drew students together as it pitted them against the system, and it was fun. Two other alumnae with determinedly positive and optimistic views of Chilocco, Irene and Marian, recall similar encounters with the system.

Irene 1929/15 Potawatomi:
I guess I did work in the dining room a little while because there was [a student] in there I didn't get along with, and I never will forget this. . . . This person that I didn't get along with got me in trouble, told on me, and anytime you got in trouble you went to [the matron] [Laughter] first. . . . I let on like I didn't know why I was being punished, but within me I kind of knew. I knew what I *felt* but, because I didn't say anything I didn't think anyone else knew. [The matron] told me, she said, "Irene, you don't have to *say* anything, it's your attitude." That made me so *mad,* to think they could read my mind. [Laughter] But she thought she'd help me, told me to work on it and helped my attitude.

Marian 1934/18 Creek:
TL: Did they still have the military system when you first started there?
    Yes, they still had it when I first got there, but then it too went by the wayside. Because I remember, I was at the last row [to march] and I was the first row to church. I know one time I had to stay home from the social, because my matron said I was flirting with my eyes [in church]. [Laughter] I didn't know what flirting was. I don't know what I was doing. And she was sitting *behind* me, how could she know?! So I just let her go, I just let her go, think what she wanted to, but I've always laughed

about that. I used to tell my daughter, I believe you're flirting with your eyes. [Laughter]

Petty authoritarianism reinforced the gulf between school personnel and even model students (from an administrator's point of view). Social forces emphasizing loyalty to the peer group above all else operated not only in student-student interactions but also in student-staff interactions. Federal policymakers did achieve some of their goals, however. Marian, for one, felt such a debt of gratitude to Chilocco that she returned there to teach for many years.

The boys reacted to Chilocco's disciplinary system much as the girls did, but since boys had more freedom and mobility, the overt resisters had more room than the girls to exercise their creativity.

Curtis 1927/9 Creek:
The army started mechanizing back in the early '30s, so they were getting rid of a lot of cavalry horses. They decided they would put some of these horses out on the Indian schools and the reservations. . . . They sent us some of 'em. We would go out in the pastures at night and catch these saddle horses, and *ride* 'em bareback, take a rope and just loop it around their chin and their lower lip to hold the horse with, and ride bareback. They had just received these [cavalry] horses so we decided we were going to check those horses out that night. We didn't know that [Kellar] was havin' a party up there behind his house, it was in the summertime. But we went out and caught some of these horses, and one of them apparently had been a troop leader's horse. [The] horse was used to being in front of the troops, could not stand to be behind another horse. And we didn't *know* that. So one of the guys got on that horse, and the rest of us got on the others, and started off down the road. And I passed this horse, and that horse just *immediately* took off, and the guy couldn't hold him, 'cause all he had was just a rope around . . . his neck, and the horse took off!

And we (were) helter-skelter right behind him. Ran right across the dam on the lake, went straight up by the gymnasium, and Kellar's house was right next to the gymnasium there on the corner. Here he had this big lawn party out there that night, he had tables out there with little lanterns, Japanese-type lanterns, strung out over these tables and all these people out there, in party dresses and the food all over the tables. And here we came thundering by the gymnasium [Laughter] and this horse was going just wild. And the guy couldn't *turn* him, and Kellar's house was right square there at the bend, and that horse went right straight through that back yard, and we were right behind him. There were about four or five of us on other horses, and . . . they're all cavalry horses, jumping was nothing to them. They went right over the tables! [Laughter] Took the lantern lines, the Japanese lanterns caught on us, and we just wiped the whole thing out! [Laughter] And the horses then cut back up through campus, and they slowed to go around the corner we all piled off, and let 'em go.

Oh, there was a big repercussion about that one, it was dark and they couldn't tell who it was. They suspected, you know, but again they were unable to prove it. They called us in and questioned us, but [Laughter] that was as far as it went. That was the *most* hilarious thing I've ever seen in my life, and Old Man Kellar, I remember going over that table and looking down, and he's standing there with his mouth wide open, his eyes as big as saucers. He was an ex-German army man, I think he thought it was the Charge of the Light Brigade! [Laughter]

The most overt resistance of all was to get out, run away, go AWOL. For decades, desertion from boarding schools plagued federal officials intent on maintaining enrollment figures. The student grapevine instantly telegraphed the news of who had run away, and who had been recaptured.

Florence 1933/7th Choctaw:
[I] went home in the summers. And it was hard to go back [to school], which I think helps to explain some of the *change* [Laughter] in enrollment [over the course of the school year]. Of course having been in schools—I've taught everything from first grade, to junior high, high school, university level—there were so many things that they *could* have done [at Chilocco], just basically a different philosophy and different approach, to have provided the kind of atmosphere that would have kept students from running away. That was a big problem, the news was always who ran away, who got caught, who was brought back, and so on.

Chilocco administrators had to maintain enrollments at capacity in order to obtain enough operating funds to survive. Funds were allocated on a per capita basis; established at the rate of $167 per student per year for many years, by 1929 the rate was raised to $225, a minimal sum to house, feed, clothe, and educate. To maintain minimum enrollment quotas the schools were overbooked at the beginning of the school year, and new students were enrolled throughout the year. Superintendent Correll explained to the commissioner of Indian Affairs in

Table 13. Enrollment Variability at Chilocco School, 1925

	Oct.	Nov.	Dec.	Total
Pupils enrolled (new)	38	61	22	121
Pupils on leave	14	24	20	58
Pupils dropped	178	32	22	232
Deserters	30	28	22	80
Deserters returned	10	16	9	35

Source: Figures compiled from Monthly Reports, October, November, December 1925, RG 75 EI B4, FRC.

1926, when questioned about overcrowding in the dormitories, that the dorm space was adequate for Chilocco's eight hundred student capacity but not for the over nine hundred currently enrolled: "It was understood that an enrollment of full 800 would have to be maintained during the year. In order to do this, it is necessary to start out with a number somewhat in excess as a considerable number sift out during the year, due to desertions, sickness in families, and other causes beyond our control."[7]

Desertion rates were high. From 1 January to 21 April 1927, eighteen girls and one hundred eleven boys went AWOL from Chilocco (813 belonged in school). (See table 13 for the anomalies in enrollment levels for the fall of the 1925–26 school year.[8]) Desertion rates were highest in the first months of the school year, when returning students and new enrollees were most homesick. Several boys deserted on 22 October 1921. It was the first Town Day of the school year, their first opportunity to draw on their funds to buy clothes and for spending money, and they took off for home. Citizens and law enforcement officials in the surrounding countryside kept their eyes open for possible runaways. Chilocco offered a reward of three to five dollars for information or assistance in returning a runaway.[9] Sometimes administrator's threats of dire consequences for desertion backfired, as a letter in 1924 from one of the agencies attested. The agent complained that the children were told that if they ran away from school they would be expelled, and that was more than sufficient encouragement for them to leave immediately.[10]

Subservient or Self-Reliant?

At first glance, the practical methods federal educators used to control and organize boarding-school students seem incapable of encouraging expressions of individuality or creativity. Military regimentation, uniformity of dress, appearance and behavior, adherence to a strict schedule of work and classes, a disciplinary system that operated by the rules with no regard for the individual, all appear antithetical to the federal rhetoric of producing self-sufficient, self-reliant citizens. Practice was more suited to producing subservience than self-reliance. Subservience did serve policy goals very directly, as the emphasis on domesticity training for girls reveals. Several alumni remark on the aftereffects of a childhood of regimentation.

Clara 1923/10 Potawatomi:
I do remember one incident where a girl was locked up in a little room for several days because she had another girl cut her hair too short, and I always thought that punishment was much too severe for the "crime." Discipline was just too strict on such insignificant things. . . . I really felt cowed down by all that strict discipline, it really made it difficult for me to just act like "normal people" out in the real world.

Juanita 1929/12 Cherokee:
TL: Did they have a schedule during the day that you had to follow?

Oh, every second, just about. [Laughter] There wasn't a lot of playtime really. You got up early in the morning and got dressed, went down in the basement and had roll call, and marched to the dining room. And then from the dining room we went back to our rooms, and we went on our way. There were schedules all *over* the place. [Laughter] You had to have a schedule or you never would know where you belonged. It was very hard when I left there because there were no schedules, there were no bells ringing and no whistles blowing: I didn't know what to do. And I didn't do very well. I couldn't stand noise, because we had to be quiet there, and what I call the white kids, Anglos—and here I sit looking like one of 'em—they were just running and free and yelling and kicking and screaming, I couldn't stand it. And they went in bunches, they didn't go two by two, [Laughter] and it drove me crazy. And nobody told me where to be at a certain time. There was no schedule made up; you had to do it yourself. And it's hard. And that was too, I think, things that Indians had to cross. A lot of 'em, it was the tribe and growing up where they did, it was hard for them to make the transition to this world. And, too, you had that training at Chilocco, that told you everything to do. That was one of the big complaints that I heard from kids that left Chilocco, especially if they spent a lot of years there.

Chilocco's regimentation made it very difficult for some students to develop direction from within. Moral development, responsibility in work, leadership were all dictated from above. Despite this disciplinary structure, the practical realities of institutional life did foster independence, self-direction, and self-sufficiency for many students. The school was simply too dependent on student labor and initiative for it to be otherwise. Students found niches in the school setting where they could express their individuality and creativity.

Trades instructors spent most of their time directing the older students, the juniors and seniors, who in turn directed the younger students. Senior boys directed work in the print shop, butcher shop, power plant or farm; girls assisted the dormitory matrons or the physical education instructor; both genders excelled on athletic teams; officers served in the military system. Within these "niches of responsibility" students developed important qualities: independent thought, independent action, a sense of responsibility, leadership, and self-sufficiency. Ironically, the exigencies of mass discipline and the excessive student labor required for institutional self-sufficiency did as much, if not more, to develop these qualities as any educational curriculum did.

The tension between disciplined regimentation and student initiative can be diagrammed along an axis of opposition. Administrators had to balance disciplinary methods deemed necessary for control against economic reality and a dependence on student labor and self-direction.

Administrative Perspective

<————————————————————————————>

Regimentation   "Ideal"   Student initiative

Characteristics of school life stemming from the military model of discipline cluster at the left end of this axis: regimentation of behavior, reliance on schedules, uniformity in dress and appearance, student organization into companies, marching and close-order drill, rules applied without exception, and an authoritarian staff. We see a constellation of factors conspiring to mass-produce a homogeneous student body free of individuality, creativity, and self-motivation but carefully programmed to follow orders. At the other end of the spectrum we see a different cluster: student supervision and leadership in the trades and farm departments, pride in knowing how to work and do a job well, and a strong system of peer group support to supplement the limited availability of sympathetic adult counselors. These latter characteristics of school life did in fact produce students who were self-motivated, self-sufficient, and independent.

From an administrative point of view, the paradigm of a "model student" lay in the middle ranges of the spectrum. The ideal student could adapt positively to the discipline rather than act out against it and could be trusted to assume a position of responsibility in his or her work. Officers fell into this category, as did trades and vocations supervisors, and athletes, who presented a positive image of the school to the general public and who focused the pride of the student body. The administration perceived themselves in alliance with these students.

A parallel schematic can be drawn from the student perspective, charting the range of students' response to discipline from accommodation through covert resistance to overt resistance.

Student Perspective

<————————————————————————————————————>

Overt Resistance	Covert Resistance	Accommodation
	"Ideal"	

Acts of active rebellion cluster at the left: drinking, stealing, making home brew, breaking curfew, sneaking off campus, and running away. The overt resisters, especially the boys' gangs, expressed the strongest loyalty to peers and adherence to a student-defined honor system. Loyalty to one's gang meant complete, reciprocal support regardless of right or wrong: when it came to a fight, you needed protection. Covert resistance, the middle ground, reinforced student allegiances. These activities ranged from home brewing to staying up and talking in the dorm rooms after lights out. Participation was not so much an active desire to break rules for the sake of breaking rules (more characteristic of overt resisters) as it was an affirmation of membership in the student group. One of the accounts of "home brewing" tells of boys who got too "tanked up" at the dances. They were maneuvered by their friends and dates to the door and escorted outside, screened by fellow students, in order to avoid drawing the attention of the disciplinarians. Students kept an eye on one another precisely in order to avoid confrontation with the authorities. Similar clandestine activities in the girls' dormitories ranged from smuggling bean sandwiches out of the dining rooms to secretive peyote ceremonies held by some of the Ponca girls.

At the accommodation end of this axis are a group of characteristics entailing a positive adaptation to Chilocco's disciplinary system. Students who accommodated were willing, even happy, to follow the rules. They often made a direct link between strict discipline experienced in the home and the direction they received at Chilocco. "Accommodators" among the girls reported close relations with the matrons in their dormitories, an indication that at least some of Chilocco's students were able to forge meaningful bonds with adults. Given the ratio of students to dormitory personnel, of course, this was not possible for all students.

The "ideal" student from the students' perspective vested his or her loyalties in his or her peers, rather than in the institution itself. Even students who could accommodate happily to Chilocco's disciplinary system broke the rules occasionally as a statement of group solidarity and a reaffirmation of their closest social relations. Loyalty to peers rather than to the institution, disapproval of "snitching," or "carrying tales," to school personnel, and some participation in activities of covert resistance were the hallmarks of a student model of ideal behavior. Students perceived as troublemakers were not really looked up to by the majority of students, although the most extreme form of rebellion, running away, was always a serious topic of conversation. It operated as an important symbol of student initiative and control even for those students who never considered it as a course of action. Conversely, students too closely allied with the authorities, who "carried tales," were not regarded well either. There was some overlap between the administration's model student and the students' model of ideal behavior (athletes were universally respected), but a crucial dichotomy separated the two conceptions. The highest value in student life was not loyalty to the institution, but peer friendship, a bond consistently referred to in later years as a family relationship closer than sibling bonds. The strong ties forged at Chilocco unite alumni, motivate alumni association gatherings, and anchor many Indian people's emotional attachment to the boarding school today.

The ties of friendship that flourished at Chilocco did not bind students in a consensus of shared experience, opinion, and behavior. Students brought diversity with them when they arrived from more than forty different tribal backgrounds, from scattered hometowns, from homes broken and intact. Students organized themselves in gangs and cliques in ways that reflected their life before coming to school and in ways that were created within the structure of the institution. The federal government classified them as Indians in an Indian school but they classified themselves much more minutely. English speakers, Creek speakers, Kiowa speakers. Eastern tribes and western tribes. Full-bloods, mixed bloods, beware the taint of African blood. Boys and girls. Baptists, Catholics, Protestants, stomp dancers, and "peyote eaters." Seniors, juniors, adults, and youngsters. Officers, enlisted men, Ironheads. Farmers, carpenters, bakers. Athletes, intellectuals, "dummy class." The permutations are nearly endless.

In the next chapter, the ties that bound and the rifts that crosscut student life are revealed most tellingly in memories of private moments, the "free" spaces within the circumscribed outlines of Chilocco. Behind closed dorm room doors, in the catalpa grove, behind the barns, in the evening along Chilocco Creek, wherever adult presence was *not*, students defined their peers according to values and criteria of their own.

The boys took what little there was and what little they had and made it into something bigger and finer and stronger than they had found.
Basil Johnston, 1989

Well, most of the things that *I* did, I wasn't really a mean kid. I got into a lot of mischief and most kids did there, there's no other way you could *survive* . . . Any time you take a bunch of kids and you put 'em together in that kind of environment and you try to control their thoughts and what they do and everything, it's impossible! Those kids are going to find *some* way to rebel and do what they want to do, and we did! We used to *deliberately* do things just to show 'em that we could do it and get away with it. It wasn't *malicious,* we did it for the *fun* of it, to let them know we could still outwit them. . . . I happened to be one that I couldn't stand somebody telling *me* what to do every minute of the day or night. That just went against my nature and everything I believed in, and I was gonna rebel come hell or high water.
Curtis, 1927/9, Creek

6

'Hm! White Boy! You Got No Business Here!'

The United States government established Indian boarding schools to detribalize and individualize Native Americans. They set out to mold a "successful" student—obedient, hardworking, Christian, punctual, clean, and neatly groomed—who would become a "successful" citizen with the same characteristics. Reality set in when school employees tried to regiment and homogenize a diverse, young, energetic student body through strict military discipline, all the while struggling to keep schools afloat that were chronically underfunded by Congress.

We need to understand the reality of school life in order to understand outcomes that policy did not foresee, for instance, that tribal and pan-Indian identity were reinforced, not diluted in Indian schools. McBeth has made the point that boarding schools in Oklahoma unconsciously structured "interaction between tribes and promoted a pan-Indian sentiment. A variety of tribal groups came into prolonged contact in these educational facilities. Tribal identity retained its significance and at the same time an inter-tribal, 'Indian' identity emerged as an important cohesive concept" (1983, 141). Evidence from Chilocco complicates McBeth's point even as it supports her.

The details of alumni memories indicate that student life was more richly textured than a simple opposition to non-Indian authority and consolidation of pan-Indian identity might indicate. Age, tribe, family life, native language, and other salient factors operated meaningfully to subdivide students while survival, shared experience, resistance to authority, and enrollment in an "Indian" school knit them together. A closely focused examination of Chilocco narratives reveals the arenas and the ways tribal identity remained central or took on new significance for students, as it reveals the circumstances that generated pan-Indian sentiments.

We can't visit real daily life at Chilocco sixty years ago, but alumni construct that reality for themselves and for others. They remember that they controlled certain times and certain spaces of student life. Private moments were the arena where gangs and cliques ruled, where tribe and/or "Indian-ness" most often mattered. These relatively free spaces existed in the interstices of regimentation and surveillance. Wherever students escaped adult supervision, students set the rules for social grouping and interaction.

Private Times, Private Places

Private moments fill treasured memories of boarding school. Students controlled their spare time away from the watchful eye of the school staff. Peer relationships were rich and complex and students organized interaction within a miniature society of their own creation. Marian describes student social control as she recalls her work detail in the school kitchen.

Marian 1934/18 Creek:
I was assigned for my first detail in the kitchen. I weighed eighty-seven pounds and I was five-one. And upon my entering the kitchen, my detail was to cook the oatmeal. Every morning, for nine hundred students. The cook, realizing that I was quite short, built me a stool to stand on, so I could stir the large, wooden ladle in the oatmeal. And then immediately after emptying the pot, my job also was to wash the pot. One day, I climbed up on my stool, to wash my pot, and being very meticulous in my dress, and grooming, one of the older girls removed my stool while I had my stomach up on the rim of it [the pot], washing the bottom of it. And then she gently pushed me into the pot. I did not call out, I did not cry. I found my way out of the pot, and with a tea towel tied on my hair, I went to the cook, and asked her if I might go back to the dormitory. She resolutely got up, and removed the tea towel from my hair, and asked me what happened. And I told her that I slipped into the pot. From then on my days on this detail were different. Because I had not elected to tell what really happened to me I guess, I was accepted, among the larger and more controlling group in the kitchen. Because in each society, there is a controlling group, and I learned that, because even at home there was a pecking order among five children.

Friendship and peer group control are certain, recurrent markers in the landscape of Chilocco's social life. Because so many alumni foreground these themes in their narratives, it is clear that student solidarity was the most influential and enduring social relationship embedded in the structure of school society. Children at Chilocco turned to one another, not to adults, to recreate and replace the close supportive ties of family and community. Given the variety of student age, tribe, hometown, personality, and gender, peer group association was a complex whole with many component parts, cliques, or gangs.

Male narratives are richer in private moment reminiscences than those of female alumnae, perhaps because female students were more closely chaperoned and not allowed free access to the outdoors and neighboring communities. Women remember life in the dorms and a more restricted range of spare-time opportunities. Men's stories are set in varied environments of group activity or private thought. Men emphasize the importance of gang membership, especially for the younger boys. The relatively weaker adult surveillance of boys allowed, or possibly encouraged, the boys' reliance on physical violence and fighting to sort out their differences.

The next few narrators map the restricted geography of the female world at Chilocco. Surrounded by 8,000 acres, girls inhabited only their dormitories and adjacent yards. Matrons chaperoned all outdoor activities and a good deal of what went on indoors.

Marian 1934/18 Creek:
Well, for fun, we were fixing up ourselves. [Laughter] We were doing our hair, we had to pass the bobby pins around, and you did your hair. When are you going to do your hair? I'm going to do my hair Thursday. O.K. then, I'll do my hair Friday, and we'd use the same bobby pins. And we sewed, we made our own little clothes, and we finally got to where we could wear our own home clothes. And we played cards, and we danced and we sang. And we could go for a walk, out on the oval, and we went to the other dorms and visited girls and played cards with 'em. Sang, group singing in the recreation room, and off and on we'd have formal teas, and we'd invite our matron in. Just your little clique. And there wasn't much to do, but that's what you did. If you ran out of that, then you got your books out. They saw to it you had plenty of homework. . . . And at nine o'clock, honey, you better be in that bed. Your light's out.

Vivian 1929/14 Choctaw:
We just went out in the yard, we'd play basketball and different games just kind of like, exercise out there, but nobody to supervise you or nothing like that [in the sense of directed physical education]. You're just on your own. And just a group would get together, some would go down in the Reading Room, they called it and people that would like to sing and play [the piano] . . . would spend hours there, let's sing this, let's sing that. It was just a lot of fun. Besides shampooing your hair [Laughter] and doing your nails.

Irene 1929/15 Potawatomie:
Evenings could be your own time. And you were allowed to go in other girls' rooms to visit, there was no law, as long as you were kind of quiet. You couldn't go in there and have a party or anything like that, but you were allowed to visit so a lot of us talked.

Noreen 1923/12 Potawatomie:
You had this little play time, about an hour, if it wasn't dark. . . . If it was already dark, and cold or raining or something like that you were allowed to play in the basement, and it was mostly things like . . . hopscotch. They let us play things like that. . . . Now like on the playground there was, there was *nothing,* just bare ground, we *played* . . . but there wasn't any equipment to play with! [Laughter]. . . . But we made our own fun, it was just a *release,* we could *yell* [Laughter] and we could laugh and we could make *noise,* which we weren't allowed to do inside the buildings, so it was pretty noisy, that hour was a pretty noisy time! [Laughter] Then we had to go back in, line up again and be dismissed and go to our rooms. And that's where we stayed until morning.
TL: So did they have lights out?
　　Oh yes, very early. But we didn't have any screens on the windows and bugs would fly in. Sometimes we'd catch a junebug, or something like that and tie paper under its legs, little pieces of paper, watch 'em fly around. Oh, it was fun. Entertained ourselves. [Laughter]

Juanita 1929/12 Cherokee:
One thing that I recall in Home 5, we had this nice kitchen. The other dormitories didn't have that, the old ones didn't have a kitchen. And the

poultry yard, which was mammoth, had lots of chickens, lots of eggs, was right near Home 5. . . . Somebody always had a boyfriend that could give you a chicken, kill you a chicken. And we would draw straws to see who was gonna go in Miss McCormick's office, get the key off the wall. . . . But her room was so close by, to unlock the kitchen, to get in there, to cook the chicken in the middle of the night. [Laughter] . . . Another thing we did, we put mattresses on the floor and we'd choke each other 'til we passed out, [Laughter] and they had the mattress there to fall over on. . . . And piercing ears. . . . That was another pastime, sort of, on Sunday afternoons, just bored stiff during quiet hour, piercing ears and . . . that falling on the mattress, that was one of our pastimes. In the wintertime, playing freeze-out, opening all the windows in those barns, snow would blow in, you know! [Laughter] It was a challenge to think of something when you were so restricted. But we had a lot to keep us occupied, we had lots of sports, Chilocco was always first. * We had arts and crafts and I can still see Edgar chasing butterflies, with a butterfly net. [Laughter] . . . Oh, we did butterfly collections and beading, and tennis, we had a lot of tennis, we had racquets and tennis courts. They didn't get a swimming pool until later years. We did an awful lot of walking up to the state line and we had a radio and music in the . . . music room.

A dirt road stretched north from the girls' dormitories a mile or so to the Kansas state line. Matrons occasionally led the girls on walks to the line, or traced a route from the central campus due east a mile to the highway.

Ellen 1927/13 Creek:
Sometimes on Sunday afternoons the matron would ask us if we wanted to go out for a walk, and she'd *go*! Walk down the road, go *clear* up to the gate, and then turn around and come back. And she'd always think we're gonna run off the road or something, but that's where we got to walk around, come back. At least you got out of the building.

Girls actively explored forbidden territory within the bounds of their restricted geography. "Wilderness" for the girls might mean the dorm kitchen or the fire escape.

Florence 1933/7th Choctaw:
You reminded me though, one time, the Home 4 had an old . . . fire escape on the outside, it was always locked. [Laughter] It was also forbid-

den, you were not supposed to get into it . . . but we found it unlocked, and we weren't up on the third floor, but we got down to the bottom of that thing and couldn't get out. But we [finally] managed to scramble back up and I remember thinking we're gonna be found here dead. [Laughter] You know wondering how many days and worrying about well how will they punish us? And then I thought well I'm gonna be dead and I won't have to worry anyway! [Laughter] It was really a frightening experience but we got back up I guess to the first floor . . . and lived. Didn't get caught even but it was just one of those crazy things that kids are going to do, I guess.

Women do not recount the same degree of overt resistance, of breaking major rules, as the men relate, but serious rule infractions such as drinking were a part of school society for girls as well as boys.

Florence 1933/7th Choctaw:
Has anyone told you, I was either in 7th or 8th grade . . . a group of the senior girls, by senior, I mean upperclassmen, got drunk on vanilla? [Laughter] . . . Oh, it was one of the funniest things, oh, it was probably pretty good vanilla, but it was a gay time for them, and I think they broke up a few things in the home ec department! [Laughter] I don't know what happened to 'em but it really made the grapevine!

Just as students found or created niches of responsibility and leadership within Chilocco's authoritarian framework, girls contrived physical spaces for free expression in their dorms and classrooms. Boys were not so hard pressed, as they had the run of the campus. Chilocco's acres were a refuge, a chance for privacy, a setting for gang membership, and a rich natural resource for hunting, trapping, and fishing. The wilderness of woods and prairies controlled by students contrasted sharply with the civilized campus controlled by staff. On evenings and weekends the boys slipped into a world of their own. It was easy.

Curtis 1927/9 Creek:
The old buildings all had big Virginia creepers, vines all over 'em, and the vines were as big as your arm. All you had to do was just slip out the window and climb down the vine, from the third floor, no problem, and go wherever you wanted to go, come back in, climb the vine, go right back into your room, your dorm. There was really no problem. You could go any time you wanted. They had bed checks every once in awhile, you just put a dummy in your bed and they never checked that.

Francis 1931/16 Cherokee:
We used to slip off to Ark City on Saturday nights, go listen to the big bands. I was in pretty good with the night watchman, I used to take turns for him, he was the one that checked the beds, so I could go to town and stay 'til one o'clock. All I had to do was tell him where I was going and when I'd be back.

Many boys were drawn to the open prairie, creek, and woods. The outdoor life figures significantly in their positive memories of the boarding school.

Albert 1926/13 Cherokee:
At Sunday noon was no duties, we were pretty much free, so we'd eat as fast as we could on Sunday noon, get out and run down to the horse barn. I think Mr. Halloway or Mr. Cobb had a hunting dog. He was a good squirrel dog, and the first one that got down there and claimed that dog, would get to hunt, hunt all up Chilocco Creek.

Curtis 1927/9 Creek:
The weekends I enjoyed, that was my time. I went hunting *every* weekend, winter, summer, whatever, went somewhere into the woods, along the creeks. Willy and I were good buddies. Willy was probably the best hunter I have ever seen. He had a knack, he didn't miss a thing in the woods. He could spot anything that had four legs or moved, and we used to go hunting all the time together. In the wintertime we'd hunt rabbits and squirrels and Willy could walk through a pasture where you had timothy hay up knee high, and snow on it and it'd form these pockets underneath, and Willy could walk along through that stuff, and just reach down and snare a rabbit right out of his *burrow*! He was something. And in the spring he and I used to go out and find baby squirrels . . . and make pets out of 'em, carry 'em around in our shirt pocket and on our shoulder, until they got big and then they'd take off.

And one year we caught some black squirrels. Willy and I saw this female black squirrel up in the sycamore tree, and so Willy shinnied up the tree and reached in the nest and pulled out two black squirrels. And so from that year on, that was the only ones we hunted for . . . we always go out and get ourselves a black squirrel every year. So, we were kind of the elite! [Laughter] . . . We'd nurse 'em on a bottle, and then start feeding 'em when they get big enough, solid food, whatever we had, nuts, any-

135

thing, and you'd go out to the walnut trees all over the place, and get walnuts and stuff, and feed 'em, crack them, and they *loved* all-day sucker candy. . . .

As far as the hunting was concerned, we used clubs and bow and arrows, and occasionally somebody would come up with a rifle, or a 4.10 shotgun. I don't know where we got these things but we always managed to scrounge one up somewhere, from some of the employees, you know, a gun that was no longer operable or that was beat up, and we'd fix it up and make it work. I remember we had a single shot .22 and the trigger mechanism was all shot. We put a rubber band around the thing and we cocked the thing and let go of it to make it work. And we used to go frog hunting in the summertime, go down to the creeks and hunt 'em, with bows and arrows and with a .22. Then rabbits you hunt 'em all winter long with bow and arrow or clubs.

The great outdoors at Chilocco was a crucial environment, where students developed and expressed mechanisms of social control. The boys' gangs were strongest there, providing mutual support and physical protection. Curtis and Edgar belonged to one of these smaller boys' gangs, and they remember their gang's territory and home.

Edgar 1929/10 Creek:
I kind of felt like I knew about every nook and cranny, every hollow tree. That ten thousand acres, we had a creek running through there that we called it Chilocco Creek. And we would get squirrels in the early spring, catch the young ones and everybody had a pet squirrel. . . . We also did a little trapping, skunks and muskrats. Many a time they moved my bed out in the hallway and left it out there, when I came in smelling like a skunk! [Laughter] . . . Also we had a little old house down in the catalpa grove where we grew our fenceposts, and real thick, thick grove. We built a little house in there and put a stove in there, and my goodness, the eggshells around there were two inches thick. Feathers, we'd go to the poultry yard and steal eggs and chickens. I never will forget N. R. [boys' advisor who had graduated from Chilocco] coming down there one time, he finally discovered that we had a place down there, so he came down and we had a great big old piece of tin, turned up on all the corners, put some grease in it, put it on top of this old homemade stove we had, and we were cooking chicken [Laughter] in that, frying it. And N. came in there and he asked

"Whatcha cooking?" We said, "Rabbit." He looked around, didn't say anything and left, and I mentioned that to him [in later years]. He said "Well, Diz, you can tell, rabbits didn't have wings." [Laughter] He knew a lot that was going on and he was a wonderful person.

Curtis 1927/9 Creek:
We even built little dugouts along some of the steep creek banks where the water didn't come up anymore, dig out a place and put a roof over it and sod it, and have a little place that we could go on our own. Even one year we tore down one of the old buildings and it was nothing but junk lumber that they were going to burn. We took that down in the woods and built a little shack, put a tin roof on it, and a little loft in it. We filled that loft with walnuts in the fall, put walnuts up in there to dry, had a little potbellied wood burning stove in there, and go down there in the wintertime and crack walnuts and sit in the warm shack. So there were a lot of little things that other kids never had that grew up otherwise. Those things I remember with great fondness. . . . They'd have stomp dances out at night, in the early years. They'd go out and build a fire, and parch corn, and then they'd make little tom-toms out of tin cans with rubber stretched over the top, and they'd have stomp dances around those fires at night, and it was a lot of fun.

The Creeks, Cherokees, and other Southeastern tribes took part in the stomp dances around the fires strung along Chilocco Creek in the evenings. Stomp dances held the boys together in a shared cultural context, and the very sociable pastime of parching corn united all tribes. Parching corn symbolized group belonging and solidarity. The "parched corn societies" were a focal point for boys' social relationships, and they stand out in warm memories of boyhood camaraderie.

Louis 1933/14 Cherokee:
In the dormitory, we were free from six to nine o'clock, to do whatever we wanted to do. Well, what are you gonna do from six to nine o'clock, when you don't have anything to do? [Laughter] So a bunch of us used to get together and I learned that we could go down to those barns down there and we'd swipe corn, and we'd take an old bucket or something, or some sort of a tin can or something, and build a fire way down by the creek, and we'd parch that corn and eat it, see, and somebody would

sneak a little butter out of the dining room and a little bit of salt. We managed to get it.

Frank 1923/14 Cherokee:
On weekends, if we were too little to make the football team. We had our own team, we went down to the picnic grounds and played football against another little organized football team. On Saturdays, and Sunday afternoons. Had a lot of fun. Had a parched corn society. . . . In the evening, you could see little fires glowing along Chilocco Creek. We had one boys' advisor in Home 3 named Mr. Lincoln, great big old thing, talked in broken English. One day had us all lined up there, and one person reported to him that we had been getting corn out of that granary down there. He said, "Been reported you boys parched half a lot of wagon, already." [Laughter]

Mason 1928/11 Cherokee:
Old Lincoln was raising cane one time. Somebody reported that the corn; well, they put it in these big hogwire circles, and they'd fill it up as they went along with those mechanical loaders, and sometimes they'd be real high. Well, of course we could get our arms through there, and the ear of corn would fall out. What they did, we'd just kind of put straw around the edges, to keep the corn from falling out, making silos out of that corn, keeping, storing it. Old Lincoln got up there, he said, "You Ironheads!" Everybody was just quiet. "You already parch a half a load of wagon!" [Laughter] "From September to October. One month! You will be expelled!" [Laughter]

Francis 1931/16 Cherokee:
We would take them dustpans, and they was pretty good dustpans, and bend up the end of 'em, stick a broomhandle in 'em, and stick a nail in 'em, just parch that corn . . . and then we'd take butter and salt, and it was good eating, it was about like popcorn, a little rougher, but when you get shut out, you could make it on a pocketful of parched corn . . . that's why Sam Lincoln got up and said, "You boys parch forty bushel wagonloads of corn."

Stomp dances and parched corn societies reinforced solidarity among the boys and delineated their separation from the school's control. The school administration never endorsed the dances but they tolerated them. No accounts, oral or archival, document the school administration taking aggressive steps to forbid or physically interfere with stomp dancing. It is an anomaly of federal policy and practice at that time.

Mason 1928/11 Cherokee:
Weekends and holidays were spent catching fur animals for hides to sell, hides were hung and dried and sold in Arkansas City, money was divided evenly with the group who had caught the hide. Fishing, stomp dancing and parching corn at the trash dump were projects candidly looked down on by faculty, but we did it.

Edgar 1929/10 Creek:
We also had, some of the Indians had their little stomp dances, Creeks particularly, we Creeks would have their little fires and at night some-times, you'd see their fire burning and their stomp dances. 'Course this was frowned on by the school authorities. As well as it was frowned on for any of the students to speak their native tongue.

There are only two references to similar activities among the girls at Chilocco.

Mary 1937/9th Cherokee:
[after discussing the boys' stomp dances along Chilocco Creek] The only time [the girls] ever, we'd do it in our basement, in the dorm. Some of those girls could do pretty good leading and singing, you know. Us green-horns, we'd just get right in there and . . . I don't know if everybody did that or not, but we did, in Home 3. I can't remember who it was that insti-gated that.

Vivian 1929/14 Choctaw:
Some of the Poncas, I remember they would get in their rooms, and I hap-pened to be in this dormitory one time, [Laughter] and it had about ten girls. Because I was late going back to school, I got put in the dormitory. I didn't have a room, and they [the other girls in the room] would have their peyote meeting in the room. All I did was sit there on my bed. [Laughter] I had never seen that, and so finally one of the girls came over and told me to come over there and sit with 'em if I wanted to. So I went over there, I set down, I didn't know what to *do,* I set down with 'em and they passed

that peyote button around, and I took a bite of it, but you know what it tasted like? Uh, a green olive. And I said, "I don't like it." And I took it out, you know, spit it out. They just laughed, didn't pay any attention to me. [Laughter] And I don't know what they were doing, they were, you know, in their own tongue, but they were all Poncas, Ponca Indians. * It sounded like they were praying, and then they'd sing and then some more, like praying, and then they'd sing, somebody was beating on a little gourdlike thing. It was quite an experience for me.

Participation in stomp dances or other covert religious activities was an important way students could retain ties to their home cultures. School authorities frowned on stomp dances but, for whatever reasons, did not stop them. Authorities were quick to clamp down on other transgressions, and some student activities seem calculated precisely to flout authority. Students followed certain courses of action because of the reaction they provoked. Alcohol production and/or consumption was guaranteed to trigger a response. The concoction of home brew, a prime undercover pastime, demanded discretion, ingenuity, and perseverance. In the conflict between acquiescence and overt or covert resistance to authority, alcohol use emerged as a potent symbol of student collaboration and radical resistance.

Edgar 1929/10 Creek:
We'd bury our beer, we'd make home brew . . . we'd find some thicket or something, we'd dig a hole, we'd put these kegs, used nail kegs, and we'd put our, oh I don't remember what-all we used, principal ingredients, yeast and malt and sugar. . . . Then we'd stretch some tote sacks over that, and it'd be buried about that much below the ground [four to five inches] and put this sack over it, real tight, and then we'd put dirt over that. And then we'd build a fire over it. This of course was an old Indian way of [hiding] where you had dug, no one would think of digging under it. * I guess the first time I got drunk I was eleven years old, and I got drunk on Sail On . . . it was vanilla extract . . . Vanilla and lemon extract, about 85 percent alcohol. . . . We'd break in the commissary and the bakery and what not and steal cases of this damn Sail On and get drunk on it. Well, there's no need telling you if you get drunk on either vanilla extract or lemon extract, how long it took you to get rid of the smell. [Laughter] . . . We thought it was something to go to the Social, with a few drinks, and some of 'em even weren't above, even kind of acting

drunk, you know. . . . There's a little peer pressure connected to it, so-and-so's drinking, so-and-so's drunk, you know, like he's really done something.

John 1931/16 Chickasaw:
One time we were up there, it was after I went back up there in '39, they were having this big farmer's party, you know? We had that farmer's party coming up so, let's see, we've got this many days, so we was getting all this stuff ready. . . . Well, we set up [our home brew] there in the dairy barn, up there in this south place where they had bundles of oats stored. We dug way down in there and we put a rag over the top of [the barrel] put a big lid on the top of it. And all this time [before the dance] them guys were throwing them bundles out in the wagon, you know, hauling 'em out and feeding 'em to the cattle. . . . So they were getting down pretty close to that [barrel] so we dug the hole down a little farther. The next kid that went out there and checked it, said, man it's really working. [Laughter] The next day or two they kept throwing the oats out of there, finally old Barslow, he was in charge of feeding them dairy cattle . . . old Barslow he backed around in there one time, he stepped down in there, he broke that thing and went down in that beer. [Laughter] And them guys, one of 'em was working up there that day that helped set the thing [up], and he said, he thought he was going to faint. [Laughter] Anyway that old Barslow had them guys pick up that old barrel we had, throw it out, so those guys come back all downhearted. I said, what happened? "Oh, old Barslow stepped in our brew." [Laughter]

Curtis 1927/9 Creek:
We got fruit, peaches, and put those in a barrel one time, and water and sugar and malt or whatever, we put in that thing and let that ferment. That stuff stank to high heaven, [Laughter] you could smell it! I don't know how, why they never found any of those things, because all you had to do was get downwind of that, and you knew what was *there*. We took raisins and did the same thing, and grapes, we went over to the orchard and got big Concord grapes and we set those up in a barrel. [Laughter] We just put cheesecloth over the top of the barrel and *butterflies*! [Laughter] You could tell a half-mile away where it was because the butterflies were swarming in on these things. We had these barrels stashed all over the

place! I don't think they ever knew about that, we were never questioned about it, anyway. . . . But that stuff was terrible, oh boy! But you got a buzz out of it. [Laughter]

School administrators were quite concerned about drinking and other crimes, and devised their own strategies to counterbalance the mischief boys got into. In the early 1930s, school staff sponsored Boy Scout troops at Chilocco as a wholesome alternative to gang activities. Superintendent Correll proudly described the scouts' accomplishments in his annual report to Washington in 1933:

> One of the big projects for the scouts last year was the completing of the scout camp which consists of three big hogans; a big, long, log council house, with a stone fireplace built in one end; many old, wooden, log footbridges across ditches and streams; a big open-air fireplace, with many tables. . . . The scout boys feel very proud of their little camp . . . and [have] done all of the things that boys of that age enjoy doing. This has not only kept their idle time occupied, but we feel like it has been largely responsible for doing away with a lot of the little, petty crimes that we have had on our campus in previous years.[1]

Curtis offers a different version of the accomplishments of Troop #2, which included Edgar and Willy.

Curtis 1927/9 Creek:
The Boy Scout camp, we built that one summer, one *year*. There was an old abandoned railway that ran through the edge of the reservation over on the west side. And there was a railroad bridge there and they got permission from the railroad . . . to have us go out there and tear that bridge down, and take the timbers and build us a Boy Scout camp. Which we did, took those big timbers and we made hogans. We had a hogan for each troop. There were about four hogans, something like that, and then we had a large meeting hogan which was long, kind of oval-shaped building and had a stone fireplace in it, and built the whole thing. They had big shake shingle roof on all of 'em. They were very nice, and well built, and that was our Boy Scout camp. We built ovens, outdoor ovens, similar to what the Hopis have only a little different. We took railroad ties and built up a big square with the railroad ties up to about waist height, and then we built the oven on top of that.

Well, we got the bright idea that we would build a whiskey still under-neath that thing. . . . I guess there were four of us, really, originally, two brothers, and then it seems to me Willy. And so I said, well, we can build a still down in the bottom of this thing, and make the logs so they swing out [and] you can crawl under. You put a little fire pot down below, put the chimney comes up through and join the oven chimney to that. So that if you build a fire in the *oven,* smoke coming out of the chimney, you go down underneath and build a fire down there and brew up, distill some whiskey. And we went out and got nail kegs, nail kegs all over the place, and we burned the inside of those nail kegs, we heard, well you had to char your kegs. [Laughter] So we charred the inside of those nail kegs and then we put a mash in there. We didn't realize you're supposed to cure your bourbon in that, but anyway, that's the way we made it. And we went out and got corn, had somebody steal the yeast from the bakery, and we got corn and sugar and whatever, I don't remember what all we put in there. I wouldn't know the first thing about making whiskey, and we didn't then but we imagined anyway.

And it fermented, and we had these kegs, we dug holes all through the forest. We put old wooden doors over 'em and then covered 'em with sod, and we set up our kegs, our mash out in the woods. And then for the still, we got a little teakettle, just a regular teakettle, got some hose and we found a copper coil that came out of a water heater, and we built this thing out of that teakettle and that copper coil. Then we'd bring our mash in and put it in that little pot, cook it, and alcohol would come out through that thing, and it wasn't really very powerful. [Laughter] We didn't know when to cut it off, you know, and the amount of alcohol that came out of that thing was infinitesimal really, [Laughter] the steam would come out along with it, kept precipitating out. We pretended that that was really booze. Oh, it had some alcohol content, but it wasn't all that strong. And then we took burnt coffee and colored it with burnt coffee! [Laughter] But we had our whiskey still. And we'd go down there and we'd build a fire down below, and then we'd build a fire up above and we'd bake biscuits, make drop biscuits and bake 'em in the oven so that they would think we were cooking, and then run off a pot, or two or three. We'd go down there sometimes and spend the whole afternoon.

One of the brothers, the younger one, I guess he got mad about some-thing so he went to Kellar and told him that there was a still. He didn't say who was in it, he didn't want to squeal on his brother, but he just told him where the still was. So they went down and found it and of course they suspected the right guys. [Laughter] They called us in and questioned us. And at that time things had changed considerably. [Kellar] was an advisor now and couldn't get as tough and as mean as he used to. They tried to pin us, but we just denied it, flat out denied it, we don't know what you're talking about. . . . They tore the oven down so that was the end of our bootlegging days.

Correll was right. The scout camp did distract the boys away from petty crime, right into major crime. As funny as this story is to tell and listen to today, we cannot ignore its serious implications. Alcohol abuse and alcoholism are pervasive tragedies among Indian families and communities. The focus on home brew, bootlegging, alcohol use, and drunkenness as important mechanisms of boarding school resistance raises difficult questions. Did the schools contribute substantially to alcoholism among Indian people? Was it a tragic consequence of students choosing a stimulus guaranteed to stir up school administrators that hurt students themselves most in the long run? Was there some element of self-destructive behavior at work for students who felt caught in a system they could not abide? Or, worse yet, could not leave? At least one tragedy at Chilocco speaks to these questions and to the further research they demand.

Curtis 1927/9 Creek:
TL: Was there any real bootlegging, with the older boys?
They went to town, there was a lot of bootleggers in Arkansas City. Particularly in the summertime there were always some of the guys coming in from town just dead drunk with that stuff. One guy even died one night, from poisoned [liquor]. I think he did it deliberately though. He had graduated from high school and he was in his twenties, had no home. I can't remember where he came from or even what tribe he was. But he had no home, no people at *all,* no relatives apparently, and they told him that he was gonna have to *leave,* because he had graduated. He didn't know where he was going or what he was gonna do; this was *home* to him. It was like kicking him out. And he came in that night, just dead drunk and died, and they think that he got, he poisoned that liquor and killed himself. I don't think they ever proved it, one way or the other, or

whether he just got hold of some bad whiskey, but I've always felt like he killed himself drinking poisoned liquor.

For this student, Chilocco was the only home he knew, or could imagine. Other students shared their own little "homes" within Chilocco, whether a facsimile of home life in the practice cottages or real, warm shacks in the catalpa grove. The wilderness of the catalpa grove was more than a safe refuge for boys in search of privacy or camaraderie. It was a social arena in contradistinction to the controlled environment of the campus; what was most strongly sanctioned there was expressed most freely here. The tribal or Indian identity, for example, suppressed by the school seemed to flourish among the catalpas.

Boarding schools were designed to eradicate Indian ethnicity and tribal affiliation while rescuing the individual, hence Pratt's famous dictum "Kill the Indian, Save the man." At best, school staff ignored tribal identity; at worst, they punished students harshly for speaking native languages or practicing native religions. It was not so easy to ignore the basic fact that Chilocco students were Indians. It was an Indian school, after all. In private spaces and private moments, students sorted out for themselves who was who and what was what. Tribal identity dominated student interaction in particular places and situations, while it lay dormant or unexpressed elsewhere. Careful attention to how tribal identity was expressed at Chilocco produces a kind of peripheral vision. Focus on ethnicity, and you glimpse things previously hidden in the shadows: distinctions among students based on gender or hometown, for instance, and the different adaptations made by older and younger students.

Indians at Chilocco

Students responded individualistically to Chilocco's regimentation. What characteristics of individual personality or experience were linked to the decisions to accommodate or resist? How did tribe, family, gender, age, language, or degree of blood influence student response? Complex questions require complex answers. Evaluation of narrative reminiscence of intertribal relations yields clues. Native language proficiency, mixed blood versus full-blood, "eastern" versus "western" tribes were balanced in a complex equation of personal identity at Chilocco. These factors, in turn, balanced with other salient disparities among students. Young students/older students, children from broken homes/ children from intact families: these distinctions made a difference for Chilocco students.

I asked Chilocco alumni, did students make friends or join gangs within their own tribe? What other factors—age, class, work details—if any, tended to define peer group association? Was there friction or hostility between tribes? Some alumni responded strongly and unequivocally, yes, tribes shaped peer association and there was friction, described in two instances as "intertribal warfare." Others responded just as strongly and unequivocally, absolutely not, there were no tribal divisions. In some cases, alumni did distinguish a salient dividing line between those of full Indian blood and those of mixed blood.

In making my own analysis of these disparate opinions, I have segregated the womens' narratives from the mens' because their discussion of private moments reveals important differences in their school experiences. The student interactions that took place in private times and places are the clearest indicators we have of student-organized peer groups and provide the clearest views of the criteria students used to sort each other into salient classes or categories. We know that girls at Chilocco were much more circumscribed than the boys; their experience of the school was different because of that. Differentiating the two genders makes it clear where men and women agree and where their accounts or perceptions diverge.

The Women Speak

Chilocco's alumnae express a wide diversity of opinion on the subject of tribal distinctiveness and/or divisiveness at the school. Clara, Maureen, Barbara, and Vivian all downplay student tensions along tribal lines. They recall group associations by age, or personality, or "status" on campus, specifically the popular athletes. Sarah agrees that Chilocco was "just one big family" but does comment on the clannishness of the Poncas.

Clara 1923/10 Potawatomie:
I really don't recall any kind of tension, or snobbery, along [tribal] lines, it seems like everyone got along together, it didn't make that much difference, were you a full-blood or mixed blood. Even those that only spoke English, and those that spoke their Indian languages seemed to get along.

Maureen 1931/14 Choctaw:
I never saw any animosity, I don't believe, between tribes. There was some infighting, a little bit. . . . But I thought as a whole, they got along pretty good.

Barbara 1928/12 Choctaw/Pawnee:
TL: Did (friendship) tend to follow tribal lines at all?

146

No, no. Not at all. It was just . . . I don't know what it would be, it would just be your personality, I guess, it must have been your personality. Because as I say, you were all in the same boat, you all wore these same clothes, and it would have to have been your personality or your background. * I think it was more class, than it was whether you were full-blood or [not] . . . well, for instance, like the basketball stars and things like that, a lot of 'em would be full-blood and very dark but still they were up there.

TL: Big men on campus?

Yes, right.

Vivian 1929/14 Choctaw:

TL: People didn't stick together just with their own [tribe]?

Oh, I didn't think they did because I had a lot of Creek friends, see I'm Choctaw [Laughter] and I married, my husband was half Creek.

Sarah 1926/12 Shawnee:

TL: Did you have some friends that you would buddy around with?

Yes, we had what they called gangs, there'd be four or five, maybe six girls in a gang. [Laughter] . . . It was probably just around your age, or maybe your classmates, something like that.

TL: So . . . people just didn't mix with their own tribe?

Some did, like the Ponca girls, they were real close among themselves, but, you know, we were just one big family . . . and they'd always help each other, whatever ways they could.

Sarah's comment about the Ponca girls agrees with other narrators' perceptions about peer groups at Chilocco. Certain tribes tended to be singled out as "clannish," but it is difficult to say today whether they were actually more or less closed than other groups at Chilocco. It may be they have come to symbolize "tribalness" to contemporary alumni. Poncas did live close to the school, and Ponca runaways had only a few miles to go to reestablish contact with their families. Perhaps this proximity strengthened their awareness of their own tribal background and ameliorated the melting-pot effects of a multitribal student body drawn together by the difficulties of being far from home. There were never more than a handful of Ponca students at Chilocco, relative to the large student body, and Ponca-ness certainly did not define the limits of tribal clannishness. Typically, native language use is the factor identified today that bound together tribal members at Chilocco.

Ellen 1927/13 Creek:
They [the girls] just mixed quite a bit but those Creeks, lot of times they got together because they'd talk to each other, some of 'em could talk in Creek, you know.

Winona 1930/10th Cherokee:
There were some of the students up there that we hardly even knew, that we just didn't even speak to them. Some of the tribes, you know, that were clannish, and that would even speak their language when they were together. Then there was students, see, that didn't want to participate in a lot of the activities that the school had. They were, well, a lot of 'em were full-blood Indians.

Winona's separation of full-bloods and mixed bloods recurs in many narratives. Juanita and Irene both recall separation or at least distinctiveness along those lines but deny that the distinction led to any kind of friction or hostility.

Juanita 1929/12 Cherokee:
TL: Did friendship follow tribal lines at all or did it cut across them?
   In my case, it cut across. Some of the full-bloods particularly that come to my mind, the Creeks, they didn't even hang out with other Creeks . . . they sort of hung together. And well I suppose there were a few Cherokees that did that, that I can recall. The rest of us, it didn't matter who was [what]. I loved the Comanches and the Cheyennes and the Arapahoes, and one of my good friends was a Choctaw. One was a Creek and one lived at the bottom of the Grand Canyon.

Irene 1929/15 Potawatomie:
TL: Did full-bloods tend to stay separate from mixed bloods?
   I think in a way it really was, but it never caused me to feel unwanted or anything, I just stayed out of the way. [Laughter] It was always just someone else you could go be with. . . . [It's] hard to help that, maybe they all came from some little community. But it never, I don't think it ever caused problems.

The proportion of full-bloods declined at Chilocco throughout the 1920s and

1930s (see table 9). Full-bloods constituted 54 percent of 954 students in the 1924–25 school year; by 1940–41 that proportion had declined to 31 percent (of 811). In the peak enrollment years of the early 1930s, the percentage of full-bloods hovered around 40 percent of over one thousand students. It seems unlikely that students knew each other's precise degree of blood as adumbrated in the schools' enrollment records, which specified ¾, ¾, ½ and ¼ Indian "blood."

Students more likely made their judgments according to a complex interplay of behavior, language proficiency, family background, and looks, especially skin color. In this latter regard, they may have been influenced by some tribes' hostility to people of African descent. School authorities were certainly ever vigilant for offspring of African-American parents trying, in federal eyes, to pass as Indians. Offspring of Indian and black parents certainly existed at the time, but the government was not interested in making a place for them in federal schools. "Too dark" was the euphemism used in school records of suspect students. At the other end of the spectrum, employees favored lighter-skinned students. Some students recall a definite rift along the faultline of complexion as well as tribe and language.

Pauline 1929/16 Cherokee:
The first year I went, I didn't get to stay with my cousin. . . . [I was in] a dormitory, I would say fifteen to twenty beds in that dormitory. And they were all full-bloods, and they were all either Poncas or Creeks, and they all talked their [own] language, they didn't talk English. I tell you, I just felt so out of place. Here I was, I was blond-headed, light-complected, and they wouldn't have anything to do with me. They wouldn't talk to me, they wouldn't tell me anything, and if they did, I couldn't understand them. [Laughter] So I was away from home, and it was a long ways, and I didn't know a soul up there but my cousin. So I went to bawling, and went down to my matron on the floor and I told her, well I'm up there in that dormitory with all those full-bloods and they won't talk to me and they won't have anything to do with me. They won't help me and tell me anything, and I asked if I could move down there with my cousin. She said yes, and she let me come downstairs, and I was happy, even though there was six of us in that room, we were all jammed in one little old room. [Laughter]
TL: Was that usual, the full-bloods sticking together or people from one tribe sticking together?

Well, it was with those Poncas. Now there was other classmates that I had that weren't all full-bloods, there were a *lot* that weren't full-blood. And I would pick one out, I could see them, you know, around through the groups, especially in my class.

Pauline's unhappiness with her roommates led her to the matron, who intervened in her behalf and assigned her to a room with her cousin. Tillie recalls that matronly intervention often came at the point of room assignments themselves and may have played a role in shaping student peer groups along lines that seemed reasonable to the matrons.

Tillie 1939/13 Cherokee:
You were assigned your roommate for the year, every year it was assigned, you didn't have a choice. They knew you after awhile, they knew what girls would fit in with what other girls, and they would put you with someone compatible. Tribes sometimes determined that, the Poncas and Pawnees stuck pretty close together, for example. Others mixed pretty well. Some of the Creek girls might have been a little clannish, and the Kiowas, and Comanches.

What seemed reasonable to the matrons as criteria for discriminating among [or against] students?

Nora 1934/10th Cherokee:
Being lighter, the employees kind of favored me. I got ribbed a lot about it, but I was always too timid to really get into any trouble.

Women remembering tribal affiliation and peer group formation at Chilocco relate perceptions ranging from little or no tribalism to specification of groups closed by tribe, native language use, or degree of blood, or by some combination of these factors. Creeks and Poncas who spoke their own languages are mentioned several times as "clannish." Juanita comments that Creeks who were native language speakers differentiated themselves from Creeks who were not. With regard to native language proficiency, the sample of alumnae interviewed is quite imbalanced. Only two of the women entered Chilocco speaking their own language. Both are Creek, and neither commented on any tribalization among the girls. Almost all the alumnae represented here think of themselves as mixed blood, roughly half a dozen as full-blood: these categories reflect family background, behavioral characteristics, contemporary place of residence, and other factors in addition to superficial considerations of looks or skin color.

Women's narratives contain other clues to tribally influenced student associations in the comments that differentiated *eastern* from *western* tribes.

Norma 1925/12 Ponca:
Seems like the tribes would divide by eastern and western, you know. Like the western people pretty well stayed together and the eastern, from Creeks to Cherokees and them, they pretty well stuck [together]. They [the eastern tribes] even had different costumes than we did. They believed in the Stomp Dances, and the Corn Dance, these kind of things, and we didn't, we had another style. So there was a little separation there, but not very much. We were pretty much all together. I had a whole lot of Creek friends, and a lot of Cherokee friends, and I guess I'm the wrong person to talk to because I had no quarrel at all.

Eastern and *western* refer here to geographical and cultural differences. Eastern tribes had been removed from the South or East to eastern Oklahoma: such as, Creek, Cherokee, Choctaw, Chickasaw, Seminole, Euchee, Delaware, Shawnee. Western tribes by culture and geography included the Southern Cheyenne, Arapaho, Comanche, Kiowa, and Apache, who were located in western Oklahoma. Several tribes who were culturally closer to the western Oklahoma Plains tribes had been assigned lands close to Chilocco, and thus close to land areas settled by the so-called Five Civilized Tribes, or eastern tribes. The Poncas, Pawnees, Otoes, Kaws, and Tonkawas were geographically eastern but culturally western and students classed them among the western tribes.

The east/west dichotomy was probably exacerbated by school staff who discounted truly Indian heritage among the eastern groups, especially the Five Civilized Tribes. Real Indians in their judgment were western Indians. In the 1930s, as new administrators in Washington directed boarding-school personnel to value Indian cultures, Chilocco established an Indian Dramatics Club under the new arts and crafts teacher. The club's members were without exception western Indians: Kiowas, Comanches, Cheyennes, and so on, with a few Caddos just to confuse the issue. School records indicate the club gave performances, mostly off-campus, to represent the "Indian School" to the surrounding American public.

The arts and crafts teacher instructed students in "crafts representative of no certain tribe" since "many of the tribes represented at Chilocco have lost their tribal arts and crafts." The crafts of no certain tribe included spinning and weaving wool; beadwork; weaving rag rugs, yarn belts, and cornhusk place-mats; and cross stitch (an art, perhaps, of the least certain tribe). In 1935, the arts and crafts teacher expressed hopes of looking up Oklahoma Indian designs. She turned for help—not to the tribes—but to the Oklahoma Historical Society and the art department at the University of Oklahoma.[2] Eastern Indians often agreed with this exotic perception of western Indians. Juanita (Cherokee) puts it eloquently:

> There's nothing in this world that will put me to sleep faster than a stomp dance . . . these Cherokees are so *colorless,* they have no feathers, no nothing . . . so now for our celebration every year we have the Plains Indians, now they can really get it on.

The Men Speak

Male narratives reveal the same broad range of opinions as the women's, from those who recall no tribal clannishness at all to those who describe intertribal "warfare." Men repeat the themes brought up by women, recalling close inter-relations among the Five Civilized tribes versus the western groups, and tribal clannishness linked with native language proficiency.

Robert 1933/15 Creek:
I've heard guys who went to school at Bacone say that the Pawnees and I guess the Creeks at Bacone always were fighting. But I didn't notice that at Chilocco. It didn't seem to me that anybody paid any attention to what tribe you were, they were just a bunch of kids. . . . If they knew you they knew what tribe you were, but it didn't make any difference. They didn't make a big deal about it. They all got along, as though they were the same tribe. I never knew of any feuds between tribes. * Might have been there and I didn't see it, but I don't remember anything like that.

Albert 1926/13 Cherokee:
I didn't notice it, really. Some of the Creeks, possibly, and some of the Choctaws that was from the [same] community at home may [have]. As far as any kind of segregation, not segregation but cliques, I didn't notice any as far as tribes or even home towns or anything. Or even relatives, everybody seemed to be up there on their own. Now I mean you had your

buddies but it was like, my close friends included a Kiowa, a Chickasaw
. . . a Creek, [and] a Choctaw boy.

Charlie 1934/9th Cherokee:
TL: Did people hang together by their different tribes?

Not a whole lot, a little bit because they were from the same locality,
generally, but other than that, no. They sort of knew each other, or they
came in together, and group dynamics will teach you that, they'll sort of
make friends on the way, and that will linger on. Other than that, no. A lot
from down in Cheyenne-Arapaho area, down by Lawton, they sort of
hung together, people over in this part of the country [near Tahlequah,
that is Cherokees] sort of hung together, but not to that extent.

The men more often recall tribe as an operative factor in determining student
associations than the women do, and they stress more the associations resulting
from hometown origin. *Hometown* in Oklahoma reflects tribal origin even today. When Indian Territory and Oklahoma Territory were consolidated into the
state of Oklahoma, tribal governments were dissolved. Reservations as protected federal trust lands had already passed largely into (non-Indian) private
ownership as a result of the Dawes Allotment Act. The eastern tribes, particularly the Five Civilized Tribes, no longer resided on reservations in the 1920s
and 30s but lived in what are known today as "historic areas." Certain small
towns in areas that had been historically designated as Creek or Cherokee or
Choctaw lands maintained a population that was heavily of that tribal origin.

Ira 1936/? Cherokee:
Two things [mattered], tribe and hometown, for the large part. Some of
the more outgoing boys, they made friends with people from all over the
place.

Louis 1933/14 Cherokee:
I think the people who had a tendency to hang together, more or less as a
group, because there were quite a few of them and that was the Kiowas
and the Creeks. Now those two tribes did, and . . . used to slip around
and try to talk their language. . . . The Poncas were pretty clannish, but
there wasn't too many of them up there, then. But the Five Tribes usually
stayed pretty close to each other, I mean, you'll find that many of the Five
Tribes intermarried into each other, quite a few of them did.

Cecil 1929/? Creek:
They'd stick pretty much so [by tribe], that's the way I seen it. I mean, a lot of them just ran in groups, most of us ran in groups.

Chester 1946/? Cherokee:
TL: Did people stick together much by their tribe?
    Well, Creeks were the most clannish. The Creeks, and Poncas. The Creeks were more friendly, but the Creeks did seem to stick together more than anybody, because more Creeks there spoke their own language.

Hometown, tribe for some students but not all, native language, eastern or western origin tended to bring the boys together in their small cliques or gangs. Although many of the boys came from rural homes, some were perceived as more backwoods than others, as Francis (1931/16 Cherokee) recalls:

They had little gangs, little clans I guess you'd call them. Like those bunch from Tahlequah and up in there, now they all stuck together pretty close. They was all hillbillies, and I mean hillbillies. [Laughter] Had to learn to wear shoes when they come down there. [Laughter] They stuck together, and they played a lot of fiddle and hoedown music. They were real good, they did jigs, Irish jigs, they get to playing music and a whole bunch of 'em would get to jigging.

There is still no clear pattern, however, among the narrators to indicate why some alumni discount tribalism as an important social factor at Chilocco and why others comment upon it. The next three narrators indicate there is a pattern of response embedded in this contradictory corpus of evidence, a pattern tied to the age boys arrived at Chilocco and to the kind of home from which they came, as well as to complexities of student interaction in a large institutional setting. Part of the reason people today have disparate memories of Chilocco is because they had disparate experiences at the school.

Little Boys, Big Boys

Edgar 1929/10 Creek:
I remember when I first came to Chilocco, we had rode on the Midland Valley train, all the way from Muskogee. Then to Arkansas City they sent a truck out to pick us up, my sister and I. As I walked up the steps of Home

2, which was the dormitory for the younger boys, old Sam Lincoln . . . Hippo, was up at the top. He looked at us, he grunted, and said, "Hm! White boy! You got no business here!" I'll never forget that, that was my first introduction: "White boy, you ain't got no business here." And I had two fights that night, before we went to bed. Of course, thereafter it was a matter of survival. Kids had to fight, but they were always fair fights. I could truthfully say that I never saw any student use a club or a knife or stomp or anything like that.

The men who speak next, Edgar, Curtis, and Mason, have some interesting things in common. They agree that tribalism was supremely important in gang membership at Chilocco. They are acutely cognizant of, and had intimate experience with, the violence among and between gangs. They emphasize how gangs physically protected their members, and the strong dichotomy between mixed bloods and full-bloods. This congruence of accounts reflects a fortuitous cluster of alumni who were closely related as students. Curtis, Edgar, and Mason are mixed bloods (Curtis and Edgar are mixed-blood Creek, Mason is mixed-blood Cherokee) who came from broken homes, with one or both parents gone. None were raised in a family with strong cultural ties to their respective tribes. They entered Chilocco as young boys (Curtis was nine, Edgar was ten, Mason was eleven) and joined small boys' gangs composed of noted troublemakers.

Curtis and Edgar ran with the same gang. Similar family backgrounds brought Curtis and Edgar to Chilocco, and similar experiences shaped their first few years as they hung out in the same gang. They rebelled strongly against the school's strict discipline and highly valued loyalty to their gang. They were in trouble a lot, and both remember that when rules were broken, they were called on the carpet as primary suspects. They were "overt resisters" par excellence. In their narratives we hear the strongest expressions of intertribal division, "intertribal warfare," and the strongest expressions of the divide between mixed blood and full-blood.

Curtis 1927/9 Creek:
There was a lot of intertribal warfare there, there was an awful lot of that went on. You belonged to one tribe, you hung out with that tribe. If you didn't have somebody to back you up, you could really get clobbered. These guys would lay for you and catch you out somewhere, so my brother and I stayed pretty close together to help each other. We got into

an *awful* lot of scraps, we both seemed to enjoy it anyway! [Laughter] Because we'd get up every morning and fight over who's gonna make the beds. [Laughter]

Edgar 1929/10 Creek:
[I had few relatives at Chilocco]. I was pretty much alone. And I was called a *stahitkey,* which in Indian means "white man," and when they called me *stahitkey,* I called them *stalustey, stalustey*'s "black man," and a fight started. The worse name that you could call me was white man, I mean to me there was nothing more despicable than to be called a white man. I was discriminated against, I guess. I had many, many fights over the fact that I was fair-skinned, and I know the reason that it was. Indians certainly would discriminate against a white person, they'd see white people discriminating against Indians, kind of a universal custom. * There were certain tribes that were clannish, that ran around together strictly because they belonged to the same tribe. That wasn't so much true *generally,* I think all the students were pretty much thrown together, and you selected your friends not upon the basis of who roomed with you, or who was in your class, because you were pretty much thrown together with everybody. Now, your friends, naturally, were the ones in your own age group, and of course later on, the ones that you worked with. But I'd say that as you grew up there, your friends pretty much were just at random throughout the school.

Curtis emphasizes tribal differences in determining relations between students, and Edgar focuses on the distinction between full-blood and mixed blood, Indian and white, but then asserts a random pattern of friendship formation. A closer look at the differences between Curtis and Edgar sheds light on their different views of tribal affiliation.

Curtis entered Chilocco in 1927. By the early 1930s, he had begun a string of unsuccessful escapes, running away from school only to be returned. By 1935, at age sixteen or seventeen, he ran away from Chilocco never to return. His tenure at the school was dominated by his affiliation with his small boys gang. He never spent appreciable time in high school at Chilocco, and he never reached a rapprochement with school authorities. He remained rebellious throughout his stay. Edgar, on the other hand, underwent something of a transformation during his years at Chilocco. He came under the influence of a visiting Baptist missionary, who convinced him of his intelligence and promise, and under her guid-

156

ance he became a star student. He graduated from high school at Chilocco at the head of his class. There is a crucial difference here between Edgar and Curtis and it has to do with age and the maturation process. Recall Edgar's statement that *"as you grew up* there, your friends pretty much were just at random throughout the school." The effect of the age difference is even more explicit in Mason's narrative.

Mason 1928/11 Cherokee:
The formative years, nine through ten, one learned he was either white—light complected; half breed—brown, light hair; or full-blood—dark. So gangs were formed, for individuals' protection, learning trust, to fight for each other, right or wrong. . . .
TL: So the gangs, the full-bloods would hang together?
Yes. You were categorized by that. That's the reason I mentioned it, you were categorized white or half breed, you were called that.
TL: Did people tend to stick together with their own tribe?
Primarily. Because the Creeks would have their little forms, Cherokees would have theirs. It went by tribal, and locality, well, locality meant you were Cherokee. That's primarily the way they were categorized. * After the tenth, eleventh grade, why you were pretty much old enough then to take care of yourself and you didn't have this business of the individuals ganging up, and they were kind of more sociable.

Mason's last comment reveals part of the pattern implicit in other answers to the ethnicity question. One of the reasons different people give such contradictory answers to the ethnicity question is because they experienced very different subcultures at Chilocco, depending on their age when they entered school. Gangs protected the smaller, younger boys and gang membership followed tribal and "blood" lines more than other criteria. This was true whether the boys came from strongly tribal homes or not. Neither Curtis nor Edgar came from homes where they had been surrounded by Creek culture. Curtis' home was in urban Wichita, and he and his brother had had almost no contact with Creeks (that is, Creeks as a tribal community, outside of immediate family) before they entered Chilocco. Yet Edgar, Curtis, and Curtis's brother joined a mixed-blood Creek gang. For these small boys, gang membership was determined by tribal affiliation and degree of Indian blood. Other narrators attest how important gangs were for mutual protection.

157

John 1931/16 Chickasaw:
Well it kind of wasn't too bad then [at the high school level], but for them little guys, they would always kind of go around in groups, and you had to join some group [for protection]. I didn't know, 'cause I went in there in the tenth grade.

Ira 1936/? Cherokee:
TL: Did you have a group of guys you hung out with?
   There was a group I hung out [away] *from*. [Laughter] I usually managed to stick around closer to friendly, older, bigger guys. I had some problems, I guess I thought I was supposed to take it and seemed like it was pretty easy for guys to pick on us, pick on me. I know quite often going to the mess hall, there'd be one on each side giving charlie horses, and they'd have me crying by the time I got there. Well, old B. H., was a big old muscle guy like Atlas, he'd say I'm going for him, and he'd grab me and he'd hold me up on his hand over his head.

Tribal affiliation did not mean the same things to older and younger students. Students who arrived at Chilocco in high school, often slightly overage for their grade, had different experiences than the young boys. Their relations with other students did in fact tend to be determined by social factors other than tribal affiliation (except for small groups of native language speakers for whom linguistic factors were important). These other social factors included class attendance, mutual work details, athletic team membership, and individual personality traits. Age when entering school and family background emerge as important correlates of a patterned response to the ethnicity question, and a partial answer to the question, "Who resisted and who accommodated?"

The link between age and family background was not accidental or circumstantial. Young children who entered the elementary grades at Chilocco in the 1920s and 1930s tended to come as orphans or from broken homes. Federal policy at this time reserved off-reservation boarding-school enrollment for students aged twelve and older, with special exceptions because of family circumstances. Children from stable families attended public schools where available in rural Oklahoma during the 1920s and 1930s and did not arrive at Chilocco until they were at least twelve years old.

Three factors emerge from this research as being important influences on (but not determinants of) response to the boarding-school environment and disciplinary system: age when entered boarding school, family background, and time when entered boarding school. Students who entered very young, in the elementary grades, from broken homes, and especially those whose attendance began in the 1920s, when military regimentation was quite strict, tend to have had a negative response to Chilocco. For boys at least, tribal affiliation dominated peer group relations, even for boys who did not come to school well versed in their own tribal culture.

Students who entered Chilocco as high school students, often slightly over-age for their grade, from strong, stable family backgrounds, especially those who attended in the 1930s, when the military aspects of discipline were being phased out, were much more likely to have made a positive accommodation to the boarding-school environment. For these students, tribal affiliation was not the most important social factor in determining peer group associations, if it was important at all. Age differences in tribally determined association are more strongly evident for boys than for girls, for reasons that remain to be elucidated in future research. None of the factors cited, either singly or in concert, operated as complete determinants of individual response. They are indications of social and cultural factors that played a role in ordering student relations at Chilocco in the 1920s and 1930s.

The 1920s and the 1930s are not the 1980s, when the stories in these pages were told, nor less the 1990s, when many of them are being read for the first time. It has been said that history and memory are natural enemies rather than allies, but perhaps some truce can be found in the story, as well as the history, of Chilocco. Alumni narratives carry historical weight, literally and figuratively. They document the reality of an existence that barely crept onto the margins of the printed pages of federal records and correspondence. These narratives also carry, even configure, personal lives. They are fifty-one people's stories of childhood, adolescence and growing up. These stories fit into larger stories that make sense of fifty-one people's whole lives. For each of them, boarding school is only part of the story. For most of them, it is an important part.

A Valuable Education

Every surviving graduate or alum of Indian boarding schools has something to say about their education. Some people valued their education in the highest degree, others look back with regret and resentment, but everyone who attended Chilocco took something immutable and everlasting with them. It might be friendships, begun in school and strengthened over the years. It might be a trade that provided lifelong employment, or the self-reliance that provided the springboard to any career. It might be strength of character forged under difficult circumstances, or remembrances of a happy time without responsibility. It might be pain and anger and loss or confidence and joy and security or most likely it's all of the above all mixed up together. Fifty-one people have looked back on their lives and found meaning in fifty-one different ways.

Although Chilocco was closed in 1980, it persists as a social reality today in many communities across Oklahoma. Local chapters of the alumni association meet monthly or on a regular basis, and annually all the chapters come together for a big reunion. Less formally, families and friends share their memories and reinforce the bonds established years ago. For many students, Chilocco was a home they shared with their family; as alumni they still keep the family together.

Florence 1933/7th Choctaw:
The thing that I remember most about it, and I think it's probably the most valuable thing I learned, or the longest lasting, is the value of friendship. [We] were *very* close friends. And you never forget, you're always concerned about them, even though you don't see them often. You can still keep in touch.
TL: Well, many people say that it was like family there.
   That's it! You develop a substitute, very close family relationship, and it's a different kind of sibling relationship.

Flora 1932/17 Creek:
TL: People have commented, they feel going to Chilocco helped them become self-sufficient. Do you feel that way?
   I think I had that self-sufficiency when I went up there, that I gained that already at the convent school. What I feel I gained from Chilocco was I gained understanding, I learned about group living, and it made working with people that much easier. I will always cherish it. The people from there are just like family, like relatives.

Students created a new kind of family life for themselves within the boarding school, which continues to have meaning today. Alumni also value other aspects of the school that were imposed on them by school authorities. In retrospect, they integrate Chilocco's discipline and work ethic with lessons learned throughout life to express an appreciation for the training they received.

160

Sarah 1926/12 Shawnee:

Yes, we used to have to march everywhere we went and we had to, just like soldiers, line up and march, call roll, every time we turned around, seemed like they had roll call. [Laughter] And at night [they would] check to see that we were there. I feel like I learned a lot there that children don't get in public schools. We learned to work, we learned that you have to work. And then on Saturdays, we had to just tear our rooms up, [Laughter] turn our mattress over, air the rooms and dust throughout the rooms, do the floors, you had to wax our floors, and shine them. Then Sunday we had inspection before we went to church . . . and some of the places they would look for dust [Laughter] it was crazy. . . . It was a clean place, it was a beautiful place.

Edward 1932/7th Cherokee, and 1929/4th Cherokee:

Rachel: I feel we got a very well-rounded education, I never made below a *B* in P.E. or home ec, although I was never that great in academics. I'm what I wanted to be, a wife and a mother, a homemaker, a good neighbor and as good a Christian as I can be.

Edward: And I got good training there: we never had to hire an electrician, or a carpenter, or a painter. There's something to being raised poor, too: you don't look to someone else to do things for you, you don't look to hire someone.

Charlie 1934/9th Cherokee:

TL: Do you think you got a good education there?

I do. Maybe my academics wasn't as high as they would have been [elsewhere] but I think I got more than that, I picked up the academics later. I had to struggle a little bit in college. I made pretty good grades, but I recognized the fact, my first year in college, that I was behind some of those in the classroom. But I gained a lot of other things that they didn't have. One of the things that made America great was perseverance, and that you learned there [at Chilocco]. That's a lost art in society today. . . . They instilled that feeling of pride. Work was honorable, and you get out and hustle for what you get, and I think later years, they didn't have that. * It was a great experience. You have a feeling of brotherhood, that you just don't have going to public schools.

School trades did not usually pan out into lifetime careers, but Chilocco alumni believe they did provide critical bridges to other employment, or simply the confidence that one could do *any* job well once one had been trained at Chilocco.

Francis 1931/16? Cherokee:
It was a good thing about that. They could learn something if they stayed with it. All walks of life come out of there. [It was good for me], I got a trade. Learned to work, and how to be skilled.

Coleman 1937/10th Delaware/Isleta:
TL: A lot of people seem to feel that . . . Chilocco made them self-sufficient.
    That's really it. . . . As I said, printing, I knew I could do that. I knew I had something, and anything else I [tried], printing would carry me. . . . Like going to college. When I went to [college] I worked in the print shop. Well I felt I was just as good as the next guy. So many times the Indian people feel degraded when they go out and try to mix with the non-Indians, but to me, printing and Chilocco gave me a crutch to adjust. To make my adjustments, until I could get on an even keel. And another thing, too, guys my age and ten years younger all had a trade. . . . All those that went to a boarding school . . . they all had a trade. They could be a carpenter, they could be a plumber, any of these trades and they could hold up their head with anybody.

Retrospective evaluation of the boarding school features other prominent themes: the kinds of social training Chilocco provided and the simple opportunity to get an education, albeit not an academically advanced education, when no other options existed. Women alumni in particular comment on the social skills they learned at Chilocco, whereas both men and women are grateful for an education they could not have gotten anywhere else. They are glad they went to Chilocco: "Otherwise, I probably, I know I wouldn't have gone to high school. [I'd] probably be back in the hills somewhere, with the squirrels" (Frank 1923/14 Cherokee).

Alice 1925/7th Cherokee:
I think though, really and honestly, the *greatest* value that the Indian schools had over the public schools was the social development of the students. It wasn't the academic program, it wasn't the vocational program, very few of those kids from Chilocco that took a Vo-Tech course worked

at it after they finished school. They went out and did something else. . . . They got the basics for life, but most of that basics was concerned with social development. * We were taught how to introduce people. Now that was one thing we had to do, because that was one thing those old ladies pounded into us. You have to know how to meet people and you have to know what to say when you get there and you have to know how to act, how to look when you get there. * Oh, my goodness yes, [Laughter] everything, everything that's happened to me has come from going to school at Chilocco, because I guess I'd still be living down in those hills [otherwise].

Nora 1943/10th Cherokee:
But I tell you, I wouldn't trade that education for all the public schools in the world. I really would not. It was really an experience, and I learned more there, maybe not academically, but overall, to take care of myself. To do on my own, and I matured. . . . Personality-wise and appearance-wise, now one rule, you *never* were seen in public with curlers in your hair, and to this day, I *cannot* go out with curlers in my hair. They really had a strong emphasis on personal appearance, and reputation.

Connie 1922/13 Cherokee:
Those are some of my happiest memories, just to be able to go to school, and the way it was run. I remember girls used to talk about rebelling, let's all just march off one day. I said "Oh, yes!" too, [Laughter] but we never did it. I think the boys fared pretty good compared to the girls. My brother-in-law's friend worked in the poultry barn and he talks about snitching eggs and chickens. . . . I wouldn't take anything for the experience I had there. I've never wanted to say anything against it. I quit in the eleventh grade and then I wouldn't go back because I couldn't stand not to graduate with my class.

Tillie 1939/13 Cherokee:
I think nothing can take the place of that mass discipline. Our parents were far away, or some didn't have parents. They sent their kids there because they wanted them to get an education. It helped many, many people, thousands of them. There weren't school buses then, or money to board kids in town, without Chilocco, so many just wouldn't have gotten

an education at all. * It really was a marvelous school; I've always felt indebted for my education there.

I believe there is a moral to the story of Chilocco, and it falls somewhere between the depiction of boarding schools as irredeemably destructive institutions
and Tillie's sentiment that Chilocco "really was a marvelous school." The
moral is that no institution is total, no power is all-seeing, no federal Indian policy has ever been efficiently and rationally translated into practice, and much of
the time practice produced unpredicted results anyway. I think that there has
probably never been an off-reservation boarding school that was all bad or all
good, all of the time (but I am still not willing to say it's impossible). We must
not, however, confuse this generic moral of an internally complex and contradictory institution with individual reality. Certainly for the young man who
drank poisoned liquor, and others, Chilocco was irredeemably destructive. It
was fatal. For Tillie, and others, it was marvelous. The institution and the institutional experience were for each individual person what that person made of it.

What did students make of Chilocco, and of themselves? Every student
came to Chilocco with knowledge, skills, beliefs, a family background, a language, a myriad complex of genetic, familial, and cultural heritage that shaped
their school experience. Many students, interacting with each other and with
school staff, created and sustained something new, a school culture that students imbued with meaning, and which in turn gave meaning back to generations of students. This celebration of personal contribution, negotiation, and
creativity must, however, be placed side by side against the limitations, the re-
pressions, and the privations built into the institutional architecture of Chilocco.

The fact that many alumni value their experience at Chilocco does not mean
they fully endorse its educational policy and practice. The majority of alumni
after all, did not or would not send their own children to such an institution, especially at a young age. The three who did send children to boarding schools,
sent them to a much-changed institution. The fact that many alumni value their
Chilocco experience does not, I believe, constitute a justification or an endorse-
ment of the school's "success." I believe it endorses the strengths and resources that students brought to, discovered at, and created within Chilocco,
through their own ingenuity and through cooperation with and reliance on each
other.

Recognition of student resourcefulness, however, should not be turned inside out into a reciprocal argument of student culpability. The obverse of the ar-

gument that Indian people were responsible for their own success during and after Indian school might be that they were also responsible for their own "failure." I abhor the twisted logic that would condemn young children who could
not or would not adapt to Chilocco, or the young victim of poisoned liquor, as
just not strong enough or creative enough to make it. The undeniable fact remains that children grew up away from their families in a very difficult, demanding, and occasionally physically violent environment. For better or for
worse, they are different people now than they would have been had they never
passed through Chilocco's doors.

Two last voices.

Robert 1933/10th Cherokee:
Like I said, I was getting a good education at a boarding school that some
millionaire would send his son back East to a place like that, wouldn't be
as good as Chilocco. That's the way I kind of looked at it. I felt like I was
really in an elite place. Everything just went like clockwork and everybody got along, course there was fights, you know kids, once in awhile
they'll have fights and so forth. * It's just something, there'll never be another one like it. It was really a marvelous place, as far as I'm concerned.
Like I said, I felt like, I never did say anything to anybody about it, but I
felt like, I'm just as well off as some kid at some prep school back East.
Everybody was interested in me, I had everything I needed. I didn't really
need any money, but of course you can always use money [Laugh-
ter]. . . . You were kind of on your own and yet you were subject to controls. You do whatever you wanted to up to a certain point, it was democratic in that sense, and at the same time, it was kind of dictatorial. You
had to march, you had to go in groups, to this and that, but it was for the
good of all, I guess. They had to do it that way. When you've got a thousand kids on the campus like that, twenty-four hours a day, seven days a
week, you got to have some controls . . . or you just have chaos. But
most of the kids enjoyed it, there's always some that just couldn't quite
make it. . . . There's always some who just felt they were being too restricted, and they broke over and then that's when they had to leave. You
knew, at least I did, you knew what the limits were and I was always able
to stay within 'em. Some of 'em could not, or didn't want to, or felt like
they were in prison. But to me, that was teaching you to, that's the way
life is. You can't just do whatever you want to do, whenever you want to
do it. You got to have some control, I think that made it easier for me,

later on. I learned there that if you stay with something long enough, pretty soon it's going to pay off for you.

Edgar 1929/10 Creek:
This school up there was certainly a great thing for all these homeless children and sometimes I think we got a little better bringing-up than some that had mothers and fathers at home. We may have lost out in some [things]. . . . I went to sleep at night crying, for various reasons, busted nose or lips . . . just so many things, you didn't have anybody to tuck you in bed, or whatever all that was. But you had so much, there was so much that was learned there on the good side. [The important thing] is this business of having to experience something, we're not going to learn other than by experience. There were things that you had to do and the discipline was such, that, it just didn't make any difference, there was no exceptions. And maybe that makes a better person out of you, at least you learn there's a lesson in all this, a *hard* lesson.

Chilocco taught hard lessons. Many students stuck with it and mined Chilocco for what it was worth. Many alumni set that worth highly today and value their experiences at the Light on the Prairie. We should value those alumni and treasure the lessons they teach us. I believe it is a tribute to the strength of Indian students that Chilocco alumni feel so strongly about their alma mater today. It is a tribute to the resilience of children, to the bonds of friendship, to creativity under duress, and to the loyalty of many lifetimes.

* * *

When Major Haworth reluctantly shouldered his responsibility to build and then fill the first school building on Chilocco Creek, he anticipated failure. Surely no federal boarding school located so close to Indian homes could survive. A product of his time and his place, he could not see a future when applications to enroll would outstrip space; when nieces and nephews and children and grandchildren would enroll; when Indian people would make Chilocco their home. Haworth's vision was not so much faulty as circumscribed, a human condition that hobbles so much prognostication. Similarly, the federal prediction of the dissolution of tribal and ethnic identity among Indians has not come completely to fruition. Close examination of student ties and cleavages has given us some clues as to how and why that is so. Family background, native language, degree of blood, hometown or home region—all interacted in a complex way as students structured school life into meaningful social units crosscut by age, tribe, gender, and individual attributes.

The story of Chilocco holds within it many stories—the shifts and vagaries of federal policy; the dedication of superintendents, teachers, and staff; the childhood of generations of Indian people; the survival of my father and our family. The story told in these pages began as many different and seemingly irreconcilable stories—accounts by female alumnae, male alumni, tribes from east or west, former employees; government documents detailing unreliable statistics and commissioners' cant. I have tried to make sense of them, and make them make sense, without suppressing or denying the kernel of truth or opinion held in each one. It is a cliché, but a true one, that I alone am responsible for the conclusions I have drawn based on these sources.

The richness, complexity, and variety of memories of boarding-school life convey to us an important message about the history of Native American education. Indian people at boarding schools were not passive consumers of an ideology or lifestyle imparted from above by federal administrators. They actively created an ongoing educational and social process. They marshaled personal and shared skills and resources to create a world within the confines of boarding-school life, and they occasionally stretched and penetrated school boundaries. In the process, an institution founded and controlled by the federal government was inhabited and possessed by those whose identities the institution was committed to erase.

Indian people made Chilocco their own.

Chilocco was an Indian school.

Epilogue: Curtis T. Carr

My father introduced me to Chilocco Indian School through the stories he told as I was growing up. He entered Chilocco as a nine-year-old boy in 1927 and he stayed there until 1935, when he ran away. The stories he told of his boyhood were stories set at Chilocco.

His mother, Cora Wynema Evans Carr, was Creek. She had grown up in northeastern Oklahoma, near a little town called Oktaha. As an adult she made her home in Wichita, Kansas, where she tried to support three children (an older boy, my father, and a younger sister) as a single mother. When economic circumstances became too severe, she enrolled the two boys at Chilocco Indian School. The sister was too young for enrollment at the time, and as she got older, Chilocco phased out the lower elementary grades so she never attended the school.

My father and his older brother entered Chilocco in 1927, at nine and ten years of age, respectively. They were placed in the lower elementary grades (third and fourth). The older brother was expelled after several years for "incorrigible behavior." He passed away in his early twenties.

Since the boys came from a broken home and family funds were not available to pay for transportation, they spent their summers as well as the academic year at Chilocco. My father finally became homesick enough to attempt to run away to Wichita; as a consequence school authorities allowed him to go home the summer he was twelve or thirteen. He had not seen his mother in the intervening years.

During that summer home he made up his mind that the strictly controlled and regimented lifestyle of Chilocco, which he had always resented and rebelled against, was not for him. His attendance during his last year or year and a half at Chilocco was sporadic, until he ran away in 1935 for the last time, at age sixteen or seventeen. Because of the prolonged separation from his mother, he did not feel at home in Wichita. He joined the hundreds of men of all ages whom the depression had forced on the road. He survived the dangers of jumping freight trains and the hobo life, traveling through the western states, California to Idaho, where he found employment cutting fire trails through national wilderness areas. In his late teens, anxious to finish his education, he settled down in Maryville, Missouri, and worked at odd jobs, including soda jerk, to put himself through high school.

While working his way through high school, he joined the Missouri National Guard. The commander of his company, also his employer in town, encouraged him to continue his education. He graduated from high school in 1939 with an Honor Society scholarship and was accepted to a small midwestern college. After he arrived on campus, a dean informed him they had no place for Indians and told him to pack his bags and go.

When World War II was declared, his National Guard unit was mobilized. He eventually enlisted in the Air Force and served in North Africa and Italy. Curtis returned home to Wichita in 1945 and began working for Cessna Aircraft. Between 1946 and 1949 he moved back and forth between Los Angeles, where he enrolled in the photojournalism program at the Art Center School of Design, and Wichita, where he worked as an engineering photographer at Boeing. Flying in an A-20 chase plane, he photographed Boeing's prototype in-flight refueling experiments.

In 1949, he married Marilyn Voth, who came from Goessel, a small German Mennonite community north of Wichita. They moved to Los Angeles until Curtis finished college on the G.I. bill, graduating from the Art Center in 1952. They returned to Kansas, where my sister and I were born. My father's business career as a salesman of business forms led us all over the Midwest, from Kansas City to Denver to Chicago to Cincinnati.

As my parents approached retirement, my Dad began to plan for and design a new home. In 1984, they retired to the mountain country near Flagstaff, Arizona. Recalling all the drafting, carpentry, and building skills learned years ago at Chilocco, he and my mother built their home by hand.

APPENDIX A

Chilocco Alumni: Research Participants

Between September 1983 and March 1984, I interviewed sixty-one people:

53 alumni of Chilocco (32 women, 21 men)

7 former employees, both academic and nonacademic staff (3 women and 4 men)

1 Chilocco alumna's husband, who did not attend Chilocco but attended other government boarding schools from age six

Note: 10 alumni (5 men, 5 women) were employed by the school in later life. Employment tenures ranged from 1 to 30 years.

Fifty-one alumni provided substantial narrative material:

41 had relatives who had attended Chilocco.

37 attended with contemporary relatives.

9 were 2d or 3d generation Chiloccoans.

3 sent children to Chilocco.

Narrators represent 14 tribal affiliations; the majority are Cherokee (see table 14).

Married couples comprise 18 of the total number interviewed:

3 couples (both alumni)

3 couples (both employees)

1 couple (both alumni and employees)

2 couples (one alumnus and one employee)

A number of factors limit the possibilities of obtaining a random, stratified sample of Chilocco alumni, in other words, a sample that would exactly corre-

Table 14. Comparison of Student and Alumni Tribal Affiliation

	1984		1925		1938	
	No.	Percent	No.	Percent	No.	Percent
Five Civilized Tribes						
Cherokee[a]	26.5[b]	55	234	26	221	29
Choctaw[c]	5.5	11	136	15	121	16
Creek[d]	7	12	105	12	139	18
Seminole	0	0	37	4	21	3
Chickasaw	1.5	3	29	3	60	8
Subtotal:	40.5	81	541	60	562	74
Other Tribes						
Apahce	0	0	3	0.3	1	0.1
Caddo	0	0	18	2	9	1
Cheyenne/Arapaho	0	0	51	6	11	1
Comanche	0	0	11	1	19	3
Delaware	.5	1	15	2	12	2
Kaw	0	0	22	2	2	0.2
Kiowa	0	0	23	3	7	0.9
Otoe	1	2	28	3	8	1
Pawnee	.5	1	35	4	13	1.7
Ponca	1	2	39	4	18	2
Potawatomie	3	6	10	1	22	3
Quapaw	1	2	0	0	0	0
Sac and Fox	1	2	24	3	27	4
Seneca	0	0	7	1	9	1
Shawnee	1	2	19	2	13	2
Wichita	0	0	13	1	7	0.9
Southwest	.5	1	1	0.1	0	0
Northwest	0	0	5	1	1	0.1
California	0	0	1	0.1	1	0.1
Other	0	0	30	3	18	2
Total for all tribes:	50	100	896	100	760	100

a. Includes North Carolina
b. The .5 designation in tribal affiliation is used for those participants who have two tribal affiliations. This designation is not intended to represent or correspond to the biological degree of Indian blood.
c. Includes Mississippi
d. Includes Euchee
Sources: Statistics for 1925 taken from report of Attendance by Tribes, 1910–25, RG 75 E65 Box 1, FRC. Statistics for 1938 compiled from Annual Reports, 1937–52, RG 75 E8 Box 5, FRC.

spond to the characteristics of the student body in the 1920s and 1930s. (These factors do not necessarily limit the possibilities of assembling a representative range of opinions and feelings about boarding-school attendance.) The population of alumni available for interviews differs from the original student population in several ways.

First of all, interviews took place some thirty-four to sixty-seven years after research participants had left Chilocco. Simple mortality has changed the population that existed at the school fifty to sixty years ago.

Secondly, the population most accessible to me were former Chiloccoans who are "successful." These people have found employment, raised families, and coped successfully with the myriad details of day-to-day decision making. There are, undoubtedly, Chilocco alumni who did not fare so well, who fell prey to chronic unemployment, to alcoholism, to the social and individual ills that haunt Native Americans as they do all Americans. Those nonsurvivors also have their stories to tell, but they did not fall easily into a group accessible to an oral historian.

There are some factors that limit the similarity between the student population of earlier decades and the alumni population of 1984, and other factors that contribute to it. Certain historical and social factors help to maintain congruence between these two populations.

In the 1920s and 1930s, Chilocco drew its student population primarily from eastern Oklahoma, with a smattering of students from the Southwest, Northwest, North Carolina (Cherokees), and Mississippi (Choctaws). Most students were from eastern Oklahoma and that is where they have remained. It was much easier to find alumni from this period in close proximity to one another than it would have been to reach alumni of the 1950s, 1960s, and 1970s, who were drawn from Alaska, the Northwest Coast, Arizona, and New Mexico. As a result, the tribal affiliations of research participants follow the tribal distribution characteristic of the student population of Chilocco in the 1920s and 1930s, except for a disproportionately greater inclusion of Cherokees in the alumni sample. The majority are Cherokee, followed by Choctaw and Creek and a variety of other, smaller tribes local to north central and northeastern Oklahoma, Kansas, and more distant states. See table 14 for a comparison of the distribution of tribal affiliations of students and alumni over time.

Chilocco's student population in the 1920s and 1930s was drawn from a cross section of Indian students of school age. Chilocco students of the 1920s and the 1930s more closely matched the general school-age population than students in later years, when admission to the school was often dependent on documentation of educational, emotional, or social problems.

Research participants were approached through personal contacts: friends, family, and the Chilocco Alumni Association. Forty-five of the sixty-one interviewees were regular or occasional affiliates of the alumni association. Membership in the alumni association does not correlate with a positive appraisal of Chilocco as an institution. It reflects loyalties to peers and lifelong friendships.

APPENDIX B

Interview Methodology

I was careful to delineate participant rights and researcher responsibilities so far as possible, guided by the institutional review procedure of Stanford University's Administrative Panel for Human Subjects in Behavioral Science Research.

Every interview began with a full explanation of my student standing, the purpose of my research, and the personal connection (my father's student experience) that grounds my interest in Chilocco Indian School. My requests to use a small Sony tape recorder during the interviews were usually accepted gracefully and without any obvious effect on narration or recall. Fifty narrators were comfortable with the tape recorder, and eleven preferred that I take notes.

At the conclusion of each interview I presented participants with several disclosure and release forms (composed with the assistance of Stanford's legal office), explaining the purpose of each form. After transcription of the taped interviews was completed, each participant received a copy of his or her own transcript for comments or revisions so that a revised copy could be prepared for each narrator (that is, each narrator receives a copy of his or her interview).

Of the 50 separate interview sessions, 36 sessions were with individuals, 13 sessions were with couples or two alumni, and 1 session was with three alumni. Almost all of the narrators were interviewed only once, in a session that lasted two to three hours. Five individuals were interviewed in two sessions each. All but three of the participants were interviewed in his or her own home or office. Of the three who were not, one participant was interviewed in a room of the Student Union at the University of Oklahoma, and the other two were present at the home of a friend or relative who was also being interviewed.

I did not use a questionnaire, but I did carry with me for my own reference an interview guide listing topics of interest to bring up (see Appendix C). Most of the narrators felt most comfortable having me ask them questions, in which case the interview followed more closely the order and sequence of topics arranged on the interview guide. In addition to the interview guide, I carried with me the school annual of 1938 and an album of pictures of the school taken in 1984. The annual proved very useful in eliciting memories and verifying names, and people also responded to the photo album. These pictures were taken on a visit to the school grounds in November 1984. My family and I obtained permission from the Bureau of Indian Affairs, Pawnee Agency, to visit the Chilocco campus. We took pictures of the older campus buildings and surroundings (some older dormitories had been demolished in the 1970s) and most interviewees enjoyed looking through this album.

Several narrators had organized what they wished to say about Chilocco. In that instance, I let them lead the conversation until they were finished, then I raised questions they had not touched upon or only mentioned in passing. Two individuals had prepared comprehensive written statements, which they first read to me, after which we switched to the question-and-answer format.

In my view, almost all of the interview sessions were relaxed and enjoyable experiences. Of the sixty-one interviews, there were only two (one with a man, one with a woman) where I could not establish any kind of rapport or communication.

APPENDIX C

Interview Guide

General:
Where was previous schooling, hometown?
Year started, age and grade when enrolled?
Tribal affiliation? Did brothers/sisters attend?
Did parents attend boarding school?
Why went to Chilocco? Homesickness?
Recall first day, first impressions?
What was the daily schedule like?
How did you make friends?
    By age, class, tribal affiliation? Were there cliques?
Did people associate in groups by tribe or other factors?

Dormitory life:
What were relations like with matrons, advisors, disciplinarians?
How did you learn rules at first: from matrons, staff, other students?
How were students disciplined?
Describe military system.
What were rules, punishments?
    belt line, rock pile, demerits, stand in hall, polish floors, bootlegging, li-
    quor, "chalk," red card
Did you ever run away?
What did you do in spare time, for fun?
    hunting, fishing, parch corn, and stomp dances
    Trunk Day

Spend summer vacations at school or home?

    visits home and family?

Ask about:

Nicknames	Dining room—food, seating
Clothing	Sports/athletics
Boy Scouts—initiation	

Slang: I back, trixing, struck on, ain't it

Town Day	Church
Commissary	Hospital

Social events: Watermelon Social, dances, Picnic Day, rabbit hunt

Clubs/societies	Describe academic classes.
Good education?	Relation with teachers?

What trade(s) did you learn? Did you use after school?

Where there trades for girls?

Describe home economics training.

Any prejudice towards Indians by staff, teachers, and so on?

    For Indian language speakers—education by peers?

How would you characterize general memories of school?

Would you recommend that schooling?

Would/did you send your own kids to similar school?

Notes

Abbreviations

FRC   Federal Archives and Regional Records Center, Fort Worth, Texas

    RG 75 Record Group 75, Records of the Bureau of Indian Affairs at the FRC

    E   Entry in RG 75

    BI/   Box number within Entry classification; if named, name follows /

    F/   Folder name within the FRC box or OHS record follows /

MONAC Museum of Native American Cultures, Spokane, Washington.

OHS   Oklahoma Historical Society records

WHC   Western History Collection, University of Oklahoma, Norman, Oklahoma.

Preface

1. Boarding-school education is discussed in generic terms in overviews such as Szasz, *Education and the American Indian* (1974) and *Indian Education in the American Colonies* (1988); and Reyhner and Eder, *History of Indian Education* (1989) for the United States, and Barman, Hébert, and McCaskill, *Indian Education in Canada,* 2 vols. (1986, 1987) for Canada. Prucha, *Churches and Indian Schools* (1979) and Berkhofer, *Salvation and the Savage* (1965) provide an excellent documentary overview of mission education. Trennert, *Phoenix Indian School* (1988); Hultgren and Molin, *To Lead and to Serve* (1989); Williams and Meredith, *Bacone Indian University* (1980); and King, *The School at Mopass* (1967) describe individual schools. Many school histories are unpublished dissertations, such as Adams, "Federal Indian Boarding School"

(1975); Lomawaima, "They Called It Prairie Light" (1987); and Ryan, "Carlisle Indian Industrial School" (1962).

2. Most evaluations of boarding-school education written by those outside the Indian Service have been critical. See the influential report by Meriam, *The Problems of Indian Administration* (1928); Fuchs and Havighurst, *To Live on This Earth* (1972); and Kennedy, *Indian Education: A National Challenge—A National Tragedy* (1969). Helen Hunt Jackson, *A Century of Dishonor* [1888] (1972) details abuses within Indian policy, including educational practice. Boarding schools have also been criticized by educational psychologists, such as Beiser, "Hazard to Mental Health" (1973); and educational researchers, such as Kleinfeld, *A Long Way from Home* (1973), and Rosenthal-Metcalf, *Effects of Boarding School on Navajo Self-Image* (1975).

3. Szasz, *Education and the American Indian* (1974) draws on interviews with approximately thirty knowledgeable Indians and non-Indians: her book is very much a history of policy and policy makers.

4. Two excellent book-length memoirs of student experiences are Francis LaFlesche, *The Middle Five* [1900] (1978), a classic account of Presbyterian mission life in the late 1800s; and Basil H. Johnston, *Indian School Days* (1989), a memoir of Canadian Catholic residential education in the 1930s. Many Native American autobiographies contain references to school life: see Brumble, *An Annotated Bibliography* (1981); Fredrickson, "School Days in Northern California" (1989); and Giago, *The Aboriginal Sin* (1978).

5. Trennert (1988) devotes a chapter to alumni reminiscences of "Student Life" in *The Phoenix Indian School* (1988) but concludes that "no one individual could be called a typical student" and that their "lives, emotional reactions, and successes or failures . . . are not easy to sort out" (148).

6. For more detailed analysis of boarding-school narratives, see Haig-Brown, *Resistance and Renewal* (1988); and McBeth, *Ethnic Identity and the Boarding School Experience* (1983). Hultgren and Molin, *To Lead and to Serve* (1989) offer a literal glimpse of student life in their exhibit catalog of Indian education at Hampton Institute (1878–1923), which includes a wonderful collection of historic photos, although the text remains dominated by a policy history perspective. Hyer has assembled an excellent montage of alumni voices and photographs in the publication and museum exhibition *One House, One Voice, One Heart* (1990) about the Santa Fe Indian School.

7. Indian resistance to the federal exercise of disciplinary power in the boarding school resembles resistance movements in other societies, such as

Dhan-Gadi (aboriginal) resistance to the Australian government's "pedagogic intervention." See Morris, *Domesticating Resistance* (1989), 112. See also James C. Scott, *Weapons of the Weak* (1985).

8. See Wallerstein, "Ethnicity and National Integration" (1960) for an instrumental approach; see DeVos and Romanucci-Ross, *Ethnic Identity* (1975) for the incorporation of psychoanalytic theory.

9. Difference equals opposition, "the essential factor in formation and development" of ethnic groups, according to Spicer, "Persistent Cultural Systems" (1971), 797.

10. See Barth, *Ethnic Groups and Boundaries* (1969), 17, where he suggests we ask "what is needed to make ethnic groups *emerge* in an area" (emphasis in the original). Roosens, *Creating Ethnicity* (1989), 14, seems to say that native groups in Canada "emerged" when "a few impecunious Indian leaders," insisting on their peoples' constitutional rights, successfully challenged the construction of a huge hydroelectric project.

11. Adams, "Fundamental Considerations" (1988); Ahern, " 'The Returned Indians': Hampton Institute and Its Indian Alumni" (1983); and Littlefield, "The B.I.A. Boarding School" (1989) apply theories of social reproduction and resistance to analyze federal policy and student experience.

12. Interviews took place from November 1983 through March 1984 and were usually conducted in alumni homes with the aid of a small tape recorder. The majority of those interviewed attended Chilocco between 1920 and 1940. Two alumni attended earlier than that, and three attended in the 1940s or 1950s. See Appendixes A, B, and C for more information on alumni and the interview process.

13. Matthews, *Friendships through the Life Course* (1986), discusses the limitations of research on friendship over the years.

14. Anthropological interest in life histories grew from 1920 through the 1940s as part of a general trend to humanize anthropological materials. See Langness, *The Life History in Anthropological Science* (1965). Scholars debated the methodological advantages or shortcomings of the genre—see Boas, "Recent Anthropology" (1943); Dollard, *Criteria for the Life History* (1935); Kluckhohn "Needed Refinements in the Biographical Approach" (1949); Kroeber, "The Use of Autobiographical Evidence in a Yurok War Reminiscence" (1945); and Sapir, "Introduction" (1938)—while its disciplinary popularity waned. Publication of life histories has expanded exponentially since the early 1970s—see Cruikshank, *Life Lived Like a Story* (1990)—as has scholar-

ship on the genre's theory, methodology, and ethics: see Crapanzano, "The Life History in Anthropological Fieldwork" (1977); Erikson, *Life History and the Historical Moment* (1975); Langness and Frank, *Lives* (1981); and Watson and Watson-Franke, *Interpreting Life Histories* (1985).

15. The difference in life course and the resultant difference in memories of boarding-school experience between survivors and "non-survivors" has been commented on by Professor Alfonso Ortiz (University of New Mexico) in an interview in the film *Another Wind Is Moving,* produced by the Kickapoo Nation School and Summit Street Productions (available through the University of California at Berkeley Media Extension Service).

16. Full transcripts of four interviews (two men, two women) are included in Lomawaima, "They Called It Prairie Light" (1987), 271–446, available through University Microfilms. The interested reader may refer to this source to see more context and the character of the exchange between interviewer and narrators.

Chapter One

1. MONAC. 1884 Superintendent of Indian Schools Report to the Secretary of the Interior, 5. Chilocco is pronounced shĭ-lŏ'-kō.

2. See Francis P. Prucha, *The Churches and the Indian Schools* (1979) for the rise of anti-Catholicism in the eastern political establishment and its effect on the withdrawal of federal funding from mission schools for Indians.

3. For the political and economic strategies of Reconstruction in the South after the Civil War and the ideology of "appropriate education" for blacks (and Indians) at Hampton, see Adams, "Education in Hues" (1977) and Anderson, "The Hampton Model" (1978).

4. In 1848, government and mission schools included 16 manual labor schools and 87 boarding and day schools. By 1879, the average attendance of Indian students at federal schools was 4,488 (U.S. Bureau of Indian Affairs, *Statistics of Indian tribes,* 1899).

5. The first federal on-reservation boarding school was founded in 1860 on the Yakima reservation in Washington. On-reservation boarding schools are defined as those located on a reservation, which educate the children of that community. The designation *off-reservation* originally indicated schools not on reservation lands, receiving Indians from various tribes and places. By 1932, the designation included schools located on reservations but enrolling students from outside the local community. In 1932, most on-reservation boarding schools were elementary schools. The off-reservation schools included junior

high grades, and eight schools granted high school degrees. Chilocco had an enrollment in 1932 of 850 in grades five through twelve (U.S. Bureau of Indian Affairs 1932) but the elementary grades at Chilocco were phased out by 1938.

6. MONAC. 1889 Report of the Superintendent of Indian Schools, 4.

7. The report was commissioned by secretary of the Interior Hubert Work and compiled by the Institute for Government Research under the direction of Dr. Lewis Meriam. The institute (referred to today as the Brookings Institution, after an early chairman, Robert S. Brookings) is an independent research organization based in Washington, D.C. In 1928, the organization described itself as an "association of citizens for cooperating with public officials in the scientific study of government with a view to promoting efficiency and economy in its operations and advancing the science of administration." Meriam, *The Problem of Indian Administration* (1928), frontispiece.

8. See Philp, *John Collier's Crusade for Indian Reform, 1920–1954* (1977) for a detailed and engrossing account of Collier's commitment to his own utopian view of communal tribal societies.

9. At Chilocco in the 1930s, the term used to refer to male attendants in the boys' dormitories was changed from *disciplinarian* to *advisor,* but personnel were not replaced.

10. Many early Chilocco records were destroyed in a fire when the commissary burned in 1909 (Letter dated 23 June 1923, RG 75 E4 BI4/1923–24, FRC). Detailed documentary records of Chilocco begin sporadically in 1902 with rather complete records available after 1904.

11. Annual Report of the Commissioner of Indian Affairs, 1891.

12. Historical synopses of Chilocco's founding in prefaces to annual yearbooks, or school publications, variously assert that Chilocco opened its doors on 15 January, 18 January, or 20 January of 1884; and that the wagon train journey of the first students lasted from one to four weeks. Initial enrollment is reported as 186 or 168. Haworth's report to the secretary of the Interior in 1884 cites an enrollment of 140 (up to 180 by February), representing seventeen tribes. Average attendance for the term through 1 July was 168.

13. MONAC. 1884 Report of the Superintendent of Schools to the Secretary of the Interior, 4.

14. Supt. McCowan to Mrs. Clarissa Mars, 8 April, 1905, F/Letters from Parents to Children, OHS.

15. In 1969, 1,100 students were enrolled at Chilocco, but during the 1970s enrollment rapidly declined. By 1979, only 140 students resided at the school,

and the final graduating class in June 1980 contained 24 members. See Wall and Wall, *Tomahawks over Chilocco* (1979), 11a.

16. Letter from Washington, 23 November, 1910, F/Curriculum 12 January, 1904–30 June, 1917, OHS.

17. By 1911, Chilocco classes were extended through the ninth grade, with five hundred students in attendance (Letter, 21 June 1911, F/Curriculum 12 January 1904–30, June 1917, OHS). By 1920, two years of high school had been added, and in 1927 the school offered grades one through twelve. By the 1919–20 school year, the first two grades of the primary division were phased out. The third grade, classified now as "Special," retained eighty-six children. The organization of the prevocational and vocational divisions did not change (F/Curriculum: Report on Promotion of Pupils, 1920, OHS).

18. The school reservation initially encompassed 1,119.06 acres, the two sections of land chosen by Major Haworth in 1882 as the site for school construction (*Chilocco: School of Opportunity* 1938, 1). Final title to the land was granted to the United States when the Cherokees sold the Cherokee Outlet in 1893. See Bradfield, "A History of Chilocco Indian School" (1963), 6–7.

19. The executive order by Chester A. Arthur for the Chilocco Industrial School Reserve, dated 12 July 1884, increased the Chilocco reservation to thirteen and a half square miles (Bradfield, 1963, 6).

It is hereby ordered that the following described tracts of country in the Indian Territory . . . are hereby reserved and set aside for the settlement of such friendly Indians belonging within the Indian Territory as have been or who may be hereafter educated at the Chilocco Indian Industrial School in the Territory" (RG 75 E5a B41/Blue Decimal 202.08-203.08 F/202.18, FRC).

20. L. E. Correll to J. B. Milam, 25 June 1947, RG 75 E5a B41 F/202.18, FRC.

21. *Indian School Journal,* 20 August 1904, RG 75 E44 B1/School Publications, FRC.

22. *Indian School Journal,* April 1906; February 1907; November 1907; and December 1907, RG 75 E44 B2/School Publications, FRC.

23. 1908 Report of the Superintendent of Indian Schools Estelle Reel, 12, MONAC.

24. Chilocco Normal Course Outline, F/Curriculum 12 January 1904–30, June 1917, OHS.

25. Ten of the alumni interviewed had careers in the Education Division of the Bureau of Indian Affairs.

26. F/Fairs 15 June 1895–31, August 1904, OHS.

27. Indian school exhibits were housed in the Hall of Revelation, where as many as twenty employees and one hundred students represented Chilocco. The domestic science department exhibited a model dining room, kitchen, and laundry, and the print shop set up at the fair produced a daily newspaper (Bradfield 1963, 69–70).

28. Report of John Francis, Jr., 15 March 1915, RG 75 EI BI/1914–15 F2/1915, FRC.

29. Home 3 was built in 1893 and housed older boys until 1923, when younger girls were moved in. In 1899, Home 1 was completed and its ten rooms occupied by the young boys. Additions were made to Home 1 in 1903, 1909, and 1923, and by 1938, it housed 150 older boys. Home 4 was built in 1903 as a girls' dormitory but burned down in 1933. It was rebuilt and in 1938 housed the tenth grade girls. Home 5, built in 1931, housed the junior and senior girls, and Home 6, built in 1932, housed the junior and senior boys.

30. A bronze plaque was affixed to the campus's central flagpole in 1924 to memorialize Chilocco's World War I losses: Bennett Lavers, David Johnson, Edward Nelson, and Simeon Mosley (Letter, 15 September 1924, RG 75 E4 BI4 F/General Accounting Office, FRC).

31. On 14 October 1918 the superintendent wired Washington, D.C., to request influenza vaccine for 75 employees; student vaccinations were not mentioned (RG 75 EI B3 F/Correspondence with Commissioner 1918, FRC). The influenza struck Chilocco on Saturday, 31 January 1920. The hospital reported 195 cases in the first week, of which eight cases developed into light pneumonia—most flu cases were reported as mild (RG 75 E4 BII/1919–21 F/1919–1920, FRC). When smallpox swept Oklahoma early in 1922, all students were vaccinated (Letter, 10 February 1922, RG 75 E4 BI2/1920–22 F/Supervisor H. B. Peairs, FRC). In 1926, five hundred smallpox vaccinations were administered (1927 *Yearbook*, RG 75 E45 BI, FRC). In 1935, when a mild measles epidemic struck Chilocco, students were also routinely vaccinated for smallpox, diphtheria, and typhoid (Annual Report 1935, RG 75 E8 B3, FRC).

32. Annual Report, 1919, RG 75 E8 BI/Records of the Superintendent, FRC.

33. *Chilocco Weekly Journal* 1, vol. 4 (8 December, 1904): RG 75 E44 BI/ School Publications, FRC.

34. F/Complaints of Students 1903–1911, OHS.

35. F/Letters From Ex-Students, 8/15/1900–4/29/1914, OHS.

36. Ibid.

37. F/Complaints of Students, 1903–11, OHS.

38. F/Letters from Ex-Students, 15 August 1900–29, April 1914, OHS.

39. Ibid.

40. Ibid.

41. Ibid.

Chapter Two

1. Indorsements, 13 August 1917, RG 75 E1 B3 F/1917–18, FRC.

2. RG 75 E8 B1/Annual Report, 1922, FRC.

3. Tuition in 1938 was $340.00 per year (*Chilocco: School of Opportunity* 1938, 12).

4. Mr. Wyly to G. W. Grayson, Principal Chief, Creek Nation, Eufaula, 20 August 1919, RG 75 E4 B11/Correspondence F/Letters, 1919–1920, FRC.

5. Letter, 16 January 1920, RG 75 E4 B11/General Correspondence F/Letters, 1919–20, FRC.

6. RG 75 E4 B11/Correspondence F/1919–21, FRC.

7. Reply to Circular #2049, 15 October 1924, RG 75 E4 B14/Correspondence F/Replies to Circular Letters 1923, FRC.

8. Letter, 15 June 1926, RG 75 E7 B1/Records of the Superintendent, FRC.

9. Age/Grade chart for September 1922, RG 75 E4 B13/Correspondence F/Supervisor Spalsbury, FRC.

10. W. C. Ryan to L. E. Correll, 2 September 1931, RG 75 E5 B18 F/820.1, FRC.

11. 1934 Annual Report, RG 75 E8 B2/Annual Reports 1928–34, FRC.

12. Ibid.

13. RG 75 E1 B4/Correspondence with the Commissioner, FRC.

14. Correll to Commissioner, 30 January 1937, RG 75 E7 B3/Reading File F/004 1937–41, FRC.

15. Correll to Danielson, 23 May 1939, RG 75 E7 B3/1926–41 Reading File F/004 1937–41, FRC.

16. RG 75 E45 B1/*Yearbook,* 1932, 1933, 1934, FRC.

17. Chilocco students shared a slang lexicon including the term *shut out* which described dining room and courtship behavior. You could be *shut out* with your girl or boyfriend by another suitor. *Struck on* meant to have a crush on another student. Senior pictures in the yearbook sometimes were captioned *Teacher of Class in Struckology* or *always struck.*

18. See LaFlesche, *The Middle Five* (1900), 71, where boys trade eighty-five Sunday cakes for one pet rabbit.

Chapter Three

1. School administrators characterized this program as a "true vocational program," a euphemism avoided by other students, who called it the "dummy class." These special classes emphasized manual skills and the three Rs for selected adolescents, age fourteen to twenty-one, judged seriously overage for their grade. Some of these students had missed opportunities to attend school as youngsters and did not deserve the labels "backward" and "retarded," which crop up in the offical documentation of the time. In 1934 the one-year "Special Vocational" course enrolled forty-four students (thirty-two boys and twelve girls), who published their own newspaper *Specials Sparkles* (Annual Report, 1933 and 1934, RG 75 E8 B2, FRC).

2. Annual Report, Trades and Industrial Departments, 1934, RG 75, FRC.

3. Report of the Superintendent of Indian Schools, James N. Haworth, to the Secretary of the Interior, 1884, MONAC, p. 5.

4. *Yearbook*, 1927, RG 75 E45 B1, FRC.

5. Annual Report, 1931, RG 75 E8 B2/1928–1934, FRC.

6. Report of the Superintendent of Indian Schools, W. N. Hailmann, to the Secretary of the Interior, 1894, MONAC, p. 9.

7. Meriam, *Problem of Indian Administration* (1928), 348–50 and RG 75 E4 B16 F/Salary Lists, FRC.

8. It should be noted that these alumni grew up during the years of the Great Depression and that undoubtedly influenced their attitudes toward work.

9. Annual Report, 1934, RG 75 E8 B2/1928–34, FRC.

10. Annual Report, 1936, RG 75 E8 B4/1936, FRC.

11. Supervisor Spalsbury to Commissioner Peairs, RG 75 E4 B16 F/Salary Lists, FRC.

12. RG 75 E44 B1, FRC. *Indian School Journal*, 1904–6, 20 August 1904.

13. Correll to Commissioner Beatty, July 1938, RG 75 E5 B18 F/820.1, FRC.

14. Ibid.

15. Annual Report, 1935, RG 75 E8 B3, FRC.

16. Correll to Commissioner, 30 November 1926, RG 75 E1 B4/Records of the Superintendent F/1, FRC.

17. Highest grade breeding stock was secured under the direction of experts from Oklahoma Agricultural and Mechanical University. Chilocco was widely

known for its quality herds of Hereford and Holstein cattle, Duroc-Jersey hogs, Percheron horses, Ramboulet sheep, and Rhode Island White poultry (Stock report, 16 August 1921, RG 75 E4 B12/Records of the Superintendent F/1920–21, FRC).

18. Blair to Commissioner, 27 April 1925, RG 75 E1 B4/Records of the Superintendent F/1, FRC; Correll to Commissioner, 13 April, 1927, ibid., F/4.

19. Correll to Cherokee Agency, 5 August 1926, RG 75 E1 B4/Records of the Superintendent F/3, FRC.

20. Blair to Comm. C. Burke, 10 July 1924, RG 75 E4 B15/Records of the Superintendent F/1924, FRC.

21. Report of the Superintendent of Indian Schools Haworth to the Secretary of the Interior, 1884, MONAC, p. 7.

22. This classic quote is a favorite among scholars of Indian policy and education. McBeth, "The Primer and the Hoe" (1984) derives her title from it; Adams (1988) uses the same text seen here, cited from Bowden, *American Indians and Christian Missions* (1981, 167). Bowden notes that the "House of Representatives Committee on Indian Affairs report of 1818 can be found in *American State Papers: Indian Affairs,* vol. 2, p. 185" (Bowden 1981, 229).

23. The school year contained no vacation breaks, and students were not permitted to go home over Christmas (RG 75 E4 B12/Records of the Superintendent F/Kiowa 1921, FRC; and letter, of 14 December 1925, ibid., B16 F/1925–26).

24. *Bullhide* was the students' nickname for the heavy, Li'l Abner–style boots that were government issue footwear produced in the prison system.

Chapter Four

1. Letter from Commissioner Cato Sells, 28 April 1917. RG 75 E1 B2/1916–17 F/Unlabeled, FRC.

2. Quoted in Adams, "Education in Hues" (1977), 174.

3. Ideals of feminine domesticity also filtered through white women's reform associations, which profoundly affected federal Indian policy. See Mathes, "Nineteenth Century Women and Reform" (1990), 1–18.

4. The philosophy of European societies' carceral systems aimed to produce "strong, skilled agricultural workers . . . in this very work, provided it is technically supervised, submissive subjects are produced and a dependable body of knowledge is built up about them." G. Ferrus, *Des prisonniers* (1850) quoted in Foucault, *Discipline and Punish* (1979), 294–95.

5. Superintendent to Supervisor for Five Civilized Tribes, Muskogee, 17 November 1925, RG 75 E4 BI6/1925–27 F/1925, FRC.

6. RG 75 E4 BI6/Records of the Superintendent. F/1925–27, FRC. Superintendent Blair was such a strong advocate of domestic training, he requested a new position in 1923, principal of the home economics department, at a salary of $1,000 a year, the absolute top of the pay scale for Indian school employees (Annual Report to the Commissioner, 1923, RG 75 E8 BI/Records of the Superintendent FRC).

7. Matrons' Report on Graduating Senior Girls, RG 75 EI B3/1917–18 F/December 1917–May 1918, FRC.

8. There are striking parallels with the education for black girls in South Africa in this century, which also stressed femininity and domesticity. Gaitskill characterizes this education as "vocational, domestic, and subservient," enforced in boarding schools that were "very much rival domestic establishment[s], giving intimate daily contact with alternative 'maternal' figures and Western cultural norms" (1988, 153, 159).

9. 17 April 1917, RG 75 EI B3/1917–18, FRC.

10. The Report of the Superintendent of Indian Schools, 20 October 1901, ERC, MONAC, p. 440.

11. Report to the Commissioner, 18 May 1906 from Riverside, Calif., on Haskell Institute (Lawrence, Kansas), MONAC.

12. Hospital Report for January 1926, RG 75 EI B4 F2/1926, FRC.

13. It was a practical consideration of the boys' trades (cattle raising, farming, carpentry, printing, and so on) that they ranged over the campus, doing much of the work necessary to support the institution. They were not under constant adult supervision, as were the girls who worked in the confines of dormitory, sewing room, and kitchen.

14. Students who had money were allowed to go into town one Saturday a month. Girls were bused as a group under a matron's supervision. They had to present a list of what they intended to buy before leaving, and the list was checked against purchases when they returned to school. Boys were unsupervised (and walked to town) but had to present the disciplinarian with proof of solvency. Boys' gangs would circulate the same fifty-cent piece so everyone could go to town. Town was Arkansas City, Kansas, seven miles to the north (not pronounced like the state Arkansas, but är-kăn'-zəs).

15. Edna Groves' Report, March 1926, RG 75 E4 BI6/1925–27 F/1926, FRC.

16. Letter of 19 September 1923, RG 75 E4 BI3/1921–23, FRC.

17. Reply to Supervisor Spalsbury's Report of 2 November, 27 November 1923, RG 75 E4 BI4/1923–24, Division Miscellaneous, FRC.

18. RG 75 E4 BI6/1925–27 F/1925, FRC.

19. Superintendent Merritt's reply to Supervisor Grove's report, 12 November 1925, RG 75 E4 BI6/1925–27 F/1925, FRC.

20. "Teaching Little Reds," *Journal* (Kansas City, Missouri) 21 October 1900, item #17, F2: Newspaper Clippings Envelope 2, 8/6/00–9/29/00, ERC, MONAC.

21. Report of the Superintendent of Indian Schools, 1901, ERC. MONAC, pp. 450–51.

22. Ibid., 452.

23. Ibid., 452–53.

24. The discrepancy between this and an earlier account of red sweaters reflects different attendance dates of the narrators.

25. We are at the juncture where Foucault calls for more than the "affirmation, pure and simple, of a 'struggle':" we must establish "concretely . . . who is engaged in struggle, what the struggle is about, and how, where, by what means and according to what rationality it evolves." Foucault, *Power/Knowledge* (1980), 164.

Chapter Five

1. Superintendent E. A. Allen to Commissioner of Indian Affairs, Response to Circular No. 590, 22 December 1911, F/Curriculum, OHS.

2. In 1923, the U.S. Army shipped 400 Krag rifles (.30 caliber Model 1898) with bayonets and scabbards from San Antonio, Texas, to Chilocco. Letters and invoices, 15 July, 17 July, and 19 September 1923, RG 75 E4 BI5/1923–24, F/Letters, FRC.

3. In September 1940, Chilocco Company C of the 180th Infantry, National Guard was mobilized for service in World War II. Chilocco staff and students also enlisted in all branches of the service, including the famous Oklahoma 45th (Thunderbird) Division of the U.S. Army. Two Chilocco students earned the Congressional Medal of Honor in World War II, Ernest Childers and Jack Montgomery. See Hale, "Uncle Sam's Warriors" (1991–92) for an overdue appreciation of Indian contributions to the American war effort in World War II, as well as a list of Oklahoma Indian medal winners, POWs, and casualties in that war.

4. Two letters, January 1907, F/Vices, OHS.

5. Jeff Mouse, assistant coach, was killed in a train-crossing accident twenty

miles south of Kingman, Kansas, while traveling with the boys' basketball team. Superintendent Correll to Commissioner, 30 January 1937, RG 75 E7 B3/1937–41 F/004, FRC.

6. From an interview with a Chilocco boxer who had a professional boxing career.

7. Correll to Commissioner, 11 October 1926, RG 75 EI B4 F/3, FRC.

8. Assistant Commissioner Merritt to Correll, 21 April 1927, March Monthly Report, RG 75 EI B4 F/4, FRC.

9. RG 75 E4 BI2 F/Supt. Locke, Muskogee, FRC. EI B4:1925–27 F/I:1925, ibid. A citizen of Newkirk, Okla., received twelve dollars for returning four runaways a distance of nine miles.

10. Letter from Fr. Cerre and Louis McDonald, 14 January 1924, RG 75 E4 BI4/Records of the Superintendent, F/General Accounting Office, FRC.

Chapter Six

1. Annual Report, 1933, RG 75 E8 B2/1928–34, FRC.

2. *Chiloccoan,* 1935, RG 75 E45 B2, FRC. See also Annual Report, 1938, ibid., E8 B5/1937–52, and ibid.

Selected Bibliography

Primary Sources

ARCHIVAL COLLECTIONS

Federal Archives and Records Center (*Fort Worth, Texas*)

When Chilocco was closed in 1980, the Bureau of Indian Affairs was directed to deposit all extant school records in the Fort Worth, Texas, regional branch of the National Archives. School records of the 1950s, 1960s, and 1970s are not nearly as wide-ranging as records of earlier decades, when record retention was more voluminous. A former Chilocco employee reported that a number of boxes of records were mistakenly sent to the dump instead of the archives. It is also possible some boxes are still at the school or forgotten in an attic of bureau offices in Anadarko or Muscogee.

The bulk of the regional archive's Chilocco records (210 shelf feet out of a total 300 plus) are personal student case files still closed to public view in 1984. The following are the relevant records.

Record Group 75: Records of the Bureau of Indian Affairs
    Records of the Anadarko Area Files
        Row 24 Box #385385 and Box #385391: Narrative and monthly reports from Chilocco Indian School, 1955–61
    Records of Chilocco Indian Agricultural School
        This partial list of Chilocco archival holdings at the Federal regional archives in Forth Worth represents records consulted by the author. For a complete index of Chilocco holdings, contact the Fort Worth Records Center.
    Records of the Superintendent:

Entry 1 Correspondence with the Office of Indian Affairs, Correspondence with the Commissioner

E4 General Correspondence

E5 White Decimal System records, 816–827

E5a Blue Decimal System records, 200.01–200.10

E7 Reading File (Letters sent), 1926–1941

E8 Annual Reports

School Publications:

E44 *The Indian School Journal,* 1904–26

E45 *Yearbook,* 1925–80

Records Relating to Students:

E59 Register of Pupils, 1884–1908

E60 Descriptive Statements of Children, 1885–1902

E61 Arrivals and Departures, 1897–1900

E62, E63, E64, E65 Records of the Superintendent, Attendance Reports

E66 Daily attendance record, 1914–22

E67 Record of Pupils by Tribe, 1902–3

E68 Miscellaneous Lists

E70 Gradebooks

E71 Checkerboard Grades, 1916–43

Museum of Native American Cultures, Spokane, Washington

Arden Sallquist Collection: Papers of Estelle Reel, Superintendent of Indian Schools, 1898–1910. In November 1991, MONAC's collections were transferred to Cheney-Cowles Museum, Spokane, Washington.

Oklahoma Historical Society (*Oklahoma City, Oklahoma*)

Earliest Chilocco records in this archive document student enrollment and attendance from 1884 to 1909 (duplicated at the Regional Archives in Fort Worth), and student enrollment from 1893 to 1918. These records seem to be all that have survived from the school's first decade and a half, and they are available from the society as microfilm publications. The bulk of the society's holdings are superintendents' records, correspondence with the commissioner of Indian Affairs from 1896 to 1907 (also available as microfilm publications). The society has prepared an inventory of all Chilocco records by topic and date (such as, Employees, 1897–1911). Most records predate 1917, and only a few extend as late as 1927.

Bibliography

Records of Chilocco Indian School:
This list of consulted records is only a portion of all records from Chilocco in the custody of the Indian Archives Division, Oklahoma Historical Society.

Activities of Ex-Students, 1904–12
Alumni Association, 1911–13
Band, 1902–22
Buildings, 1900–25
Carlisle Indian School, 1900–17
Cattle and Pastures, 1902–19
Cemetery, 1911–12
Census, 1906–15
Classification of Students, 1893–1906
Complaints from Students, 1903–11
Curriculum, 1904–17
Deaths, 1901–26
Fairs, 1895–1904
Indians, AWOL, 1903–13
Indian Celebration, 1904–11
Indian Courts, 1903–18
Indian Dances, 1903–9
Letters from Ex-students, 1900–14
Thefts, 1904–13
Vices, 1902–25

Secondary Sources

FEDERAL PUBLICATIONS (INCLUDING CHILOCCO PUBLICATIONS)

U.S. Bureau of Indian Affairs. 1899. *Statistics of Indian Tribes, Indian Agencies, and Indian Schools*. Washington, D.C.: Government Printing Office.

———. 1890–1940. Annual Reports of the Commissioner of Indian Affairs. (Between 1897 and 1963 this report appeared in the U.S. Department of the Interior, Annual Report of the Secretary of the Interior.)

———. 1932. *Indian Schools and Education*. Washington, D.C.: Government Printing Office.

———. 1938. *Chilocco: School of Opportunity for Indian Youth: A Book of Useful Information about Chilocco, the School of Opportunity*. Chilocco, Okla.: Chilocco Printing Department.

———. 1938a. *The Chiloccoan*. Senior Class Annual. Chilocco Indian School: Chilocco Press.

Bibliography

———. 1972. *The Chiloccoan*. Vol. 72. Chilocco Indian School: Chilocco Press.

———. 1980. *The Chiloccoan*. Vol. 80. Chilocco Indian School: Chilocco Press.

BOOKS AND ARTICLES

Adams, David W. 1975. "The Federal Indian Boarding School: A Study of Environment and Response, 1879–1918." Ed.D. diss., Indiana University.

———. 1977. "Education in Hues: Red and Black at Hampton Institute, 1878–1893." *The South Atlantic Quarterly* 76 (2): 159–76.

———. 1988. "Fundamental Considerations: The Deep Meaning of Native American Schooling, 1880–1900." *Harvard Educational Review* 58 (1): 1–28.

Ahern, Wilbert H. 1983. "'The Returned Indians': Hampton Institute and Its Indian Alumni, 1879–1893." *The Journal of Ethnic Studies* 10 (4): 101–24.

Anderson, James D. 1978. "The Hampton Model of Normal School Industrial Education, 1868–1900." In *New Perspectives on Black Educational History,* ed. V. Franklin and J. Anderson, 61–96. Lexington, Mass.: G. K. Hall.

———. 1982. "The Historical Development of Black Vocational Education." In *Work, Youth, and Schooling,* ed. H. Kantor and D. B. Tyack. Stanford: Stanford University Press.

Armstrong, Samuel C. 1883. *The Indian Question*. Hampton, Va.: Normal School Steam Press.

Barman, Jean, Y. Hébert, and D. McCaskill, eds. 1986, 1987. *Indian Education in Canada*. 2 vols. Vancouver: University of British Columbia Press.

Barth, Fredrik. 1969. *Ethnic Groups and Boundaries: The Social Organization of Culture Differences*. Boston: Little, Brown.

Beecher, Catharine E. 1846. *A Treatise on Domestic Economy, for the Use of Young Ladies at Home, and at School*. 3d ed. New York: Harper & Brothers.

Beiser, M. 1973. "A Hazard to Mental Health: Indian Boarding Schools." *American Journal of Psychiatry* 131:305–308.

Berkhofer, Robert F., Jr. 1965. *Salvation and the Savage: An Analysis of Protestant Missions and American Indian Response, 1787–1862*. Lexington: University of Kentucky Press.

Boas, Franz. 1943. "Recent Anthropology." *Science* 98:311–37.

Bourdieu, Pierre. 1977. *Outline of a Theory of Practice*. Cambridge: Cambridge University Press.

Bowden, Henry W. 1981. *American Indians and Christian Missions: Studies in Cultural Conflict*. Chicago: University of Chicago Press.

Bibliography

Bradfield, Larry L. 1963. "A History of Chilocco Indian School." Master's Thesis, History Department, University of Oklahoma.

Brumble, H. David. 1981. *An Annotated Bibliography of American Indian and Eskimo Autobiographies*. Lincoln: University of Nebraska Press.

Crapanzano, Vincent. 1977. "The Life History in Anthropological Fieldwork." *Anthropology and Humanism Quarterly* 2 (2–3): 3–7.

Cremin, Lawrence A. 1980. *American Education: The National Experience, 1783–1876*. New York: Harper & Row.

Cruikshank, Julie, in collaboration with Angela Sidney, Kitty Smith, and Annie Ned. 1990. *Life Lived Like a Story: Life Stories of Three Yukon Native Elders*. Lincoln: University of Nebraska Press.

DeVos, George, and Lola Romanucci-Ross. 1975. *Ethnic Identity*. Palo Alto: Mayfield.

Dollard, John. 1935. *Criteria for the Life History*. New Haven: Yale University Press.

Ehrenreich, Barbara, and Deirdre English. 1978. *For Her Own Good: 150 Years of the Experts' Advice to Women*. New York: Anchor Press/Doubleday.

Erikson, Erik. 1975. *Life History and the Historical Moment*. New York: Norton.

Foucault, Michel. 1979. *Discipline and Punish: The Birth of the Prison*. Trans. Alan Sheridan. New York: Vintage Books.

———. 1980. *Power/Knowledge: Selected Interviews and Other Writings, 1972–1977*. Ed. Colin Gordon. New York: Pantheon Books.

Fredrickson, Vera Mae, ed. 1989. "School Days in Northern California: The Accounts of Six Pomo Women." *News from Native California* 4 (1): 40–45.

Fuchs, Estelle, and Robert Havighurst. 1972. *To Live on This Earth*. New York: Doubleday.

Gaitskill, Deborah. 1988. "Race, Gender, and Imperialism: A Century of Black Girls' Education in South Africa." In *"Benefits Bestowed?" Education and British Imperialism*, ed. J. A. Mangan, 150–73. Manchester: Manchester University Press.

Giago, Tim A., Jr. 1978. *The Aboriginal Sin: Reflections on the Holy Rosary Mission School*. San Francisco: The Indian Historian Press.

Gould, Charles N. 1933. *Oklahoma Place Names*. Norman: University of Oklahoma Press.

Haig-Brown, Celia. 1988. *Resistance and Renewal: Surviving the Indian Residential School*. Vancouver: Tillacum Library.

Hale, Duane K. 1991–92. "Uncle Sam's Warriors: American Indians in World War II." *The Chronicles of Oklahoma* 69 (4): 408–29.

Hultgren, M. L., and P. Molin. 1989. *To Lead and to Serve: American Indian Education at Hampton Institute*. Virginia Beach, Va.: Virginia Foundation for the Humanities and Public Policy.

Hyer, Sally. 1990. *One House, One Voice, One Heart: Native American Education at Santa Fe Indian School*. Santa Fe: Museum of New Mexico Press.

"Indian Education at Hampton and Carlisle." 1881. *Harper's New Monthly Magazine* 42 (371): 659–75.

Jackson, Helen Hunt. [1888] 1972. *A Century of Dishonor: A Sketch of the United States Government's Dealings with Some of the Indian Tribes*. New York: Scholarly Press.

Johnston, Basil H. 1989. *Indian School Days*. Norman, Okla.: University of Oklahoma Press.

Kantor, Harvey, and David Tyack, eds. 1982. *Work, Youth, and Schooling: Historical Perspectives on Vocationalism in American Education*. Stanford: Stanford University Press.

Kappler, Charles J. 1975. *Indian Affairs, Laws, and Treaties*. Vol. 1. Washington, D.C.: U.S. Department of the Interior.

Kennedy, Edward M. 1969. *Indian Education: A National Tragedy—A National Challenge*. Report of the U.S. Senate Committee on Labor and Public Welfare, Special Subcommittee on Indian Education. Senate Report #91–501. Washington, D.C.: U.S. Government Printing Office.

King, A. Richard. 1967. *The School at Mopass: A Problem of Identity*. Case Studies in Education and Culture, edited by G. and L. Spindler. New York: Holt, Rinehart, & Winston.

Kleinfeld, Judith. 1973. *A Long Way from Home: Effects of Public High Schools on Village Children away from Home*. Fairbanks, Alaska: Center for Northern Educational Research.

Kluckhohn, Clyde. 1949. Needed Refinements in the Biographical Approach. In *Culture and Personality,* eds. S. Stansfeld Sargent and Marian W. Smith. New York: The Viking Fund.

Kroeber, Alfred L. 1945. "The Use of Autobiographical Evidence in a Yurok War Reminiscence." *Southwestern Journal of Anthropology* 1 (3): 318–22.

LaFlesche, Francis. [1900] 1978. *The Middle Five*. Lincoln: University of Nebraska Press.

Langness, L. L. 1965. *The Life History in Anthropological Science*. New York: Holt, Rinehart, & Winston.

Langness, L. L., and Gelya Frank. 1981. *Lives: An Anthropological Approach to Biography*. Novato, Calif.: Chandler & Sharp.

Littlefield, Alice. 1989. The B.I.A. Boarding School: Theories of Resistance and Social Reproduction. *Humanity and Society* 13 (4): 428–41.

Lomawaima, K. Tsianina. 1987. " 'They Called It Prairie Light': Oral Histories from Chilocco Indian Agricultural School, 1920–1940." Ph.D. diss., Anthropology Department, Stanford University.

Lopez, Barry. 1990. Introduction to *Bighorse, the Warrior*. Ed. Noel Bennett. Tucson, Ariz.: University of Arizona Press.

Mathes, Valerie S. 1990. "Nineteenth Century Women and Reform: The Women's National Indian Association." *American Indian Quarterly* 14 (1): 1–18.

Matthews, Sarah M. 1986. *Friendships through the Life Course: Oral Biographies in Old Age*. Sage Library of Social Research, vol. 161. Beverly Hills, Calif.: Sage Publications.

McBeth, Sally. 1983. *Ethnic Identity and the Boarding School Experience of West-Central Oklahoma American Indians*. Washington, D.C.: University Press of America.

———. 1984. "The Primer and the Hoe." *Natural History* 93 (8): 4–13.

Meriam, Lewis. 1928. *The Problem of Indian Administration*. Institute for Government Research. Baltimore: Johns Hopkins Press.

Millett, Kate. 1970. The Debate over Women: Ruskin versus Mill. *Victorian Studies* 14 (1): 63–87.

Minnesota Public Radio. 1991. "Learning the White People Way." Aired May 15. St. Paul, MN.

Morris, Barry. 1989. *Domesticating Resistance: The Dhan-Gadi Aborigines and the Australian State*. Oxford: Berg Publishers.

Myerhoff, Barbara G. 1980. "Telling One's Story." *The Center Magazine* 13 (2): 22–40.

Philp, Kenneth R. 1977. *John Collier's Crusade for Indian Reform, 1920–1954*. Tucson, Ariz.: University of Arizona Press.

Prucha, Francis P. 1979. *The Churches and the Indian Schools*. Lincoln: University of Nebraska Press.

———. 1986. *The Great Father: The United States Government and the American Indians*. Abridged edition. Lincoln: University of Nebraska Press.

Reyhner, Jon, and Jeanne Eder. 1989. *A History of Indian Education*. Billings: Eastern Montana College.

Richards, Josephine E. 1900. "The Training of the Indian Girl as the Uplifter of the Home." In *Journal of Proceedings and Addresses*. National Education Association. Chicago: University of Chicago Press.

Roosens, Eugeen E. 1989. *Creating Ethnicity: The Process of Ethnogenesis.* Frontiers of Anthropology, vol. 5. Newbury Park, Calif.: Sage Publications.

Rosenthal-Metcalf, Ann H. 1975. "The Effects of Boarding School on Navajo Self-Image and Maternal Behavior." Ph.D. diss., Anthropology Department, Stanford University.

Ryan, Carmelita S. 1962. "The Carlisle Indian Industrial School." Ph.D. diss., History Department, Georgetown University.

Sapir, Edward. 1938. "Introduction." In *Son of Old Man Hat,* Walter Dyk. Lincoln: University of Nebraska Press.

Savage, William M., Jr. 1972. "Intruders at Chilocco." *The Chronicles of Oklahoma* 50 (2): 199–204.

Scott, James C. 1985. *Weapons of the Weak: Everyday Forms of Peasant Resistance.* New Haven: Yale University Press.

Sleeth, Emma DeKnight. 1906. "Reminiscences of Chilocco." *Indian School Journal* (September).

———. 1907. "Received in Full Membership." *Indian School Journal* (December).

Speelman, Margaret. 1924. *A Pageant of Oklahoma.* Pageant program held in the Western History Collection, University of Oklahoma (Norman, Oklahoma).

Spicer, Edward H. 1971. "Persistent Cultural Systems." *Science* 174: 795–800.

Szasz, Margaret. 1974. *Education and the American Indian: The Road to Self-Determination, 1928–1973.* Albuquerque: University of New Mexico Press.

———. 1977. "Federal Boarding Schools and the Indian Child, 1920–1960." *South Dakota History* 7 (4): 371–84.

———. 1988. *Indian Education in the American Colonies, 1607–1783.* Albuquerque: University of New Mexico Press.

Trennert, Robert. 1988. *The Phoenix Indian School: Forced Assimilation in Arizona.* Norman: University of Oklahoma Press.

Tyler, Samuel L. 1973. *A History of Indian Policy.* Washington, D.C.: U.S. Department of the Interior.

Utley, Robert, ed. 1964. *Battlefield and Classroom: Four Decades with the American Indian, the Memoirs of Richard H. Pratt.* New Haven: Yale University Press.

Van Well, Sister Mary S. 1942. *The Educational Aspects of the Missions in the Southwest.* Milwaukee, Wisc.: Marquette University Press.

Wall, C. Leon, and Beulah W. Wall. 1979. *Tomahawks over Chilocco.* Oklahoma City: Kin Lichee Press.

Wallerstein, Immanuel. 1960. "Ethnicity and National Integration." *Cahiers d'etudes africaines* 1 (3): 129–39.

Bibliography

Watson, Lawrence C., and Maria-Barbara Watson-Franke. 1985. *Interpreting Life Histories: An Anthropological Inquiry*. New Brunswick, N.J.: Rutgers University Press.

Wilkinson, Charles. 1987. *American Indians, Time, and the Law: Native Societies in a Modern Constitutional Democracy*. New Haven: Yale University Press.

Williams, John, and Howard L. Meredith. 1980. *Bacone Indian University*. Oklahoma City: Western Heritage Books.

Willis, Paul. 1977. *Learning to Labor: How Working Class Kids get Working Class Jobs*. Westmead, England: Saxon House.

Index

Winners of the North American Indian Prose Award

Boarding School Seasons
American Indian Families, 1900–1940
Brenda J. Child

Listening to Our Grandmothers' Stories
The Bloomfield Academy for Chickasaw Females, 1852–1949
Amanda J. Cobb

Claiming Breath
Diane Glancy

They Called It Prairie Light
The Story of Chilocco Indian School
K. Tsianina Lomawaima

Son of Two Bloods
Vincent L. Mendoza

All My Sins Are Relatives
W. S. Penn

Completing the Circle
Virginia Driving Hawk Sneve

Year in Nam
A Native American Soldier's Story
Leroy TeCube